RECONSIDERING INFORMALITY
Perspectives from Urban Africa

Edited by
Karen Tranberg Hansen and Mariken Vaa

D1614002

Nordiska Afrikainstitutet 2004

Indexing terms

Informal economy
Land use
Livelihoods
Planning
Urban housing
Congo-Brazzaville
Guinea-Bissau
Kenya
Lesotho
Mozambique
South Africa
Tanzania
Zambia
Zimbabwe

Cover photo: Karen Tranberg Hansen (2002)
Long distance bus leaving Chipata (on the Malawian border) for Lusaka.

Language checking: Elaine Almén

Index: Margaret Binns

© the authors and Nordiska Afrikainstitutet, 2004

ISBN 91-7106-518-0

Printed in Spain by Grafilur Artes Gráficas, 2004

Contents

Preface 5

CHAPTER 1   *Karen Tranberg Hansen and Mariken Vaa*
Introduction 7

SECTION I: LOCALITY, PLACE, AND SPACE. 25

CHAPTER 2   *Gabriel Tati*
Sharing Public Space in Pointe-Noire, Congo-Brazzaville:
Immigrant Fishermen and a Multinational Oil Company 28

CHAPTER 3   *Knut G. Nustad*
The Right to Stay in Cato Crest: Formality and
Informality in a South African Development Project 45

CHAPTER 4   *Karen Tranberg Hansen*
Who Rules the Streets? The Politics of Vending Space
in Lusaka 62

SECTION II: ECONOMY, WORK, AND LIVELIHOODS. 81

CHAPTER 5   *Ilda Lourenço-Lindell*
Trade and the Politics of Informalization in Bissau,
Guinea-Bissau 84

CHAPTER 6   *Barbara Mwila Kazimbaya-Senkwe*
Home Based Enterprises in a Period of Economic
Restructuring in Zambia 99

CHAPTER 7   *Amin Y. Kamete*
Home Industries and the Formal City in Harare,
Zimbabwe. 120

SECTION III: LAND, HOUSING, AND PLANNING 139

CHAPTER 8   *Marco Burra*
Land Use Planning and Governance in Dar es Salaam:
A Case Study from Tanzania 143

CHAPTER 9   *Rose Gatabaki-Kamau and Sara Karirah-Gitau*
Actors and Interests: The Development of an Informal
Settlement in Nairobi, Kenya 158

CHAPTER 10   *Resetselemang Clement Leduka*
The Law and Access to Land for Housing in Maseru,
Lesotho. 176

CHAPTER 11   *John Abbott*
Upgrading an Informal Settlement in Cape Town,
South Africa 193

CHAPTER 12   *Paul Jenkins*
Beyond the Formal/Informal Dichotomy: Access to Land
in Maputo, Mozambique 210

Abbreviations 227
Biographical Notes 229
Index 231

Preface

The second conference under the auspices of the research programme *Cities, Governance and Civil Society in Africa* (1997–2002) was convened in Copenhagen, Denmark in June 2000. The conference was entitled "The Formal and the Informal City—What Happens at the Interface?" and was organized by the Nordic Africa Institute in conjunction with the Department of Human Settlements of the Copenhagen School of Architecture.

The thematic background to the conference was the co-existence and interaction of a formal and an informal set of rules and institutions in the cities of the developing world, a phenomenon which is particularly conspicuous in Africa. *The informal city* consists of extra-legal housing and unregistered economic activities. In contrast, the *formal city* consists of the city government and its agents and institutions, and rules and regulations that over time have been introduced in order to control the urban space. The formal and the informal city meet at a series of interfaces, as when regulatory frameworks are adjusted and readjusted in response to the widening boundaries of informalities, or when government agents arbitrarily enforce some rules but not others. In many cases, some activities are formally extra-legal, but considered legitimate by the actors concerned.

One preliminary observation based on the response to the call for papers and the papers presented in Copenhagen is that in African urban studies, the relationship between the formal and the informal city is an active and fruitful field of research. At the conference, there were 47 participants, 25 from Africa, 20 from the Nordic countries and 2 from the United Kingdom. In all, 23 papers had been prepared, drawing on material from 15 different African countries. Of the 12 chapters in this book, 11 are revised versions of papers presented in Copenhagen, while Chapter 1 and the introductions to the sub-sections were written after the conference was held.

Many people contributed towards making the conference a success, first and foremost, the authors of papers, the discussants and the other participants. On the practical side, thanks are due to the conference secretaries Ingrid Andersson and Kirsten Ditlev. We would also like to thank the Danish Ministry of Foreign Affairs for providing supplementary funding for the conference.

The preparation and publication of this book involves the efforts of many people. First, we would like to thank the contributors for their industry and, as time went by, their patience in responding to yet another set of suggestions for the revision of their chapters from the editors. Elaine Almén did a language check of the whole manuscript. Ingrid Andersson, assistant to the programme *Cities, Governance and Civil Society in Africa* has performed a variety of tasks. Among other things, she has kept track of authors and manuscripts and checked bibliographical references. She also drew up the list of Abbreviations. The index has been constructed with the help of Margaret Binns. Finally, two anonymous referees for our publication department have contributed many insightful comments and suggestions. They have all been carefully considered in a final round of revisions.

Evanston and Oslo, July 2003

Karen Tranberg Hansen and Mariken Vaa

CHAPTER 1

Introduction

Karen Tranberg Hansen and Mariken Vaa

At the turn of the millennium, Africa's cities were driven predominantly by informal practices in such vital areas as work, shelter, land use, transportation, and a variety of social services (Stren and Halfani 2001:474). The significance of these developments invites close attention by scholars and policy makers to explain how African urban livelihoods are made in order to improve generally falling standards of living. It is only recently that major multinational and bilateral development organizations have turned their focus on the rapidly growing cities in the developing world (UNCHS 1996, Milbert and Peat 1999, UNCHS 2001). There is no doubt that this shift reflects concerns about the political and economic ramifications of demographic projections that point to dramatic urban population growth in some of the poorest parts of the world. Over the last 15 years, influential actors in development policy and practice, such as the World Bank, have also with increasing insistence argued that cities are engines of macro-economic growth (World Bank 1991, 2000a; Harris 1992).

According to the UN's urban demographic projections, the developing world alone will be adding almost 2 billion people to its existing cities and towns by 2030 (UNCHS 2001:271). Although Africa is the least urbanized of all the continents African cities have grown at a faster pace than cities in most other parts of the world since the 1960s (Stren and Halfani 2001:479). What can concerns about what we will term the informal city contribute to our understanding of how African urban residents are negotiating their journeys toward what they hope will be a better tomorrow?

THE INFORMAL CITY

In this book, we consider extra-legal housing and unregistered economic activities as constituting the informal city. A large, if varying, proportion of Africa's urban population is housed in unauthorized and unserviced settlements, and increasing numbers find their livelihood in the informal economy. In some cities, up to 90 per cent of the new housing stock has been provided informally and more than half of the adult population is in unregistered employment. What is more, workers in the formal economy are increasingly supplementing their income by engaging in informal activities (Meagher 1995). Informal activities and practices may be illegal or extra-legal but are not necessarily perceived as illegitimate by the actors concerned. It is likely that many urban residents consider what from the official standpoint is illegal or irregular as not only functioning but normal and legitimate practices.

In contrast to the informal city, the *formal city* consists of the urban government and its agents, institutions and rules and regulations that over time have been introduced in order to control urban space and economic life. The registered segments of the urban economy and buildings and infrastructure that have been established legally, are also part of the formal city. The formal and the informal city meet at a series of interfaces, for instance when regulatory frameworks are adjusted and readjusted in response to powerful citizens' demands for flexibility, or when government agents arbitrarily enforce some rules but not others. Although some activities may be extra-legal in formal terms, the actors concerned consider them as legitimate. Sometimes, formal authorization may be obtained or provided informally. Thus, urban space is not so much a product of an overall regulatory system as it is a dynamic field of interaction for economic, social, cultural and political processes.

With this book's focus on the informal city we bring together two bodies of social science scholarship that have tended to be separated in most work on urban Africa. One category of research focuses on subjects related to urban land use and housing while the other category is concerned with production and reproduction in the informal economy. Regardless of the specific focus, scholarship frequently claims that there is a close relationship between poverty, informal housing and informal income generation (Gilbert and Gugler 1992, ch 3 and 4). Yet, even if they often overlap, poverty, expressed by low incomes and substandard shelter, and extra-legality of income generation and housing are two distinct phenomena. In effect, there may well be mutually reinforcing relationships between extra-legality, poverty and wealth in African cities in which government policies and practice towards the informal city are important.

In themselves, work and reproduction in the informal economy and the role of regulatory frameworks are important research themes. So are patterns of land acquisition, property relations, urban land use, planning and service provision. To examine sectors as important as housing and work together, in relation to law, regulatory frameworks and social practices of the government as well as the governed may provide a basis for more productive and less exclusionary urban reforms than the patterns of urban management that are current in many cities today.

There are strong policy reasons for examining the role of illegality or extra-legality in producing and maintaining high levels of poverty. This is particularly so because the informal city is not exclusively the domain of the poor. Better off segments of the urban population also engage in illegal land occupation and construction, at times reaping extraordinarily high profits from sub-letting very sub-standard housing. Informal production and trade of goods and services offer opportunities for better off entrepreneurs for rapid enrichment while their employees work under highly exploitative conditions with little job security and no legal protection.

The Interface between the Formal and the Informal City

A dictionary definition of interface describes it as a surface that forms a common boundary between two parts or areas, or a point of communication between two different systems (Penguin's Wordmaster Dictionary 1987). The word is used largely as a technical term in system theory and computer sciences, but does occasionally appear in social science works (e.g., Baker and Pedersen 1992; Guyer 1995). Guyer's definition is close to that of the dictionaries, but she adds the dynamics of exchange and subsequent change: "[the interface is] a point of meeting where difference [is] maintained, albeit on changing bases and with changing terms" (1995:8).

In this book we use the notion of interface to highlight encounters between entities or processes that are governed by different rules; the outcomes may be neutral, implying non-recognition or accommodation, or they may entail conflict or cooperation. These meetings may include individuals or groups, practices and beliefs, institutions or systems. They take place in public places and courtrooms, spontaneous and planned encounters, households and networks, and in people's minds.

Informal Settlements

There is a vast gap between the number of housing units produced by the formal sector and the growth of urban populations in most African cities. New unauthorized settlements are appearing at the same time as the older ones continue to grow. Most African countries inherited and have kept a legal framework for urban development that was designed to contain settlement rather than to deal with rapid growth. Even if blatantly repressive aspects such as pass laws were abolished at independence, zoning laws, building standards, and many other planning regulations have remained on the books in several countries. These regulations restrict the provision of housing affordable to the poor and the not-so-poor. The result is the emergence of unauthorized, or illegal settlements.

There are considerable variations in legal contexts between African countries, and in the *de facto* recognition or acceptance of unauthorized settlements in the same city. Illegality or extra-legality of unauthorized settlements takes three principal forms. The first is illegal occupation of land that infringes on communal or individual property rights. The second is illegal or clandestine subdivision of land in conflict with planning regulations, and the third is construction or use of houses without permission and in contravention of building codes. Often, the first and the second forms of illegality overlap with the third, but not necessarily.

Shelter standards and incomes in such settlements vary considerably. Both case studies of individual settlements and city-wide studies have documented that the populations of unauthorized settlements in many respects are as heterogeneous as the rest of the city (Antoine et al. 1987; van Westen 1995; Durand-Lasserve 1998). Income levels are varied, but lower than city averages, indicating an over-representation of the poor and the very poor. Residents of irregular settlements pursue many types of activities, making their living both in formal and informal work. Because of poverty, and because they may face legal or other constraints in the formal housing market, many *de facto* and *de jure* women-headed households seek shelter as tenants in the cheapest sections of the unauthorized settlements. Some are able to secure a house there making a living from letting out rooms (Moser 1987; *Environment and Urbanization* 1991; Schlyter 1991; Hansen 1997). In recent years, an increasing number of middle and high standard housing areas have developed informally, as illegal forms of land occupation and un-authorized subdivision of land (Fernandes and Varley 1998).

A major difference in living conditions between informal settlements and the rest of the city concerns social and physical infrastructure. Unless some legaliza-tion process or donor-funded upgrading project is anticipated, city authorities may be both unwilling and financially unable to provide water, sanitation and drainage, pave roads, collect garbage, build schools and clinics in informal set-tlements. As we have already pointed out, unauthorized settlements do not con-sist solely of self-help, owner-occupied housing. Housing in many informal settlements has become commercialized and a variety of housing sub-markets has emerged (Amis and Lloyd 1990). Both small scale and large scale landlord-ism are important components; indeed in some settlements, rental accommo-dation is the major form of tenancy (Andreasen 1989; Amis 1996). Yet, international agencies have only recently included rental housing on their agen-da, and few governments have a housing policy that makes any reference to rental housing (UNCHS 1993).

The Informal Economy

The term the informal economy was first coined by the British anthropologist Keith Hart (1973) in a study from Accra, Ghana. The terms formal/informal gained wide currency in the early 1970s, when the International Labour Office (ILO) adopted this terminology in its city case studies under the World Employ-ment Programme. According to ILO usage, the formal sector consists of enu-merated, large scale, capital intensive firms, while the informal sector is composed of the unenumerated self-employed, mainly providing a livelihood for new entrants into the cities. One of the most widely used classifications stems from the ILO report on Kenya. The informal sector is here characterized by its ease of entry, reliance on indigenous resources, family ownership of enterprises, small scale of operations, labour-intensive and adapted technology, skills ac-quired outside the formal school system and unregulated and competitive mar-kets (ILO 1972). A later summing up of studies undertaken under ILO auspices emphasized the small scale of operations and the importance of the informal sec-tor in creating employment and incomes (Sethuraman 1981:17).

An alternative approach to that of ILO characterizes informal economic activ-ities by one central feature, their extra-legality (Castells and Portes 1989:12). From this perspective, the informal economy is a near universal phenomenon, present in countries and regions at very different levels of economic development and not confined to a set of survival activities performed by destitute people on the margins of society. The forms of unregulated production, distribution and service provision, the incomes they yield and their position in relation to legal codes and law enforcement may vary widely both between countries but also within the same city. Their degree of legitimacy and illegitimacy and the extent to which better-off segments of the urban population are involved also varies between cities and countries. Given the increasing heterogeneity of informal activities in Africa's urban economies and the fact that the well-to-do as well as the poor seek livelihoods and profit from them, we prefer the term the informal economy rather than the informal sector. From this perspective, it is their extra-legality that is the salient characteristic of informal economic activities, not the type or size of the enterprises nor the incomes earned there.[1]

TRANSFORMATION OF URBAN SPACE

Why should we reconsider Africa's urban housing and work dynamics at this point in time? After all, it has been recognized for a long time that both economic livelihoods and physical shelter are provided informally for a large proportion of Africa's urban populations. Numerous research efforts and publications testify to the growth of these activities in many African urban settings in the period following independence (e.g., King 1996; Tripp, 1997). If we should be misled by this wealth of information to consider informalization to be a product of post-colonial developments, scholarship on colonial urban history will convince us about the longevity of some of these processes (Balandier 1985; Clark 1994; Hansen 1997:21–82; Martin 1995; Robertson 1997; van Onselen 1982). But what is at issue are not linear progressions from the past to the present. The economic, political, and social conditions in African cities at the turn of the century differ significantly from those of previous eras. Aside from providing the rationale for this book, this situation has important implications for urban policy both at the national and international level. In short, this is a strategic moment to reconsider informality.

When the idea of the informal economy was launched in the early 1970s, many of Africa's newly emergent states were seeking to organize the economy with development policies aimed at regulating the proliferation of informal activities. The collapse of the state in many countries has led in turn to a general informalization of the economy. Keith Hart has linked this process to the widespread crisis of state capitalism after the Cold War (1992). In the wake of this crisis, the conjuncture of neo-liberal reforms since the early 1990s and two decades of Structural Adjustment Programmes (SAP) has been transforming urban space, affecting both the distribution of social groups and activities throughout specific cities and among cities in Africa and globally (Guyer et al. 2002; Mulenga 2001; Zeleza 1999). The human costs of SAP have been enormous because of the inability or failure of many governments to provide jobs and housing, and because of growing poverty, low or declining levels of educa-

---

1. It is interesting to note that in a report to the 90th session of the International Labour Conference in 2002, the International Labour Office (ILO) prefers the term "the informal economy" to "the informal sector" (ILO 2002).

tion, and poor health that in eastern and southern Africa is adversely affected by high exposure to HIV/AIDS (Poku 2001). As we discuss below, neo-liberal political and economic reforms from the early 1990s are exacerbating this grim situation in many countries, making social inequality across urban space more visibly than ever before.

Shifts in Power

These ongoing transformations of urban space are set into motion by a combination of processes that testify to the decreasing sovereignty of central governments. State power is being de-institutionalized and decentralized under internal demands for democratization and external pressure for economic liberalization. Everyday urban life in some countries continues to take place against a backdrop of internal wars and violence. In such situations, for instance during the recurrent upheavals in Congo-Brazzaville since the early 1990s, political conflicts have become urbanized, with ethnic and outright xenophobic distinctions accentuated (Geschiere and Nyamnjoh 2001). Taken together, factors such as central governments' lack of resources, misappropriation and patronage are pushing a variety of initiatives on to civic associations and NGOs, fuelling the informalization of services that the state is unable to provide (Balala 2001; Tostensen et al. 2001). New actors and models of participation are appearing in the process, including women and youth (Dauda 2001).

In the wake of neo-liberal reforms, changes in land value are transforming both the place and nature of commercial space and affecting access to housing and its location. One strategy pursued in some countries, privatising housing markets through the sale of municipal or state-owned housing units to sitting tenants, easily favours better-off persons who in turn push previous tenants onto the informal housing market because of their financial inability to buy or rent formal housing. As a result, privatising the housing stock may in fact promote a sort of gentrification process that not only extends the housing gap between poor and rich but also is gender biased (Schlyter 2002). A recent study from Zambia's Copperbelt, for instance, indicates that far fewer women tenants than men were able to purchase their dwellings (Chellah 2001). Women's access to formal credit was limited and they had to rely on financial assistance from relatives and friends.

The lack of appropriate finance systems makes it difficult for government authorities and municipal councils to meet the low-income population's demand for land and housing (Durand-Lasserve 1998:236). Where privatization of housing markets takes place without the construction of low-cost housing by governments or private developers, the vast majority of urban populations is forced to live in housing built without authorization. It is not surprising that the most effective supply of housing takes place outside the law. In many cities planned by British colonial authorities, especially in former settler regions, the urban system is still residentially segregated, formerly along racial lines and now along class lines, and by rigid zoning of land use activities. As a result, the search for shelter by the poor often pushes them onto the periphery where infrastructure and amenities are in short supply. In such areas, inadequate provision of electricity, water, and transport reduces the exploitation of economic options in both services and small scale manufacturing activities. The possibilities for spatial expansion are often limited because of adjacent developments on peri-urban land, such as commercial farms and airports. The result is overcrowding in existing informal settlements whose population growth is accommodated on subdivided plots in a proliferation of rented rooms (Potts and Mutambirwa 1991). Sometimes customary tenure co-exists with a liberalized land market, for instance in peri-urban Kampala, Accra, Gaborone, Maseru and Bamako (Payne 1997; van Westen 1995; Vaa 2000; Mbiba 2001).

Where foreign investment has taken place it is often concentrated in commerce and finance rather than in manufacturing. Across much of southern Africa, for example, South African firms are exploiting the institutional and financial weaknesses of countries in the region, establishing commercial outlets in cities from Lesotho to Mozambique. In the wake of such investments, a variety of economic activities are becoming restructured with new patterns of spatial segregation as a result. A highly visible consequence is the displacement of small scale trading and service activities from the centre of the city to areas on the periphery to yield space, for example, to shopping malls and upscale boutiques. Violent confrontations between urban authorities and street vendors over the commercial use of public space are recurrent events in many African cities. Urban authorities frequently seek to remove street vendors, dismissing them as untidy, disruptive of established business, and allege that they are illegal immigrants if not criminals. Yet the truce on the street is often of short duration because street vendors need to make a living.

Demographic Implications

If crowding in informal housing areas is one visible effect of the processes described above, a youth bulge in the urban demographic pyramid is another. Almost everywhere in Africa, children and young people are comprising a growing proportion of the overall urban population. At the same time, declining life expectancy and employment prospects are challenging age and gender ideals that used to guide the social organization of households. This is manifesting itself in increasing household dependency rates, more tenancy relations, depressed marriage rates, increasing experiences of unmarried motherhood, and male frustration and violence (Ashforth 1999). In some African urban settings dependency rates are already overstretched, particularly when affected by HIV/AIDS, fuelling the growth of a population of orphans and propelling young people into the streets.

This transformed urban space gives young women and men from poor economic backgrounds fewer economic options in the city centre than those their parents' generation enjoyed. The reorientation toward the periphery that results from these transformations is also evident in cultural space and in how, where, and with whom young people spend their time away from home: on streets, in markets, barber shops and hair saloons, video parlours, drinking places, revivalist churches, and other forms of associational life. We do not have much sub-stantive knowledge about these interactions although there is no shortage of assertions about the proliferation of new forms of social ties, networks, and sol-idarities (e.g., Simone 1998). Without a doubt, given the changing processes at work in the informal economy, new ways of doing things are emerging, turning conventional social organizational practices on their head or reinventing them in new disguises of generation, gender, and globalization.

Youth and space are part of an urban research agenda that so far seems to have stimulated scholarship in areas that are obviously visible in public space, namely violence, media use, sports and fashion (De Boek and Honwana 2000). Youth preoccupations with media representations from the West in music, film, sport, and fashion, among other things, show an extent of globalization that perhaps was hidden by the command economy of the one-party states. "Free market" policy and the removal of trade barriers are revealing how urban resi-dents connect their local experiences of "being in the world" (Friedman 1994:12–16) with their desires for going elsewhere.

The recent extensive growth of informalization across urban Africa demon-strates new modalities in the diversification and supply of goods and services and the expanded regional and global scope of a previous era's suitcase trade. Interregional diasporas within the continent have a long history and now in-clude South Africa as a desirable migration location for Africans from countries that were never part of the apartheid era's migrant labour system, for example Senegal and Nigeria (McDonald et al. 1999). European and American cities are among the destinations to which increasing numbers of Africans migrate in or-der to enhance family livelihoods at home (MacGaffey and Bazenguissa-Ganga 2000; Stoller 2002). Interregional and transnational migration coupled with global influences that African urban residents contend with in everyday life pro-vides rich evidence of the interaction of urban residents who are citizens of the world as well of their own locality.

AID AGENCIES AND CITIES

In the second half of the twentieth century, Africa's newly independent govern-ments did not approach urban growth as a development issue but rather as a problem to be contained. International and bilateral donors have until recently concerned themselves only to a limited degree with urban processes. In develop-ment economics, it is only recently that the importance of cities for economic development has been recognized. In fact, multilateral and bilateral agencies only slowly formulated strategies for urban development. Unauthorized settle-ments were either ignored or demolished, and informal income generation was considered to be a passing phenomenon, linked to high rural-urban migration. Habitat I, the United Nations Conference on Human Settlements held in Vancou-ver in 1976, indicated that governments' attitudes towards slum and squatter set-tlements were beginning to change. The overwhelming majority of governments participating in the conference officially recognized the necessity of improving uncontrolled settlements and integrating their inhabitants into the national development process.

Enablement

In the following decade, the United Nations agency principally concerned with the urban sector, the United Nations Centre for Human Settlements (UNCHS/ Habitat), formulated a new role for governments in housing development and service provision in cities. Its *Global Strategy for Shelter to the Year 2000* from 1988, later adopted by the UN General Assembly, stated that it was not the task of governments to construct shelter and provide services but to be facilitators or "enablers". The Strategy recommended that governments concentrate on creating incentives for householders, NGOs and the private sector to provide shelter and services. In subsequent publications, "enablement" has been developed further to mean the provision of legislative, institutional and financial frameworks to effectively develop the urban housing sector through initiative and entrepreneurship in markets, communities and in households (Pugh 1995:358).

The second United Nations Conference on Human Settlements (Habitat II) held in Istanbul in 1996 had two principal themes: "Adequate shelter for all" and "Sustainable human settlement development in an urbanizing world". Again, "enablement" was a pivotal concept. The participating governments committed themselves "to the strategy of enabling all key actors in the public, private and community sectors to play an effective role—at national, state/provincial metropolitan and local levels—in human settlement and shelter development" (UNCHS 1996, Chapter III, para. 44). In a number of other paragraphs that bear directly on improvement of extra-legal shelter, the Habitat Agenda advocates among other things transparency, decentralization, strong local government, citizen participation and empowerment, access to credit, regularization of self-built housing, and revision of institutional and legal frameworks. The Habitat II Agenda not only reflects the anti-statist and neo-liberal political economy that became fashionable during the 1990s, but also the alternative housing strategy that has become orthodoxy in international thinking. The role of governments is not to build houses, but to provide inexpensive land, basic services and security of tenure. It remains to be seen if these policies will expand the access of the urban poor to adequate shelter and improved shelter security. Although a number of governments at Habitat I in Vancouver had already endorsed the recommended policies of assisted self-help and upgrading, they continued to pursue their established policies of demolishing settlements that they deemed substandard and building subsidized apartments for the not-so-poor.

Multilateral Agencies and the World Bank

In 1991, the World Bank and the UNDP produced new strategy papers for urban development. The new UNDP urban agenda had four points: poverty alleviation; infrastructure and services provision for the poor; improvement of the environment; and promotion of the private sector and NGOs (UNDP 1991).

While stressing the need for poverty alleviation and improvement of the environment, the World Bank also advocated improving over-all urban productivity and called for a reassessment of the linkages between the urban economy and macroeconomic performance (World Bank 1991). Both the UNDP and World Bank strategy formulations stress how past programme and project approaches rarely had city wide impacts and largely bypassed the poorest. This observation applies to the financing of site-and-services and upgrading of unauthorized settlements as well as to the building of urban infrastructure more generally. These programmes divided cities into specific projects, aimed at improving individual neighbourhoods without affecting the prevailing urban policies and institutional framework (Cohen 2001). In 2000, the World Bank formulated a new urban strategy entitled *Cities in Transition* (World Bank 2000b), with the following chief goals: assisting the formulation of national urban strategies, facilitating city development strategies, scaling up programmes to provide services to the poor and assisting capacity building (Kamete et al. 2001:74).

In 2001, the United Nations held a special session in New York, dubbed Istanbul + 5, to assess achievements on the Habitat Agenda and the Plan of Action five years after Habitat II. The reports to the conference noted some progress, but less than expected. Habitat, or the UN Centre for Human Settlements was in late 2002 given programme status, on a par with the UN Environment Programme, as the principal advocacy agency within the UN system for cities and human settlements with a special focus on urban poverty (Tostensen 2002:10). It has been renamed UN-HABITAT.

Urban employment creation and production have been promoted by the International Labour Organization (ILO) through its World Employment Programme. In a number of cities in Africa and elsewhere, the programme has provided assistance with management skills, improved technologies, tools and equipment, marketing and product design for micro-enterprises (Maldonado et al. 1988). In 1990, the ILO also formulated a more comprehensive programme aimed at enabling countries to create appropriate policy and institutional environment to favour growth of output and employment in the informal sector (ILO 1990). The organization also recognized what it has termed 'the dilemma of the informal sector': should the informal sector be promoted as a provider of employment and incomes or should regulation and social protection be extended to it, thereby possibly reducing its capacity to provide jobs and incomes?

> ... there can be no question of the ILO helping to 'promote' or 'develop' an informal sector as a convenient, low-cost way of creating employment unless there is at the same time an equal determination to eliminate progressively the worst aspects of exploitation and inhuman working conditions in the sector. (ILO 1991:58)

Legality and extra-legality of land use, shelter production and work in African cities are not straightforward matters. Legal systems are rarely single and unitary with courts that are positioned to be the sole judges of what is legal and what is illegal. But ignoring the complexities of law, including informal law, is no solution. Already in the early 1990s, an international expert on legal land questions, Patrick McAuslan of UNCHS, proposed that urban reforms should start with a thorough survey of the legal situation. He argued that, without such a survey "it is not possible to know whether the problem is too much law, too little law, out-of-date law, ignorance of law, law at variance with practice, customs and beliefs, a reasonable law unreasonably administered, law needing wholesale reform, or law needing minor adjustments" (McAuslan 1993:248). In our view, such surveys should not be confined to urban land, property and use of space, but include legal matters pertaining to the informal economy, such as commercial law, tax law, labour relations and environmental legislation.

Bilateral Agencies and Non Governmental Organizations

Very few bilateral agencies have formulated policies to assist urban development. Orthodox thinking until recently was that development had to start with agriculture and that the growth of cities in developing countries was somehow pathological. Aid to urban development was usually not called that, but aid to transport, housing or infrastructure. More recently, several agencies, notably SIDA (Sweden), SNV (Netherlands), CIDA (Canada) and DFID (United Kingdom) have formulated urban development strategies, based on a recognition that urbanization not only is unstoppable and irreversible but that cities are engines of economic growth. Reducing urban poverty, improving the urban environment, promoting urban economic growth and improved urban governance are singled out as principal objectives by these agencies (Kamete et al. 2001:56–71).

Bilateral aid agencies, regional development banks and non-governmental agencies have for the last couple of decades given support to informal economic activities in cities, though not necessarily under that label. Strategy and programme documents refer to credit schemes, support to micro-enterprises, the importance of home based enterprises (HBE) and small and medium enterprises (SMEs, sometimes MSEs) in creating employment and promoting economic growth with increasing frequency. But micro-enterprises encompass a range of activities that draw on widely diverse means of access and may require different types of resources and inputs. Unless the economic and social nature of such activities is accounted for in more specific terms, development assistance risks being restrictive, thus jeopardizing the very goals of expanding employment and income generation that it seeks to promote (Hansen 2001). In short, there are serious discrepancies between aid agencies' rhetoric about the importance of micro-enterprises and credit schemes and the actual support devoted to such programmes.

INFORMALITY, URBAN CHANGE AND DEVELOPMENT

Viewing it as a democratic alternative to state-led economic development, neo-liberal perspectives on the informal economy in African and other Third World cities emphasize its potential for employment creation and growth (de Soto 1989). This view has been espoused by both the World Bank and the ILO. In their advocacy for support to what they until recently persistently labelled the informal sector, efforts to disengage the state from the economy are a recurrent theme. This celebratory view underplays the heterogeneity and exploitative work conditions and insecurity that characterize many informal economic activities. An alternative perspective can be found in a structuralist 'informalization' approach, that regards the expansion of informal activity as part of the response of the formal economy and the state to economic crisis (Meagher 1995).

Regardless of perspective, it is often asserted that there is a wealth of knowledge regarding informal economic activities. To be sure, over the last 25 years, considerable research has been done, both by the ILO and other agencies, and by independent researchers. Most of these studies consist of small scale surveys, and even more comprehensive studies do not offer detailed information about the size of urban informal economies, their composition, organization, competitiveness and links to formal economies.

Some other important knowledge gaps have also been identified. Discussing research priorities in African urban studies. Mohamed Halfani (1997:32) has pointed to the lack of serious studies on the productive capacity and competitiveness of African cities, in relation to the twin processes of marginalization and globalization. Among other things, he notes how the current understanding of poverty and inequality is rather sketchy. While some statistical information is available, it is highly aggregated, often out of date, and pertaining to only a handful of cities. Studies of the urban informal economy abound with generalizations. Such generalizations tend to be drawn from scattered case studies that make use of different types of observations and hence are rarely comparable.

The informal production of shelter and typical features of living conditions in unauthorized settlements are probably better documented than the informal economies of African cities. The burdens that informality places on residents of un-serviced settlements in terms of crowding, shelter cost and high levels of morbidity and mortality have been documented again and again. There is also a growing body of scholarship on the significance of illegality or extra-legality in providing access to land and shelter and how such practices are not exclusively associated with the urban poor (McAuslan 1993; Fernandes and Varley 1998; Rakodi 1997). The research record is less impressive when it comes to assessing the importance of the informal economy for the overall functioning of cities.

Urban Crisis and Urban Development

There is a growing awareness that African cities are in crisis. Access to employment, shelter and services is precarious for most urban residents. The failure of existing systems of governance to cope with the challenges of rapid urban growth is also well documented. The inherited legal, institutional and financial arrangements for managing urban development have proven their inadequacy (Rakodi 1997:568). Over the last decade, multilateral and bilateral aid agencies have begun to develop insights and approaches that view the cities more holistically than the project-by-project approach to urban development of the 1970s and 80s. But given the immensity of the need for institutional reforms and investment, widespread ambivalence about urbanization and the drying up of development aid, it is unlikely that foreign technical and financial assistance will play any major role in the future development of Africa's cities. The task rests squarely with city dwellers and their governments and leaders, who are facing the challenge to find ways of incorporating the informal city into city urban management and governance.

The Need for Knowledge

To address the role of research in urban development, an ambitious comparative project was launched in the early 1990s at the University of Toronto, supported by the Ford Foundation and later the World Bank. Regional teams, commissioned papers and meetings presented important research on the cities of the developing world (of particular relevance for Africa are Stren 1994; Stren and Kjellberg Bell 1995; McCarney 1996; Swilling 1997). The Nigerian geographer Akin Mabogunje made interesting observations regarding the role of research based knowledge in urban development in Africa. According to Mabogunje, the relationship between researchers and policy-makers is far from cordial or close in most African countries. Many decisions affecting urban development and day-to-day urban management are made without appropriate information that researchers might have provided if policy-makers had enlisted their cooperation. This lack of cooperation means that there are no well articulated national urban policies to facilitate the identification of national priorities in urban development. Most African governments approach the problems of the city in a piecemeal and project-oriented way (Mabogunje 1994:38). Regardless of whether urban development projects are funded by local governments or assisted from abroad, their lack of success or outright failure is often due to their lack of prior consideration of the prevailing legal and institutional frameworks.

We argue that empirically based, substantive research is necessary in order to understand ongoing processes of change in African cities and to promote urban development. The deteriorating living conditions facing most of Africa's urban residents and the often hostile encounters between the formal and the informal city demonstrate that African cities are in critical need of improved urban management and governance systems. Yet urban space, as we noted at the outset, is not only a product of an overall regulatory system but also constitutes a dynamic field of interaction for economic, social and political processes. Contextualized research has an important contribution to make in order to cast light on local complexities and is a necessary basis for understanding them as well. This book's focus on the informal city as comprised of extra-legal housing and unregistered economic activities provides a step in that direction. Bringing together two distinct bodies of scholarship, on informal housing and the informal economy, the contributors to this book cast unusual light on the nature of Africa's urban transformations and by doing so, they open up a fresh research agenda.

Looking back at research from the 1970s, Keith Hart recently reminded us that the informal economy "was nothing less than the self-organized energies of people, biding their time to escape from the strictures of state rule" (2001:157). Along with the decline of state economic power, widespread informalization of the world economy has taken place in recent years as evidenced in the international trade in drugs, diamonds, armaments, and finance, among others. Hart describes the informal economy as being "the entire economy" in countries like the Democratic Republic of the Congo and Jamaica (2001:154–55). He goes on to suggest that when so much of the economy is "informal", we are "entitled to ask whether the term has outgrown its usefulness" (2001:155). We suggest that the idea of an informal economy remains constructive by revealing how livelihoods are made when from a reading of standard statistical indicators there are very few resources with which to make a living. Because Africa's future will be increasingly urban and driven to a great extent by the kind of processes that are at the core of this book, we advocate a continuous reconsideration of Africa's urban informal economies and the dynamics they are fuelled by in the context of unfolding shifts in the world economy.

References

Aldrich, B.C., and R.S. Sandhu (eds), 1995, *Housing the Urban Poor*. London: Zed Books.

Amis, Philip, 1996, "Long-run trends in Nairobi's informal housing market", *Third World Planning Review* 18:3, pp. 271–85.

Amis, Philip and Peter Lloyd (eds), 1990, *Housing Africa's Urban Poor*. Manchester: Manchester University Press.

Andreasen, Jorgen, 1989, "The poor don't squat: The case of Thika, Kenya", *Environment and Urbanization*, Vol. 1, No. 2, October, pp. 16–26.

Antoine, Philippe, Alain Dubresson and Anni Manou-Savina, 1987, *Abidjan "coté-cours"*. Paris: Karthala.

Ashforth, Adam, 1999, "Weighing Manhood in Soweto", *CODESRIA Bulletin* 3 and 4, pp. 51–58.

Balala, Najib, 2001, "Challenges of Local Governance: The Experiences of One Mayor" in Freire, Mila and Richard Stren (eds), *The Challenge of Urban Government: Policies and Practices*. Washington DC: The World Bank Foundation.

Baker, Jonathan and Poul Ove Pedersen (eds), 1992, *The Rural-Urban Interface in Africa*. Seminar Proceedings No 27. Uppsala: The Scandinavian Institute of African Studies.

Balandier, George, 1985, *Sociologie des Brazzavilles Noires*. Paris: Presses de la fondation nationale des sciences politiques.

Chellah, Hilda A., 2001, *The Gender Dimension of Property Rights and House Accommodation of Ndola City Council on the Copperbelt, Zambia*. MA dissertation in Gender Studies, University of Zambia.

Castells, Manuel and Alejandro Portes, 1989, "World Underneath: The Origins, Dynamics and Effects of the Informal Economy" in Portes et al. 1989, pp. 11–40.

Cohen, Michael, 2001, "Urban assistance and the material world. Learning by doing at the World Bank", *Environment and Urbanization*, Vol. 13, No. 1, pp. 37–60.

Clark, Gracia, 1994, *Onions Are My Husband: Survival and Accumulation by West African Market Women*. Chicago: University of Chicago Press.

Dauda, Carol L., 2001, "Preparing the Grounds for a New Local Politics: The Case of Women in Two African Municipalities", *Canadian Journal of African Studies* 32(2), pp. 246–81.

De Boek, Filip and Alcinda Honwana (eds), 2000, "Enfants, Jeunes et Politique", *Politique Africaine* 80, pp. 5–11.

Durand-Lasserve, Alain, 1998, "Law and Urban Change in Developing Countries: Trends and Issues" in Fernandes and Varley, 1998, pp. 233–87.

Environment and Urbanization, 1991, Vol. 3, No. 2, (Special Issue on Women in Environment and Urbanization: Strategies for Action and the Potential for Change).

Friedman, Jonathan, 1994, *Cultural Identity and Global Process*. Thousand Oaks: Sage Publications.

Fernandes, Edésio and Ann Varley (eds), 1998, *Illegal Cities: Law and urban change in developing countries*, pp. 18–52. London and New York: Zed Books Ltd.

Geschiere, Peter and Francis Nyamnjoh, 2001, "Capitalism and Autochtony: The Seesaw of Mobility and Belonging" in Comaroff, Jean and John L. Comaroff (eds), *Millennial Capitalism and the Culture of Neoliberalism*, pp. 160–90. Durham: Duke University Press.

Gilbert, Alan and Josef Gugler, 1992, *Cities, Poverty and Development*. Second Edition. Oxford: Oxford University Press.

Gombay, Christine, 1994, "Eating Cities: Urban Management and Markets in Kampala", *Cities* 11(2), pp. 86–94.

Guyer, Jane I., 1995, "Introduction: The Currency Interface and Its Dynamics" in Guyer, Jane I. (ed.), *Money Matters: Instability, Values and Social Payments in the Modern History of West African Communities*, pp. 1–33. Portsmouth NH and London: Heinemann and James Currey.

Guyer, Jane I., LaRay Denzer and Adigun Agbaje (eds), 2002, *Money Struggles and City Life: Devaluation in Ibadan and other Urban Centers in Southern Nigeria, 1986–1996*. Portsmouth NH: Heinemann.

Halfani, Mohamed, 1997, "The Challenge of Urban Governance in Africa. Institutional Change and Knowledge Gaps" in Swilling 1997, pp. 13–34.

—, 1996, "The Challenge of Urban Governance in East Africa: Responding to an Unrelenting Crisis" in McCarney 1996, pp. 183–203.

Hansen, Karen Tranberg, 2001, "Informal Sector", *International Encyclopedia of the Social and Behavioural Sciences*, pp. 7450–53. Amsterdam: Elsvier.

— 1997, *Keeping House in Lusaka*. New York: Columbia University Press.

Harris, Nigel (ed.), 1992, *Cities in the 1990s*. London: UCL Press Ltd.

Hart, Keith, and His Memory Bank, 2001, *Money in an Unequal World*. New York: Texere.

—, 1992, "Market and State after the Cold War: The Informal Economy Reconsidered" in Dilley, Roy (ed.), *Contesting Markets: Analyses of Ideology, Discourse and Practice*, pp. 214–27. Edinburgh: Edinburgh University Press.

—, 1973, "Informal Income Opportunities and Urban Employment in Ghana", *Journal of Modern African Studies* 11:1, pp. 61–89.

International Labour Office (ILO), 2002, *Decent work and the informal economy*. International Labour Conference, 90th session, 2002. Report IV. Geneva: ILO.

—, 1991, *The dilemma of the informal sector*. Report of the Director General, International Labour Conference, 78th Session.Geneva: ILO.

—, 1990, *Informal sector and urban employment*. Geneva: World Employment Programme, Technology and Employment Branch, ILO.

—, 1972, *Employment, incomes and equality: A strategy for increasing productive employment in Kenya*. Geneva: ILO.

Kamete, Amin Y., Arne Tostensen and Inge Tvedten, 2001, *From Global Village to Urban Globe. Urbanization and Poverty in Africa: Implications for Norwegian Aid Policy*. Report 2001:2. Bergen: Chr. Michelsen Institute.

King, Kenneth, 1996, *Jua Kali Kenya: Change and Development in an Informal Economy 1970–95*. London: James Currey.

Mabogunje, Akin L., 1994, "Overview of Research Priorities in Africa" in Stren, 1994, pp. 21–45.

MacGaffey, Janet and Remy Bazenguissa-Ganga, 2000, *Congo-Paris: Transnational Traders on the Margins of the Law*. Bloomington: Indiana University Press.

Manji, Ambreena, 2001, "Land Reform in the Shadow of the State: The Implementation of New Land Laws in Sub-Saharan Africa", *Third World Quarterly* 22(3), pp. 327–42.

Maldonado, Carlos et al., 1988, *Petits producteurs urbains d'Afrique francophone—Analyse et politiques d'appui*. Geneva: ILO.

Martin, Phyllis, 1995, *Leisure and Society in Colonial Brazzaville*. Cambridge: Cambridge University Press.

Mbiba, Beacon, 2001, *Review of Urban and Peri-Urban Transformations and Livelihoods in East and Southern Africa*. Peri-NET Working Paper 1–6. London: Peri-Urban Research Network, South Bank University.

McAuslan, Patrick, 1993, "The role of law in urban planning" in Devas, Nick and Carole Rakodi (eds), *Managing Fast Growing Cities*. Essex and New York: Longman and John Wiley and Sons.

McCarney, Patricia L., 1996, "Considerations on the Notion of 'Governance'—New Directions for Cities in the Developing World" in McCarney, 1996, pp. 3–20.

— (ed.), 1996, *Cities and Governance: New Directions in Latin America, Asia and Africa*. Toronto: Centre for Urban and Community Studies, University of Toronto.

McDonald, David A., Lephophotho Mashike and Celia Golden, 1999, *The Lives and Times of African Migrants and Immigrants in Post-Apartheid South Africa*. Migration Policy Series No. 13. Cape Town: Southern African Migration Project.

Meagher, Kate, 1995, "Crisis, Informalization and the Urban Informal Sector in Sub-Saharan Africa", *Development and Change*, Vol. 26, pp. 259–83.

Milbert, Isabelle with Vanessa Peat, 1999, *What Future for Urban Co-operation? Assessment of post Habitat II Strategies*. Bern: Swiss Agency for Development and Co-operation.

Moser, Caroline, 1987, "Women, human settlements and housing: A conceptual framework for analysis and policy-making" in Moser and Peake 1987, pp. 12–32.

Moser, Caroline and Linda Peake (eds), 1987, *Women, Human Settlements and Housing*. London: Tavistock Publications.

Mulenga, Chileshe L., 2001, *Peri-Urban Transformations and Livelihoods in the Context of Globalization in Lusaka, Zambia*. Peri-Urban Research Network, Working Paper 3. London: Faculty of the Built Environment, South Bank University.

Payne, Geoffrey, 1997, *Urban Land Tenure and Property Rights in Developing Countries. A Review*. London: IT Publications/ODA.

Poku, Nana K., 2001, "Africa's AIDS Crisis in Context: 'How the Poor Are Dying'", *Third World Quarterly* 22(2), pp. 191–204.

Portes, Alejandro, Manuel Castells and Lauren A. Benton, 1989, *The Informal Economy*. Baltimore and London: The Johns Hopkins University Press.

Potts, Deborah with C.C. Mutambirwa, 1991, "High-Density Housing in Harare: Commodification and Overcrowding", *Third World Planning Review* 13(1), pp. 1–55.

Pugh, Cedric, 1995, "The Role of the World Bank in Housing" in Aldrich and Sandhu 1995, pp. 34–92.

Rakodi, Carole (ed.), 1997, *The Urban Challenge in Africa: Growth and Management of Its Large Cities*. Tokyo: United Nations University Press.

Robertson, Claire C., 1997, *Trouble Showed the Way: Women, Men, and Trade in the Nairobi Area, 1890–1990*. Bloomington: Indiana University Press.

Schlyter, Ann, 2002, "Privatization of housing and the exclusion of women" in Matseliso Mapetla and Ann Schlyter (eds), *Gender and Housing in Southern Africa: Emerging Issues*. Roma: Institute for Southern African Studies, University of Lesotho.

—, 1991, *Twenty Years of Development in George, Zambia*. Stockholm: Swedish Council for Building Research.

Sethuraman, S.W. (ed.), 1981, *The Urban Informal Sector in Developing Countries*. Geneva: ILO.

Simone, AbdouMaliq, 1998, *Urban Processes and Change in Africa*. CODESRIA Working Papers 3/97.

Soto, Hernando de, 1989, *The Other Path: The invisible revolution in the Third World*. New York: Harper and Row.

Stoller, Paul, 2002, *Money Has No Smell: The Africanization of New York City*. Chicago: University of Chicago Press.

Stren, Richard (ed.), 1994, *Africa. Urban Research in the Developing World, Vol. 2*. Toronto: Centre of Urban and Community Studies, University of Toronto.

Stren, Richard and Mohamed Halfani, 2001, "The Cities of Sub-Saharan Africa: From Dependency to Marginality" in Paddison, Ronan (ed.), *Handbook of Urban Studies*, pp. 466–85. Thousand Oaks: Sage Publications.

Stren, Richard and Judith Kjellberg Bell (eds), 1995, *Perspectives on the City Urban Research in the Developing World, Vol. 4*. Toronto: Centre of Urban and Community Studies, University of Toronto.

Swilling, Mark (ed.), 1997, *Governing Africa's Cities*. Johannesburg: Witwatersrand University Press.

Tostensen, Arne, 2002, *Urban Dimensions of Donors' Poverty-Reduction Strategies*. Working Paper R 2002:5. Bergen: Chr. Michelsen Institute.

Tostensen, Arne, Inge Tvedten and Mariken Vaa (eds), 2001, *Associational Life in African Cities: Popular Responses to the Urban Crises*. Uppsala: Nordiska Afrikainstitutet.

Tripp, Aili, 1997, *Changing the Rules: The Politics of Liberalization and the Urban Informal Economy in Tanzania*. Berkeley: University of California Press.

UNCHS, 2001, *Cities in a Globalizing World*. London and Sterling: UNCHS (Habitat) and Earthscan.

—, 1996, *An Urbanising World: Global Report on Human Settlements 1996*. Oxford: Oxford University Press.

—, 1995, *Shelter Provision and Employment Generation*. Nairobi and Geneva: UNCHS and ILO.

—, 1993, *Support Measures to Promote Rental Housing for Low-Income Countries*. Nairobi.

UNDP, 1991, *Cities, People and Poverty: Urban Development Cooperation for the 1990s*. UNDP Strategy Paper 1991. New York: UNDP.

Vaa, Mariken, 2000, "Housing policy after political transition: The case of Bamako", *Environment and Urbanization*, Vol. 12, April 2000, pp. 27–34.

—, 1995, "Issues and Policies in the Development of Unauthorized Settlements", *Norsk Geografisk Tidsskrift*, Vol. 49 (4), pp. 187–95.

Van Onselen, Charles, 1982, *Studies in the Social and Economic History of the Witwatersrand 1886–1914. Volume 2, New Nineveh*. London: Longman.

Van Westen, A.C.M., 1995, "Unsettled low-income housing and mobility in Bamako, Mali", *Nederlandse Geografische Studies* 187. Universiteit Utrecht.

World Bank, 2000a, *Entering the 21st Century: World Development Report 1999/2000*. Oxford: Oxford University Press: The World Bank.

—, 2000b, *Cities in Transition: World Bank and Local Government Strategy*. Washington DC: The World Bank.

—, 1991, *Urban Policy and Economic Development*. Washington DC: The World Bank.

Zeleza, Paul T., 1999, "The Spatial Economy of Structural Adjustment in African Cities" in Zeleza, Paul T. and Ezekiel Kalipeni (eds), *Sacred Spaces and Public Quarrels: African Cultural and Economic Landscapes*, pp. 43–72. Trenton: Africa World Press, Inc.

SECTION I
LOCALITY, PLACE, AND SPACE

The rapid growth of African cities is accompanied by confrontations over the use of urban space. Subdivisions of land, squatting, construction, street vending and productive activities take place in defiance of existing legal regulations and governments' attempts at enforcing them. Local and state authorities have responded in various ways to the massive processes of informalization that have taken place, from laissez-faire and co-optation to coercion. Ambitious initiatives for urban economic and social development may founder when faced with economic realities and urban civil society. Contestations over access to and use of space occur not only between city residents and representatives of law and order. Sometimes, different segments of the urban population make claims to the same locality, and local authorities become observers or mediators rather than effective controllers.

The chapters in this section illustrate various types of informal appropriation of space, of land acquisition and use to which local and state authorities respond in ways that reflect not only their perception of how the informal city should be harnessed and governed, but also their limited capacity to do so.

Gabriel Tati reports on a longitudinal study of migrant West African fishermen who have successfully installed themselves just outside the city of Pointe-Noire on the coast of Congo-Brazzaville. Their economic success is based on their occupational skills and appropriation of coastal space for productive and housing purposes. The site originally chosen was advantageous both because of its proximity to the fishing grounds and to the city market. Some public facilities also existed, such as water and access roads. From the start, this appropriation was not negotiated with relevant authorities or local landowners. An informal settlement of successful fishermen simply emerged side by side with an already existing settlement of migrants from the Congolese countryside, some of whom had obtained land from a local family claiming to be customary landowners. However, this use of the coastal site soon became contested. In 1980, the Congolese government authorized the installation of a multinational oil company on the beach, for the development of an industrial site in support of oceanic oil extraction. This required a large part of the beach land, in conflict with the spatial requirement of the growing settlement and the economic activities based there. The local authority attempted to evict the fishermen and other residents of the settlement and relocate them to a section of the beach far from the city. However, this was vigorously opposed by the residents, who joined together in a committee that successfully negotiated relocation to a site close to the one they were evicted from. The local authority soon found itself cast in the role of mediator between the residents' committee and the oil company.

Authorization to settle on the new site has been granted on a temporary basis, but the allocation of a site for resettlement was regarded by the fishermen as a legitimization of their occupation of land. Economic success in fisheries and fish processing have resulted in investments in permanent housing, constructed without occupancy or construction permits. The actors involved no longer perceive this as inviting eviction, but as a symbolic expression of possession of space. Ambiguities in mandate among local authorities are skilfully navigated by the fishermen's community. They have avoided direct confrontation with the oil company over the threat its presence poses to fisheries, while successfully demonstrating their contribution to the city economy both through the fish production and processing and through offering employment opportunities for local youth. They also participate in local social and political manifestations. The result is a climate of tolerance towards migrant fishermen that is rare in West Africa.

Knut Nustad's chapter takes us to what has been one of the most violently contested urban areas in South Africa. It is called Cato Manor, situated within five miles of the centre of Durban. After the apartheid regime had evicted its 120,000 occupants in the late 1950s and early 1960s, Cato Manor was a wasteland for almost thirty years. Towards the end of the 1980s, people began moving into the area and erecting shacks there. Cato Crest, the site of Nustad's study, is a squatter settlement within Cato Manor. During a few months in 1993, its population grew from a few hundred people to over twenty thousand as a result of pre-election violence in KwaZulu/Natal, the province where Durban is located.

In the early period of resettlement of Cato Manor, local community organizations fought for recognition and the right to stay. Thus the first civic organizations were set up by squatters with a long history of political activism and many were African National Congress (ANC) members. The population continued to grow and it soon became obvious that it would not be possible for the local authorities to remove them forcibly. In 1992, an umbrella organization (CMDA) was established, which was to guide the development of the whole of Cato Manor. It comprised local branches of political parties, local civics, squatter committees, government bodies and NGOs. In post-apartheid South Africa, a top-down approach to development was impossible. The association chose a participatory approach, working with community structures. Inclusiveness and participation were central concepts.

Participatory development of settlements presupposes collaboration with local representative bodies. In Cato Crest, however, the local leadership from early on established factions that fought each other for control of positions as community representatives, which meant access to outside resources. Converting a position in a community organization to material gains and power took a variety of forms, such as allocation of jobs to dependants and followers, appropriation of money and equipment or trading registration numbers which were issued to guarantee access to plots. Local factionalism culminated in a "taxi war", when a group of ex-combatants backed by a faction of the local leadership attempted to take over the minibus taxi industry linking Cato Crest to central Durban.

In Nustad's analysis, informal activities can only be understood in relation to a conception of the formal. The form imposed on Cato Crest for development of the settlement only captured a part of the dynamics of social life in Cato Crest, and the local leadership was able to deflect outside resources to its own advantage.

Karen Tranberg Hansen's chapter analyses the contests over public places in Lusaka, Zambia, between street vendors and the authorities as a meeting between "free market" policies and poverty-fuelled informalization. During the 1990s street vendors had invaded most public places in central Lusaka. Retrenchment both in the private and the public sector made more and more people dependent on informal activities, particularly retail trade. Street vending had been illegal from the colonial period, but continued and grew in contravention of existing regulations. Attempts by the local authority to remove it met with little success.

For a few years after the regime change and shift to economic liberalization in 1991, informal traders enjoyed political protection from the President, and street trading flourished as never before. At the same time, the government opened the economy to foreign investors and accepted external funding for improving urban infrastructure, including upgrading of urban markets. A new city market opened in 1997 but remained nearly empty for several years. Traders claimed the fees were too high and the congestion in the streets continued.

In early 1999, the City Council with the help of police and paramilitary personnel razed temporary stalls and chased thousands of vendors off the streets. This happened in all urban centres throughout the country. Vendors were told to move to designated market sites where the work environment would be healthier and necessary amenities installed. It is uncertain how many complied, but in Lusaka, the vendors did not return to the streets immediately as they had done earlier. They have slowly appeared again, although not in as large numbers as before. Since 2000, they have been facing periodic crackdowns and the daily enforcement of new laws that prohibit both buying and selling outside designated markets.

While attempting to control the environment within which vendors operated, the government has not proposed any consistent or substantive policy to improve the opportunities for the thousands of people involved. Rather, the issue for the government is a Zambian version of "free market" policy to open up the economy for investments. Its implementation required, in fact, not freedom but institutional control.

CHAPTER 2

Sharing Public Space in Pointe-Noire, Congo-Brazzaville: Immigrant Fishermen and a Multinational Oil Company

Gabriel Tati

Over the past two decades, migrant fishermen from West Africa, particularly from Benin, Togo and Ghana, have been remarkably successful in artisanal fisheries off the Congolese coast. Their economic success has been accompanied by an appropriation of public space for both economic and housing purposes. This chapter highlights how the development of fishing enterprises by African migrants to the coastal area of the city of Pointe-Noire (Congo-Brazzaville) has resulted in informal space appropriation. It deals first with the ways in which immigrant fishermen together with Congolese co-residents negotiated the occupancy of a coastal site they had so far shared with a multinational company. Thereafter the study identifies the changing relations that have emerged between fishermen operating in the informal sector and the multinational company operating in the formal sector. The mediating role of public authorities is also examined.

Fuelled by the type of chain migration and ethnic networks that have been well documented in other parts of the world (Light et al. 1993), the fishermen community in Pointe-Noire has grown rapidly. A census conducted in 1984 indicated a population of 449 fishermen, while the author counted 1,100 fishermen there in 1998. Since then, the number has probably doubled. Housing and household enterprises within this community have grown so rapidly that their settlement has been recently designated as a new ward of the city, and is served by several buses operating at the city level. However, by its very nature the settlement remains informal despite this recognition. The potential for growth in artisanal fisheries is high, but a major physical constraint to the expansion of the settlement is the industrial site developed on the beach by Elf-Congo, a branch of the French multinational oil company Elf Aquitaine, installed here since the early 1980s. Relations between grassroots communities and multinational companies have been frequently depicted as being marked by conflicts, violence and resistance from the former (see, for example, Guha 1989; Peluso 1992). In the present case, the growth of the fishermen's settlement and the proliferation of canoes in the space close to the company formed the basis of conflictual relations. However, the problems associated with this space sharing have not until now been carefully assessed in research.

With a population approximating 498,832 inhabitants in 1998, Pointe-Noire is ranked as the second largest city of Congo-Brazzaville. Available information indicates that since the early 1980s, the city has experienced the fastest annual population growth rate within the national urban structure, averaging 7.4 per cent (Tati 1993). Forestry, services and fishery industries used to be its most important economic activities, but today, the economy of the city is predominantly oil-based.

ARTISANAL FISHERIES

Previous research on this community has described patterns in the social organization of artisanal fisheries in the coastal area of the city. Jul-Larsen documented the development of the artisanal fishery industry among the first waves of African immigrants who settled there for that purpose (Jul-Larsen 1994). The focus of this work was on the internal organization of fishing canoes as productive units and it did not examine the relationships between the development of informal fishing enterprises and space appropriation for housing the fishermen and their families. Recently, Bøe has documented the economic organization of the immigrant community (Bøe 1999). Taking the household as the unit of analysis, she emphasizes transactions between the fishermen and their wives. The transactions consisted mainly in the fishermen selling fish to their wives at a low price. In turn, the women, after processing and re-selling the fish, re-invested in their husbands' fishing activities.

Like Jul-Larsen, Bøe's work did not consider housing space in the dynamics of fishing activities development. Implicitly, the transactions along the gender lines highlighted by Bøe suggest that the housing unit has indeed an important economic dimension as it also serves as the premises for women's enterprises. The acquisition of housing units and land became important in the fishery economics as a major prerequisite for the family enterprise of fish smoking. From a community perspective, this is where the social logic of space appropriation finds its dominant driving force.

Some recent studies on informal economic activities have stressed the need to understand the spatial logic of migrant entrepreneurship. For example, Kesteloot and Meert (1999) have argued that although there has been a proliferation of studies on informal activities, little research has been conducted into the spatial patterning of these activities. Zeleza and Kalipeni have adopted similar lines to emphasise the place of space and spatiality in the understanding of social phenomena in an African context (Zeleza and Kalipeni 1999). These authors have also claimed that spatiality is key to the formulation of social theory that posits space as a social construct. In the present case study, both physical and socio-economic spaces, fit within the perspective suggested by Zeleza and Kalipeni. They suggest that "all spaces are socially produced and they produce the social, that is, in as much as space is socially constructed the social is spatially constructed too, for all social phenomena, activities, and relations have a spatial form and a relative spatial location" (Zeleza and Kalipeni 1999:2).

Conceptual Framework

In line with this theoretical assertion, the purpose of this chapter is to show how space is transformed at the micro-spatial level. The central question is about the ways public space, in this case coastal space, is being appropriated both domestically and economically by African migrant fishermen, and how this appropriation interacts with the legal system constituted by both the public authorities and the multinational oil company. I am primarily interested in explaining this social process through the daily activities of fishermen, as social actors, as they bring about or submit to, changes in socio-spatial patterns. From a conceptual perspective, these changes entail a process of appropriation of space through which migrant fishermen build, produce, transform, and attach significance to their livelihoods. This appropriation involves illegal dwellings for two reasons. First, a large number of them have been built with permanent materials on public beaches, while the authorization to settle there was granted on a temporary basis. Second, houses have been constructed without occupancy or construction permits.

The appropriation of space through the transformation of the built environment is a dialectic process that largely depends upon the capacity of fishermen to act strategically. Whether it involves conflict or not, this appropriation of space allows fishermen to express their identity and to realize their projects. Through this process, the migrant community takes symbolic possession of space by expressing community values or personal achievements. Culture and the economics of space are underlying dimensions of this appropriation.

On the other hand, establishing a dwelling is a cultural process because it includes shaping a space and giving it a form according to specific tastes and aesthetic criteria, and establishing a social network inside a local community. Indeed, because culture implies communication and processing identities and projects, it is at the heart of the appropriation of space.

Sources of Information

The chapter draws on data from a research project that was initiated in 1995 and is still in progress. The aims of this project are to conduct longitudinal observations documenting the changing dynamics of African migration and its impacts on the development of artisanal fishery in the coastal area of the city of Pointe-Noire. One aspect of the research is concerned with the transfer of know-how in fishing techniques between immigrant fishermen and local fishermen (Tati 1996). Another aspect is the rapid housing development and the changes in livelihoods generated by the proximity of the fishermen's settlement to the multinational company.

Data for the story told here were collected during several field visits from 1994 to 1999. During these visits, observations were made of the fishing activities, housing development and physical expansion of the site. Conversations and semi-structured interviews were also part of the information collected. Informants were either fishermen or civil servants linked through their profes-

sional functions to coastal resources management. I also gathered some historical information regarding the patterns in the resettlement of fishermen after the
development of the industrial site by the oil company. Casual conversations
were held with some fishermen working on the canoes surveyed.

PATTERNS IN THE SETTLEMENT OF FISHERMEN

The population size of the settlement formed by the fishery community, comprising men, women and children, is difficult to establish as no census has been
conducted in this locality. For the same reason, the exact number of fishermen
operating in the coastal fishery is difficult to establish. Statistics on branches of
activity derived from the 1984 national population census provide an estimate
for setting the number of fishermen at 449 individuals. My research in April
1998 provided an estimation of 1,100 fishermen. These figures however under-
estimate the real number of persons participating in the fishing activity as wom-
en and children are not included. Although women are not involved in catching
fish at sea, they are active operators in the chain of fish processing and marketing.

According to some, the first waves of migrant fishermen go back to the end
of the 1960s. Over the past few years, the fishermen community has increased
considerably in size with the continuous arrivals of new migrants in the area.
Chain migration was motivated by income-generative opportunities present in
the artisanal fishery (Chan Kwok Bun and Ong Jin Hui 1995). The economic
success of the first settlers motivated other fishermen to migrate to Pointe-Noire.
In addition to this chain migration, family formation through marriage with
women of the same place of origin gained in force among fishermen, reflecting
a tendency toward a more permanent residence in the area. The family regroup-
ing itself contributed to a natural increase within the fishermen community. The
arrival of new fishermen and family formation became indirectly the accompanying demographic mechanisms of the appropriation of the physical and economic spaces, corroborating the commonly held view that the larger the size of
the community, the stronger the community's voice for any claim.

The coastal land on which fishermen settled had some locational advantages.
Proximity to the main market places in the city was among those advantages.
The site also allowed migrants to benefit from the existence of public facilities
available in the vicinity of the area where they settled, such as roads to the other
major places of the city, an outlet for water supply and two nearby primary
schools. The presence of a grammar school and two military posts were also
among the public services close to the settlement of fishermen. The military
posts including a *gendarmerie* base were viewed as protective institutions, which
was important in the ethnic clashes in Congo in 1977–1978.

Some of these locational advantages probably also motivated a multinational
oil company to choose the site for the development of an important industrial
infrastructure. This development was initiated in 1980, following an authorization granted by the government. This resulted in an attempt at forced eviction
by the local authority, but was opposed by local residents. The nature of this

contestation is recapitulated here as it indicates the genesis of informal occupancy of the area.

A Negotiated Relocation

In the early 1980s, the oil company undertook the construction of a chemical laboratory to conduct analyses needed for the tapping of off-shore oil. In addition, it developed an industrial unit for the construction of metallic jackets used for deep sea oil-platforms. The development of the industrial site required a very large space on the beach. As indicated above, the company wanted to take advantage of the infrastructure that was already there, such as good access roads, electricity and water supply, as well as the proximity of the site to the city harbour. The harbour of Pointe-Noire is regarded as one of the most important harbours along the Atlantic coastal line of Africa. From the point of view of security, the site offered the advantage of being located close to military bases. The proximity to these military bases was undoubtedly a major factor in the company's decision to locate there.

With development about to take place on the site, the local authority decided to evict all the land occupiers from the area. The city authorities ordered the occupiers including the fishermen to resettle on another site designated for them. This site was very far away from the one occupied at that time. Because the beach was public property that fell under the harbour authority, the eviction was planned without financial compensation. Most dwellers in the area did not possess titles to their land, although they were house owners. In the course of the eviction being implemented, some resistance emerged from these dwellers. The oil company had to negotiate with local residents in order to deal with different interest groups among residents in the area. The local authority mediated between the oil company, which required a very large area of the beach for future industrial expansion, and the demands put forward by the various groupings in the settlement. There was particularly strong resistance from non-fishermen living in the area where the eviction was intended.

The non-fishermen were mostly Congolese nationals who had migrated from rural areas and installed themselves with their families on the beach land. A few were refugees from the neighbouring oil-rich enclave of Cabinda. These people settled in the area long before the arrival of fishermen from other West African countries. Other nationals were individuals who, some five years before the eviction, had acquired land for housing from a local family claiming to be the customary landowners. This family had kinship and social ties to other affluent persons in the local authority apparatus, especially with the port authority in charge of managing and approving any transformation related to coastal zone development. These ties were used to support claims for ownership of beach land and subsequently to seek support from authorities in negotiating financial compensation from the oil company. Among the non-fishermen, many ran grocery shops, food stalls and bars, thriving on the steady growth of the settlement. Quite a few house-owners worked in the formal sector, either as civil servants or employees in city-based private enterprises. The fishermen outnumbered the non-fishermen in the area. This is one of the reasons why an alliance with the fishermen community was essential when they made their claims to the local authority.

These non-fishermen vigorously rejected any form of compensatory scheme other than relocation in an area very close to the major centres of economic activity in the city. To make their claims heard, they engaged in collective action with the purpose of achieving a positive outcome in the negotiations, and set up a Beach Committee. As part of their strategy, emphasis was placed on the important role of fisheries in satisfying the food demand of the urban population. More specifically, the group stressed the importance for the fishery activity to have easy access to the main market places of the city. In the negotiation process, it was also argued that difficult access to facilities and road infrastructure might have disruptive effects on the fishermen's families. For all these reasons, these spokesmen for the settlement concentrated their demands on resettling on a site close to the one where the eviction was being implemented.

The migrant fishermen for their part agreed with this view. Relocation in a remote area would lead to increased costs in the transportation of fish to the major market places and a substantial reduction in customers who had been buying fish daily on the beach. The security-related concerns mentioned above also motivated migrant fishermen to reject the relocation on a site proposed by the city authority. A resettlement on a part of the beach on the urban periphery would have meant greater physical vulnerability in situations of unrest. The leaders of the fishermen community expressed this concern in the negotiations. In their view, a relocation in a remote area as proposed by both the city authority and the oil company would badly affect the performance of their fishing activities. The representatives of the collective action backed this concern as it supported their own claim for a site close to the one they had occupied before the industrial development by the oil company. This common ground cemented a coalition between migrant fishermen and the beach committee representatives in the bargaining process over resettlement. In the end, this coalition revealed itself as an effective instrument of negotiation with both the city authorities and the oil company. An important concession was then made. Emphasising the importance of fisheries for the city, the authorities permitted the fishermen to relocate both their housing and economic activity to the space they had been bargaining for. The authorization was granted on provisional terms, and this marked the starting point of the development of housing on the site. The eviction of the original site was initiated and implemented from 1981 onwards and was completed by 1983.

SPACE APPROPRIATION AFTER THE RESETTLEMENT

The permission to resettle on a site favourable to their fishing activities stimulated space ownership within the community of fishermen in various ways. In a way it was the starting point of the community identity formation associated with the expression of some claims to citizenship. First, proximity to the oil company was perceived by the community as a protecting element as were the two military bases mentioned earlier. Also, although granted on provisional terms, the foreign fisherman perceived the relocation in that space both as an official recognition of their community, and their fishing activity. They regarded the new site as a permanent place of settlement for the pursuit of livelihoods. The decision of a few Congolese fishermen who were sharing the former site with them to move with them to the site allocated by the city authorities to fishermen, partly reinforced their attitude. Expression of cultural identity gained in force, and housing became a prominent feature of this expression. It was also the mechanism through which the informal space appropriation was driven, and this process is still in progress.

Informality in Land Allocation and Housing Development

The architectural design of a typical house within the foreign community has changed considerably since the resettlement. From a single one-room hut standing without a fence, it has evolved to a courtyard containing two or more well-constructed houses with several rooms. Housing conditions have also changed as a consequence of zoning and some service provision. Gradually, the new site has become a reflection of the fishermen's cultural identity and a space for both production and reproduction. These developments have taken several forms, and only some salient actions are reported here.

Following the outcome of the negotiations, the beach committee conducted a land zoning exercise without official authorization from the municipality. The objective of the zoning was to allocate plots of land to fishermen taking into account the spatial configuration of their previous settlement. It was also intended to facilitate the identification of plot owners as a way of monitoring the fees for land occupancy. But the allocation of plots to foreign fishermen was not done properly. Rather it was dominated by corruption and exclusion that left many fishermen landless. Only canoe owners and community leaders were allocated plots. A fisherman working in a canoe owned by another fishermen had only the option of living on the property of his employer or renting a room elsewhere. This mode of plot allocation was a reflection of the distribution of assets among the fishermen.

Following this land zoning, the number of courtyards increased in the area. Rooms around courtyards (*concession* in French) is a typical urban housing form in many West African countries. A courtyard generally shelters a mix of individuals linked to each other through a variety of ties. Many households may be found inside the same courtyard though one particular individual is generally reckoned as the head of the courtyard. In this particular case, courtyards also provide sites for production, as the smoking of fish takes place there.

The development of courtyards was accompanied by the supply of water and electricity by the two state companies. The supply of these commodities illustrates the commitment fishermen had toward the improvement of their living conditions in their new site. Yet, not all concessions have had water or electricity, as some fishermen could not afford the fees for connection to the networks. Individuals living in a courtyard without water can obtain it from another courtyard where it is available. As for electricity, in exchange for a fee, some obtain illegal access from a nearby house that is legally connected to the power network.

Most fishermen tend to avoid formal subscription to these public utilities for a number of reasons. As stipulated by Leitmann and Bahatoglu (1998:110) who studied informal rules in relation to service provision in Turkey's spontaneous settlements, illegal utility connections are made because they are low-cost and because there may be no legal alternative to obtain the service. Yet, in the case of Ponte-Noire, the issue of affordability raises some doubts as their fishery activities generate substantial incomes. The proliferation of illegal electricity connections may be due to the fact that fishermen who want to use this utility have no legal access to it as their claim to the plot they occupy is not legally recognized. A number of bars have appeared in the settlement, most of them also with an illegal supply of electricity. These bars, owned by members of the beach committee or residents in the city, serve as recreational spaces for the fishermen. Some wealthy fishermen have also invested in this business.

Inside courtyards, two distinct types of houses may be found, reflecting changing attitudes toward space ownership among migrant fishermen. The first type may be considered permanent housing. Houses are constructed in permanent materials like cement, and supplied with water and electricity. The owners are generally wealthy canoe owners who have spent several years in Pointe-Noire. These houses are quite spacious, and the various individuals living in them are usually related. Quite often, the house owner rents out one or two rooms to fishermen who have recently arrived, and are working with him in his canoe. A courtyard is delimited by a cement wall that *de facto* attributes a sense of land ownership to households living inside.

The second type of housing is the one still sheltering the majority of fishermen. Despite the substantial income derived from the fishing activity, many fishermen and their families still live in wooden houses surrounded by fences made with thin planks. Those who live in this type of housing are not necessarily poor. Rather, they often perceive the construction of a house with permanent material as an insecure investment. When a house owner does not have legal title to the land, there is a real risk of demolition.

Differences in the type of housing have not created social cleavages. Fishing practices constitute the cultural foci shaping the social relationships among fishermen, regardless of their housing status or wealth. There seems to be no residential segregation in the area, in the sense that there is on one side a residential area for housing built in permanent materials, and, on another side, a deprived area for wooden housing. This is not to say that the exterior of a courtyard, or that of any house which is inside, has no symbolic importance. In the same way that the boat is generally used by fishermen as an architectural symbol (Lewcock and Gerald 1975:112), modern housing may also be used to communicate to the world outside the community the social status of the inhabitants. A similar social attitude has been reported in Robben (1989:166–77) in his study on the fishermen of Camurim, a small coastal town in Brazil.

Within the settlement, a strong ethnic cohesion prevails, as there is a shared awareness about the risk of eviction by the public authorities. This awareness has given rise to collective action among members in order to avoid eviction. Meetings are frequently held to discuss matters regarding land occupancy. Also, as a way of claiming citizenship, the residents of the settlement increasingly participate in cultural and other popular events taking place in the city. Not only has this participation increased the cultural visibility of the settlement, it has also shaped the sense of belonging to the city and reduced the social marginalization of its members. In a way, this participation is a reflection of a collective strategy aimed at facilitating the transition of the settlement from informality to formality.

The Economic Role of Women

The division of labour within the immigrant community is strongly gendered. Women occupy a central position in the running of the fishing enterprise, with the courtyard as their base. The courtyard thus takes on a symbolic meaning which is acknowledged by male fishermen. While the sea and the beach symbolize the territory of men, the courtyard is the territory of women. In economic terms, it is the place where women run their economic enterprises. These enterprises present a great deal of diversity, such as fish smoking, baking cakes and preparing dishes for sale.

The internal setting of a courtyard convincingly reveals the involvement of women in the running of micro-enterprises. The dominant enterprise is the fish smoking as it is by far the most lucrative. The fish most commonly smoked is herring. Catches are abundant, particularly during the dry season, from May to September. The excess of fresh fish is recycled through smoking and is sold in the various market places of the city. The smoking is done in a traditional way with wood and sawdust, using old metal barrels for smoking chambers. Every courtyard has two to four units for smoking fish. Manual operators of this equipment are recruited among young Congolese who come on the beach every day to look for casual work. With inflation and the growth of urban demand, this activity has become so lucrative that the earnings from smoked fish are sometimes higher than those derived from fresh fish.

In addition to fish smoking, women have diversified their sources of income. Some women have become petty retailers for basic household products (cooking oil, sugar, salt, petrol). Other women have opted for open-air restaurants inside the courtyard, selling a variety of food adapted to the culinary tastes of fishermen. Stalls selling basic manufactured products or food are generally placed at the front door of the courtyard on the sidewalk of the street. While the market for smoked fish is city- and nation-wide, the market for goods from these other types of micro-enterprises is more local. Children, particularly girls, are frequently employed in this petty trade on the street. Older girls may also work in bigger enterprises such as open-air restaurants. Because women themselves are heavily involved in fish smoking, they use children as helpers in their other activities. The children may address them as "Mama", but they are not necessarily the children of these women. Most of them are sent by relatives in the country of origin. Together, women and children constitute the workforce in the off-sea enterprises taking place inside the courtyard.

The fish smoking does not affect the selling of other food and retail products. The equipment used is designed in such a manner that smoke is released not only slowly but also in a small quantity. In fact, keeping (or recycling) the smoke as long as possible inside the smoking chamber is essential to this fish processing. Furthermore, the smoking is actually located either in the backyard or at a reasonable distance from where most trading activities take place, because of the heat emanating from it.

Smoking the fish adds a substantial value to what it would cost if sold as fresh fish, and it is sold not only locally, but also at the main market places in the city. During a visit to the settlement in December 2002 I discovered that women have developed a market place on their own where smoked fish is traded to wholesalers. The market appears to have obtained some formal recognition from the municipal authority, since this official sign was fixed at the entrance: *Marché de la Plage—Arrondissement 4 MvouMvou* (Beach Market, Fourth District, MvouMvou).

The income generated by women from their enterprises has an important economic function in the development of fishing activities. For foreign fishermen, women are key economic agents and they play a crucial role in their search for fortune. In turn, once a spouse has joined her husband in Pointe-Noire, she first becomes involved in fish smoking in order to earn money for herself and for the fishing activity of her husband. In domestic relations, the emphasis is on obligation and transaction rather than consideration and affection. The fishing activity of men at sea has increasingly become linked to the economic activity of women inside the courtyard. The latter partially provide the financial capital needed for the acquisition of additional technical capital.

The interconnectedness of fishing at sea and the smoking of fish in the courtyard entails an overlap of obligations. The responsibilities of a fisherman at sea are related to the funds received from his wife at home. Poor economic performance harms the household, and insufficient financial resources generated from the fish smoking reduce the profits from the fishing enterprise. Fishermen sell their fish to their wives at a price below the local market price. The wives process the fish (through smoking) and re-sell it in close and distant markets, making a profit they mainly re-invest in their husbands' fishing activities. This arrangement impels both men and women to work hard in order to make the most of their respective enterprises. This is the reason why it is important for the migrant fisherman to acquire a plot of land for housing as this provides the premises for fish smoking. Land acquisition is therefore an accompanying feature of fishery development. In short, the forces driving the informal housing development in the area arise from household economics.

THE PROXIMITY TO THE OIL COMPANY

The proximity to the oil company has induced significant changes in the livelihoods of the community. Some of the changes are reflected in the adoption of
more intensive fishing techniques, whilst others are evident in the level of congestion in the near-shore maritime space shared by the fishermen's community
and the oil company. Before the development of the industrial site, the fishing
took place near the shore. Seine fishing was widely used by both foreign and
Congolese fishermen to take advantage of various fishing grounds along the
beach.[1] Large quantities of herring, sardine, mackerel and crabs were easily
caught with this technique. The moderate size of waves and the ecosystem in
general were appropriate to seine fishing. Seine fishing has a long standing as it
allows fishermen to generate cash quickly. It does not involve as much risk as
when fishing is conducted far from the coast. And it is less costly in regard to
expenses associated with the acquisition of nets and a motorised canoe.

The presence of the oil company has affected the fishing practices in many
ways. First, as the activities conducted on the industrial site have generated an
intense ship and boat traffic, the movement of fishermen's canoes has been considerably hindered. The situation is particularly critical in the evening when fishermen go out. Frequently, fishing canoes leaving the shore have collided with
ships in the same space. Ships have sometimes had to use an alarm in order to
alert the fishermen not to get close to them. Also, there have been a number of
accidents with boats ruining nets on their course over the fishing grounds near
the shore. In order to make the nets more visible, canoe fishermen adopted colourful floating signals with lights attached to different parts of the nets. This
method seemingly gave the impression of stakes protecting private property
against intruders, of legitimising ownership in a frontier territory. The damage
to nets diminished but did not cease altogether. The oil company has complained about the congestion and has asked the city authorities to prevent fishermen from casting their nets right in the middle of the boat routes. While the
fishermen see the sea as common property, the oil company does not share this
view, and suggests that the fishermen put their nets somewhere else. The tension
has diminished in recent years. Fishermen try to place their nets at a distance
from the boats' routes. They have claimed that damaged nets were not reim-
bursed while the oil company's executives simply deny that boats caused harm
to nets. The absence of dialogue between the oil company and the fishermen has
made it difficult to investigate these claims.

The second source of disturbance for the fishing activity lies in the noise produced by the engines of boats coming to or leaving the site. According to fishermen, the noise, combined with the vibrations made by ship engines, has
disrupted the colonies of fish generally found close to the shore, causing them

---

1. A seine is a fishing-net for encircling fish, with floats at the top and weights at the bottom edge,
   which is hauled ashore or into boats. In the coastal area of Pointe-Noire, the most frequently used
   method of seine fishing is with purse seine locally called "tchissoko". The purse seine is a fishing
   net used to encircle surface-dwelling fish, usually landed aboard a boat rather than beached. The
   net may be up to 1km in length and 300m in depth and is used to encircle surface-schooling fish
   such as mackerel, sardines, crabs, trevally and skipjack tuna.

to move to other grounds. The proximity to the oil company has also brought about some environmental change that has caused great concern among fishermen. The pollution of seawater is visible, as the water near the plant looks greasy and is darker than it is a few miles further along the shore. A fisherman I interviewed about the increasing pollution, explicitly mentioned the colour of the water: "Before this company came here, the sea was green and sometimes blue, you could see the sand and the fish beneath the surface, now the water is like a river, you can't see anything. Even kids dare not swim at this place, as the colour gives the impression that the waters are very deep".

Coastal environment protection has been permanently absent from the agenda of the public authorities concerned with this issue. There is no institutional mechanism set up by the local authority allowing for the monitoring of the oil company's behaviour with regard to the quality of the marine environment in the area. What seems to prevail is a unilateral declaration made by the representatives of the company that their activities are not harmful to the marine ecosystem in the area. Although the fishermen are well aware of how the industrial activities conducted by the nearby oil company have affected the stocks of fish available in the area, they have tended not to complain overtly about it. Their status as foreign migrants temporally occupying a public space is the major factor restraining any collective action against the oil company, as they have not been granted long term right of occupancy. There is a fear of being evicted by the municipal authorities if any complaint is addressed against the company. As long as they can travel a long distance from the coast, and catch the volume of fish that allows them to make profits, some fishermen do not regard the intrusion of the oil company into their space of livelihoods as being a threat. In fact, some fishermen perceive the environmental problem related to the pollution of waters as being of secondary concern. The locational advantages associated with their site of settlement are strong incentives for minimizing the effects of pollution.

High sea fishing is being gradually affected by the offshore oil extraction. As the fishermen are pushing their fishing territory further from the coast, they get closer to the field of oil platforms. According to the fishermen, the lighting coming from the oil platforms is so bright that it disturbs the fish and makes catching it difficult. Bands of fish that used to move on the surface of the water are threatened by the lighting, and have moved to other places. Fishermen have had to continuously redefine their fishing territory and locate new fishing grounds where abundant catches can be found. Some of them are now advocating the fishing of sharks or giant skates that abound in the waters at a distance from the coast. In the past the fishing of these species was not economically advantageous, as consumer demand was low.

Because of the abundant colonies, catching sharks or skates does not require fishermen to spend a long time at sea. But this specialization in shark catching is costly as sharks often damage fishing nets. This has resulted in fishermen spending more time on land mending nets on the beach. To remedy the damage frequently caused by sharks to the nets, the use of appropriate nets for this kind of fish has now been widely adopted. This required important investments, and ethnic solidarity within the community was invoked. It is important to note that shark fishing has always taken place in the area. However, it significantly increased in magnitude with the growing number of migrant fishermen becoming involved in this type of fishing. Persistent declines in the catches of other species, largely caused by oil-related industrial activities in the fishing territories, forced fishermen to shift to intense shark fishing in order to compensate for losses.[1]

The effects of the proximity to the industrial site are reflected in the price of fish sold to consumers. The price has over the past few years increased rapidly in the local markets. Even species like herring and shark that in the past were affordable to low-income urban households, are now beyond the purchasing power of most of them. In addition, the quantity of fish retailed in the market place has declined. In short, the consumers seem to be the most affected by the rising price of fish.

INSTITUTIONAL RESPONSES TO THE INFORMAL APPROPRIATION OF SPACE

The expansion of informal housing built with durable materials in the area has been accompanied by an attitude of laissez-faire from the public authorities. This attitude partly stems from the fact that the settlement has always been regarded as temporary. For the authorities, the site occupied by the fishermen remains first and foremost public property and it can be claimed back at any time. Even though awareness has been mounting at the city authority level about the rapid growth of the settlement, no action has been taken in order to regulate the construction of houses, but some concerns have been voiced about the environmental problems related to waste disposal, sanitation and crowding.

Informal housing developed by fishermen has tended to spread outside the limits permitted by the authorities. The oil company has up till now managed to contain the growth of the settlement within the site boundaries defined at the time the provisional authorization was granted. The company seeks to prevent the informal housing settlement from expanding closer to the industrial premises. In the last five years, the security department of the oil company has repeatedly expressed concerns about the risk of the outbreak of fire represented in the proliferation of informal housing units. Along the same lines, the department has complained that no safety measures are being observed with regard to the connection of electricity lines from house to house. The oil company has constantly renewed its demand about relocating fishermen to a coastal area distant from the industrial premises. Surprisingly, despite the company's power to persuade the local authority to satisfy its demands, the *status quo* has prevailed.

To some extent, the evidence on the spatial dynamics of housing lends support to these concerns. The lack of regulation from the official authorities partly results from the confusion prevailing between the city council and the harbour

---

1. In July 2001, the Congolese government, in line with the international convention promulgated under the auspices of the Food and Agricultural Organization of the United Nations (FAO), enacted a law prohibiting the shark fishing as this species was classified in the category of fish threatened by extinction due to over-fishing.

authority as to which institution bears responsibility for the management of the coastal area. From a legal viewpoint, the harbour authority in the city of Pointe-Noire is the institution in charge of managing or planning the development of this area. Its responsibility covers both the sea and the beach line. However, the authorities in charge of the municipality of Pointe-Noire, and particularly the city council, perform a supervisory function with regard to the management of the coastal area. Apart from the financial gains that can be derived from some coastal activities, the city council is not properly speaking involved in the day-to-day supervision of activities taking place on the beach.

The institutional confusion has been recently reinforced by the decision made by the *Chambre de Commerce et d' Industrie* (Chamber of Commerce and Industry) to impose the payment of taxes on the fishing activity run by African migrants, thereby indirectly giving some legitimacy to the informal settlement. Among the functions of the Chamber of Commerce and Industry is to monitor institutional procedures regarding the framework within which a particular profit-making enterprise is authorized to operate. It also elaborates taxation schemes applicable to different types of commercial and industrial establishments. In line with this, its role is to assess whether a given profit-making establishment is taxable and under what form or scheme taxation is applicable. The Chamber of Commerce and Industry works in conjunction with other public services in charge of collecting taxes, including services from the municipality and the Ministry of Finances.

At the time when data for this chapter were collected, the decision to impose legal taxes on the fishing activity had just been made. What was envisaged in a first phase is the registration of all the fishing canoes as profit-making enterprises that, taken individually, require, like any other business, a commercial licence including the payment of fishing tax. The argument underlying this fiscal decision rests on the view that a fishing enterprise is like any other enterprise and therefore needs to pay tax. Thus, while confusion seems to prevail between the city council and the harbour authority as to which institution has supervisory power over housing development in the area, the Chamber of Commerce and Industry has chosen to recognize the mushrooming fishing activity for fiscal purposes.

The overlapping of authorities has resulted in an institutional vacuum with regard to the enforcement of rules to guide the occupancy and preserve a healthy environment within the settlement. Meanwhile, the beach committee, lacking legal status, has taken advantage of the demand for plots by allocating beach land to foreign fishermen. Under the supervision of the beach committee, plots are illegally allocated to migrant fishermen. The beneficiaries are the representatives of the beach committee, all Congolese nationals. The allocation of a plot of land on the beach often involves large amounts of money, and corruption is a dominant feature of land transactions. To any fisherman, land acquisition is the starting point of any plan for setting up an enterprise for fish smoking run by his wife. In the prevailing situation, the city authorities have very limited control over land transactions within the community of fishermen.

CONCLUDING COMMENTS

This chapter has shed light on the patterns prevailing in the informal space occupancy of housing and their linkages to the development of migrant enterprises in coastal artisanal fisheries. The findings have highlighted how fishermen have collectively constructed their space for livelihoods close to a multinational oil company. The gradual appropriation of space has been made possible thanks to the resources and the power migrant fishermen have had in the framework either of the existing laws, rules and norms, or the informal rules and norms they have elaborated specifically for the purpose of sustaining their resettlement on the site they have shared with the oil company. Ethnic know-how in fishery techniques, financial means and collective action have been used in the dialogue with the formal institutions to consolidate the possession of space. The temporary authorization granted by the city council and the institutional vacuum with regard to coastal regulation have been strategically used by the community in the formation of claims to ownership of land. The interface between the informal actors, the migrant fishermen on the one hand, and the formal institutions, the public authorities and the oil company on the other, has provided an arena for the fishermen where they have been able to apply their own interpretative and strategic frameworks. For instance, the fishermen have tended to avoid making overt complaints against the oil company with regard to pollution or destruction of fishing nets. Far from being a reflection of a weak position, this collective attitude can be regarded as a strategy to avoid direct confrontation with the company in order to preserve control over the disputed coastal site. An open confrontation could have resulted in a threat of eviction from the site that offers them locational advantages.

In the course of this public space appropriation, the relations emerging at the interface between the informal and formal actors involved are dynamic. These relations are shaped by changing circumstances, themselves dictated by local economic and social practices. The dialectic character of these relations is reflected in the overlapping of diverse considerations. Changing fishing practices, housing transformation, the growth of the settlement, rising security concerns and non-compliance with formal subscription to utilities are all expressions of control, avoidance and circumvention amongst migrant fishermen. Taken together, these considerations are the dynamic forms of space appropriation. To migrant fishermen, informality in housing development is no longer perceived as a risk inviting eviction, but as an instrument of symbolic possession of space through the cultural expression of community values or personal achievements. Thus migrant fishermen build, produce, transform, and attach signification to their site, through a relatively hidden collective action to express community rights over public space, making it their legitimate territory.

This informal space appropriation departs from the dramatic situations the migrant fishermen experienced in the past. Despite the illegal character of land ownership and the volatile social environment, the social integration of the fishermen community has been impressive. Until the early 1980s, the experience of African foreigners with running a business in Congo was frequently marked by social tension and violent conflicts perpetrated by the authorities. As in many other African countries, African immigrant entrepreneurs were confronted in the past with attitudes of xenophobia from local populations. They were expelled from the country in a violent manner by the military forces, and their property was either destroyed, looted or confiscated without compensation. Before the industrial site development, events of this kind occurred twice. Surprisingly, since the resettlement took place at the end of the 1980s, the growing migrant entrepreneurship in fisheries parallel with illegal appropriation of coastal space seems not have generated xenophobic attitudes. Rather, an attitude of tolerance has tended to prevail toward migrant fishermen. This might be a strong indication of a real change in the way migrant fishermen are perceived by local populations.

It must be underscored that the tolerant attitude towards migrant fishermen on the part of the local population has over the years gained ground from different perspectives. First the alliance that was formed between the migrant fishermen and the non-fishermen at the time of eviction in 1981–1983, subsequently served as an informal institutional framework for designing and implementing collaborative initiatives on matters regarding the residents' welfare and the physical development of the area. From that date, the participation of migrant fishermen in both local decision making and collective bargaining with municipal authorities gained momentum. Second, as emphasized elsewhere, the allocation of a site for resettlement by the local authority was regarded by the fishermen, most of them being undocumented migrants, as a legitimization of their informal occupancy of land for housing. Along the same lines, it also gave some kind of public testimony of the importance of their fishing activities for the city economy.

The combination of all these elements with a certain political willingness to appease potential tensions between foreigners and nationals, contributed, in some respects, to increased confidence within the migrant community. Parallel to this, the formation of claims within the migrant community for greater access to basic social services also facilitated the expression of collective identity and integration. One channel through which identity was expressed was through local cultural initiatives and at political events at the city or national level. This was manifested in the setting up of committees on different local matters and taking part in cultural and political events at the city level.

On a different note, migrant fishermen and their families, demonstrated strong willingness to learn and communicate with the local population in one of the national languages *kikongo*, widely spoken in the city. Most importantly, their know-how and industrial organization contributed to the recognition of their growing importance as economic actors in fish production for the local market. Their entrepreneurial success generated jobs, though of a casual nature, for many young Congolese. In the final analysis, migrant fishermen were not posing major threats to the stock of jobs and housing available to the local population. All these elements have contributed to fostering a climate of tolerance toward migrant fishermen.

In this regard, adequate policies need to be set up in order to consolidate this climate of tolerance. The community of immigrant fishermen make an important contribution to the local economy. There is also an urgent need to formulate appropriate public actions with regard to informal coastal land occupancy and to monitor the spread of the settlement and the growing environmental problems generated by crowding and lack of services.

References

Bøe, Turid, 1999, *Access Regime and Institutions: The Economic Organization of the Migrant Popo Fishermen of Pointe-Noire, Congo.* Working paper, 1999:8. Bergen: Chr. Michelsen Institute.

Chan Kwok Bun and Ong Jin Hui, 1995, "The many faces of immigrant entrepreneurship" in Cohen, Robin (ed), *The Cambridge Survey of World Migration*, pp. 523–31. Cambridge: Cambridge University Press.

Guha, R., 1989, *The Unquiet Woods: Ecological Change and Peasant Resistance in the Himalaya.* Dehli: Oxford University Press

Jul-Larsen, Eyolf, 1994, *Migrant Fishermen in Congo: Tradition and Modernity.* Report 1994:6. Bergen: Chr. Michelsen Institute.

Kesteloot, Christian and Henk Meert, 1999, "Informal Spaces: The Geography of Informal Economic Activities in Brussels", *International Journal of Urban and Regional Studies* 23, 2, pp. 232–51.

Leitmann, Josef and Deniz Bahatoglu, 1998, "Informal Rules. Using Institutional Economics to Understand Service Provision in Turkey's Spontaneous Settlement", *The Journal of Development Studies* 34(5), pp. 98–122.

Lewcock, Ronald and Brans Gerald, 1975, "The Boat as an Architectural Symbol" in Paul, Oliver (ed.), *Shelter, Sign and Symbol*, pp. 107–16. London: Barrie and Jenkins.

Light, Ivan, Parminder Bhachu and Stavros Karageorgis, 1993, "Migration Networks and Immigrant Entrepreneurship" in Light, Ivan and Parminder Bhachu (eds), *Immigration and Entrepreneurship: Culture, Capital, and Ethnic Networks*, pp. 25–50. New Brunswick: Transaction Publishers.

Peluso, H.L., 1992, *Rich Forests, Poor People: Resource Control and Resistance in Java.* Berkeley: University of California Press.

Robben, Antonius C.G.M., 1989, *Sons of the Sea Goddess. Economic Practice and Discursive Conflict in Brazil.* New York: Columbia University Press.

Tati, Gabriel, 1996, "Migration Interafricain. Transfert de Savoir-Faire et Développement Local en Afrique: le Cas du Congo". Paper presented at the international colloquium on "The Work of Cheikh Anta Diop: Africa's Renaissance on the Threshold of the Third Millennium", Dakar-Caytu, February 26–March 2, 1996.

—, 1993, *Migration, Urbanization et Développement au Congo.* Cahiers de l'IFORD no 5. Yaoundé: IFORD and CEPED.

Zeleza, Paul T. and Ezethel Kalipeni, 1999, "Introduction" in Zeleza, Paul T. and Ezethel Kalipeni (eds), *Sacred Spaces and Public Quarrels. African Cultural and Economic Landscapes*, pp.1–13. Trenton: Africa World Press.

CHAPTER 3

The Right to Stay in Cato Crest:
Formality and Informality in a South African Development Project

Knut G. Nustad

The labelling of some social phenomena as 'informal' received widespread popularity in the 1970s, after Keith Hart (1973) coined the term 'informal economy', one of a few concepts which have originated in anthropology and then been taken up by economists. Today, it seems self-evident what the 'formal' and 'informal' denote. But this simple dichotomy has sparked much controversy in the past. Shortly after the concept was launched, the informal economy was embraced by the ILO as an important target for efforts, and seen by policy makers as proof of an entrepreneurial spirit among the poor that could be boosted to advance the economy. Marxist oriented writers, on the other hand, argued that it was a bourgeois term that covered up class relations. After initially embracing the concept, a number of social scientists began arguing that the dichotomy was not really helpful at all: actual cases of informal economy activity proved to be closely tied to the formal economy, and this undermined, it was argued, the usefulness of maintaining the dichotomy (e.g. Skar 1985).

Hart conducted fieldwork in Nima, a huge settlement outside Accra between 1965 and 1968 (Hart 1973). According to official figures, over half of Nima's population was self-employed, non-wage earning, and unemployed. In fact, almost a quarter of the population was listed as 'not economically active' (Hart 1973:62). This, Hart recognized, was an observation devoid of meaning. Clearly there was a lot of economic activity going on, but a substantial part of this activity took place outside the structures of the state, and escaped the abstractions and analytical categories of economic models. It was these activities that Hart labelled the 'informal economy'.

The term 'the informal economy', then, was originally meant to draw attention to the limitations of a certain approach to understanding economic activities: the application of economic models that rested on an understanding of economic activities as rationalized and thereby open to enumeration. The informal was coined as a term for acts and processes that escaped these models: all the activities that were not captured by the economists' understanding of what economic activities entailed. Thus, 'informality' is not in itself a characteristic of an activity; it only signifies that it has been left out by a definition that is 'formal'. But, as the history of this concept clearly demonstrates, in naming there lies a peril: 'the informal', instead of denoting the flux of social practices, was instead encompassed by formal models as a residual category for everything which escaped the conceptual grid of administrators and academics. Despite this fate, I believe that the informal/formal dichotomy can act as a useful tool for analysing attempts by bureaucrats at ordering the world according to their models and people's responses to these attempts. The concepts 'formal' and 'informal' are useful as long as one recognizes that informal practices are both constituted by, and must be analysed in relation to, formal practices.

The first part of the chapter will examine these practices, and show that of necessity, bureaucrats construct a model of the social field in which they want to intervene. This model is thus the basis for a formal understanding of a social field. This formal understanding necessarily cuts away large chunks of the social field, highlighting only those aspects that are open to enumeration and manipulation. This conception of the formal/informal will be used to analyse a South African urban development project, where the formal abstractions made by the developers as a precondition for controlling the development process also created spaces in which relationally defined informal practices were established.

EARLY MOBILIZATION

The area in which Cato Crest is situated, Cato Manor, has been one of the most violently contested urban areas in South Africa. It is a huge area of land that covers 1,800 hectares and is situated within five miles of the centre of Durban, a city of 3 million people. Originally owned by a white landowner, George Christopher Cato, the land was partitioned in the 1930s and sold to Indian workers who had completed their tenure, as well as to other Indian immigrants (Edwards 1994). With the great influx to the city during the Second World War, many of the Indian landowners sublet to black workers and the first years after the war saw a vibrant mixed settlement emerging. All was not harmony however. Conflict between Indian landowners and black tenants erupted into violent conflict in 1949 and set in motion plans to regulate the area for white occupation. Cato Manor fell prey to apartheid development, and by the mid-1960s, all its inhabitants had been forcibly removed to the new townships outside Durban. The destruction of Cato Manor, which affected the lives of 120,000 people, came to epitomize the brutality of apartheid development.

After its black and Indian occupants were forcibly removed in the late 1950s and early 1960s, Cato Manor was a wasteland for almost thirty years. Towards the end of the 1980s, when it became increasingly clear that change in the political regime was imminent, people began moving into Cato Manor, erecting shacks well out of sight of the relatively affluent neighbouring suburbs of Bellair, Manor Gardens, Sherwood and Westville. The influx of people continued, despite attempts by the authorities to halt it. In 1995 it was estimated that more than twenty thousand people lived in the squatter settlement of Cato Crest alone (Makhathini and Xaba 1995).

In an attempt to mobilize against the government's demolition teams, the squatters formed a neighbourhood association, of the type referred to in South

Africa as a civic. This organization, and those that followed, were named by residents after the order in which they were established. Thus people spoke of the first, second, and third civic. Later, amalgamations of these groups, as well as other organizations such as the local branches of the African National Congress (ANC) were created by development interventions and variously called the General Council, the Executive Committee, Cato Crest Development Committee, Devco etc. These organizations for the most part consisted of the same people, and I will in what follows refer to them collectively as the local leadership.

Neighbourhood organizations have existed in black townships from their creation, and they functioned as foci of organized political opposition through the ANC in the 1940s and 50s. During the 1960s, they declined in importance as a result of repression, but re-emerged in the late 1970s and reached a prominent position in the mid-1980s (Seekings 1997). Somewhat idealistically, they can be defined as 'localized grassroots organizational structures that are accountable to local constituencies, seek to address the local grievances that residents have with their conditions of daily living, and are located outside formal governmental, party-political or development agency institutions' (Swilling 1993:16). The issues around which they organize are 'civic' issues, as opposed to party issues, such as housing, services, land, education, health, transport and community facilities (Swilling, Cobbett et al. 1991:187).

But in the mid-1980s they took on a more political role and became important local structures in the resistance against apartheid. When the apartheid state granted 'self-determination' to black townships in the early 1980s they set up a system of Black Local Authorities (Coovadia 1991:335). In 1982 the Black Local Authorities were given the power to control local affairs such as housing, rent and services. But the economic crisis continued and there were a huge number of unemployed people in the urban black townships. The Black Local Authorities sought to balance their books by increasing taxation, which only escalated the crisis. Resistance to these new structures was strong. In 1983, the United Democratic Front (UDF) was formed to oppose the tri-cameral constitution of which the Black Local Authorities were a part. The campaign was effective and the turnout for the elections to the Indian and coloured parliaments was low (Tsenoli 1994:32).

An important factor in the growth of the civic movement was the banning of the ANC. Local civics became a focal point of the political struggle, organizing resistance campaigns, mobilizing for the release of political prisoners and the lifting of the state of emergency (Heymans 1993:5). During the mid-1980s, civic organizations were targeted by the state, which believed that they were attempting to make South Africa ungovernable (Heymans 1993:6). The civics sought to strengthen themselves by forming wider networks. An attempt was made in 1984 to construct a national organization of civics as part of the UDF, but it failed because of state repression which saw many of the civics banned and their leaders jailed or detained under emergency regulations. It was not until after the unbanning of political organizations that a national civic organization would be established. This occurred in 1992, when the South Africa National Civic

Organization (SANCO) was formed. The civics were, after this, no longer independent organizations but branches of SANCO (Swilling 1993:17).

From that time, however, the importance of both civics generally and SANCO specifically has declined rapidly (Seekings 1997). The unbanning of the ANC and other opposition parties had by now raised the question of what role the civics should play when they were no longer needed as foci of opposition. This debate continued throughout the 1990s. Heymans (1993) argues that they have a role to play in the transition to democracy, but that they need to become 'non-partisan' and more 'development orientated'. Mayekiso (1993), an organizer at the Alexandra Civic Organization, takes Seekings (1992) to task for his prediction that, once legitimate local government structures are in place, civics will have a limited role to play. Mayekiso argues that civics will be needed as watchdogs in the democratization process and for building participatory democracy (Mayekiso 1993:25). Shubane (1994) links the issue of civics explicitly to development, as does Smit (2001), who believes that civics, which he equates with 'civil society', will have an important part to play in development projects. The recent trend towards people-centred development, he argues, has led developers to seek out local civic organizations before commencing their work. But, as Shubane points out, 'organizations of the marignalized and the marginalized themselves might in many circumstances not be the same thing' (Shubane 1994:36). Steven Friedman (1993) was one of the first to caution against this. He questions the assumption that civics can meaningfully be said to represent the larger community, and whether in fact such an entity can be said to exist. 'Communities' consist of a multiplicity of interests, and a past history of creating unity in opposition to apartheid does not in itself qualify for the role as a legitimate expression of the interests of a community (Friedman and Reitzes 1996). Mayekiso (1995) argues against such a distinction, and holds that protest is inseparable from development. The problem, however, is that developers need a representative body with which to negotiate, something that easily leads to the question of legitimacy and representativeness being played down. This was, as will become clear, the case in Cato Crest.

Besides the civics, other organizations also involved themselves with the plight of the squatters, among them the Cato Manor Residents' Association (CMRA), which represented the Indian landowners who had been forcibly removed in the 1960s. From 1979 this organization had successfully fought off attempts to develop Cato Manor for white housing. The CMRA, together with other organizations, established a Development Forum in 1992. In 1993, the Forum launched the Cato Manor Development Association (CMDA), with a mandate to guide the development of the whole of Cato Manor.

From the outset the CMDA set out to find alternatives to the top-down planning of the apartheid government. They chose a participatory approach which entailed close collaboration with community structures, and which rested on an assumption of the representativeness of these structures vis-à-vis the wider community. This, then, was the formal understanding of the situation on which the developers based their interaction with the community.

THE DEVELOPMENT INTERVENTION

I have followed the developments in Cato Crest during two periods of fieldwork, the first from November 1994 until June 1995, and the second from May 1996 until April 1997. The period described below covers the period from roughly 1990 until April 1997, which means that to a large extent I had to base my information on past events on interviews. These were conducted with as many people in the leadership as possible.

Most of the information I received on sensitive issues, such as the trading of land and registration numbers, came from a limited number of people. For obvious reasons, I could not discuss these issues with people that I did not know very well. I therefore conducted a series of structured interviews to establish the extent to which commerce in land and registration numbers had taken place. The list of events was also checked against interviews with people outside Cato Crest, and against newspaper articles and official documents. Many of these documents I obtained from the Cato Manor Development Association's information centre. Another important source was the Local History Museum (for the old Cato Manor), the Natal Provincial Administration and the library of the University of Natal, Durban. In addition to interviewing members of the old leadership and attending community events, I spoke to all those who had been working with development-related issues in Cato Crest.

My material shows that most of the people who settled in Cato Crest from the late 1980s were not new arrivals in Durban. Most had lived in the formal townships surrounding the city. But Cato Crest appeared to many people as an ideal location in which to live. Nearness to the city centre meant that job opportunities were much closer at hand. Since transportation is expensive, the possibility of walking into the centre was important to many. In addition, many evoked the historical significance of the place when they told me why they had chosen to settle in Cato Crest. One woman, who later became a prominent figure in the local leadership, told me that she had grown up in the old Cato Manor and saw the changing political climate in the late 1980s as an opportunity for claiming her stake in the area. Cato Crest soon established a reputation as an ANC stronghold, and this was the reason why so many chose to settle there in the mid-1990s, when the conflict between Inkatha and the ANC made many townships unsafe.

In the early period of the settlement, when there was a constant risk of eviction, the local community organizations fought for recognition and right to stay. Thus the first civic organization was set up by squatters with a long history of personal involvement as political activists and ANC members. They successfully mobilized progressive whites, local NGOs and the media to create pressure on the local government to let them stay. The authorities tried various strategies, such as extending recognition to those squatters already on the site, on the condition that they kept others out. To no avail, as demonstrated by the desperation in this warning issued by the private construction company, National Investment Corporation Ltd. (NIC), that had secured the right to build middle-class houses in the area:

NIC appeals once again to all people who are building in this area to *stop immediately* and commence dismantling their structures. The only people who are permitted to remain are those who possess notices who's (sic) shacks were numbered by NIC a few days ago. *DO NOT IGNORE THIS NOTICE* if you do your structure will be demolished by NIC for you. If you resist you will be charged with trespassing. NIC repeats *DO NOT IGNORE THIS NOTICE* if you do your structure will be demolished by NIC for you. If you resist you will be charged with trespassing. By order[1]... . (National Investment Corporation Ltd. 1991, original emphasis.)

The population continued to grow to such a size that it became increasingly impossible for the government to remove them forcibly. While squatter settlements were established in other parts of Cato Manor as well, none reached the size of Cato Crest and it was thus to this area that the attention of authorities was drawn. One of the officers responsible for keeping the land free from squatters complained to his superiors: 'The squatters are moving in and building shacks all over the area. There is no control over the influx of squatters in the area'.[2]

On 23 April 1993 the Cato Manor Development Association was launched in an embryonic form (CMDA 1994:1). It grew out of the Cato Manor Development Forum which comprised 31 organizations, including political parties (amongst others the Democratic Party, the National Party, and the ANC), government bodies, community organizations such as the previously mentioned CMRA which represented the Indian landowners, squatters' committees, and NGOs. It was governed by a board of twelve directors, comprising ten members of the Association and two specialists (Robinson 1994). As Robinson put it, this embryonic structure 'was to encounter a severe baptism of fire in its first year of operation' which 'took the form of a seemingly endless series of challenges, some to the very existence of the CMDA' (Robinson 1994:9). One of the main obstacles to development were the 'land invasions' in Cato Crest. From a population of less than a hundred, Cato Crest evolved into a squatter settlement of over two thousand households over a few weeks, and to one of almost four thousand in the following months (Robinson 1994:10).

In early 1994 the board and an executive staff were in place and a business plan was formulated. Here, it is stated that the 'mission of Cato Manor Development Association is to facilitate the development of Cato Manor in a manner consistent with the vision statement' which reads:

Cato Manor will be developed as a symbol of urban reconstruction in South Africa and as a clear departure from the apartheid planning of the past. The area will be a vibrant mixed-use area with a mix of incomes. Special emphasis will however be placed on the provision of affordable housing for low-income people and on the creation of job opportunities ... . (CMDA 1994:8)

The CMDA defined its role as a facilitator, and only in the last resort would it take on the role of a developer. In 1995, the CMDA produced a Structure Plan (CMDA 1995b) based on the Policy Framework which marked the end of the project's planning stage (Robinson and Forster 1996). Here, comprehensive and

---

1. 'Demolition Notice Warning', 11 April 1991. National Investment Corporation Ltd.
2. 'Re: Squatter Count Cato Crest', 4 April 1991. Report from Brown, S.P.A.C, Department of Land Affairs, Durban, to D.P. De Beer, S.P.A.O, Department of Land Affairs, Durban.

ambitious plans were drawn up for construction of housing and communal facilities (CMDA 1995b).

The board was restructured in July 1994, after the first democratic elections,
to exclude defunct apartheid-era bodies such as the House of Assembly and the
House of Delegates.[1] In 1995, the CMDA became a Special Presidential Lead
Project under the new South African regime's *Reconstruction and Development
Programme* (RDP), and a new body, the Provincial Special Presidential Projects
Committee was set up to oversee and monitor its implementation. This Projects
Committee was jointly chaired by the Provincial Minister of Local Government
and Housing and the Minister of Economic Affairs and Tourism, and it included
members from the Metropolitan and Local Councils. In July 1996, after the first
democratic elections for local government structures, the CMDA board was re-
constituted to strengthen the presence of local government. The board now included members from Provincial Government, Metropolitan and Local Councils, a group of experts appointed by the outgoing board as well as local communities.

In December 1997, shortly after I left the area, control over the project shifted from the Provincial Government to the Durban Metropolitan Council. The
CMDA now effectively became an agent of this body for the development of
Cato Manor. This had the effect of strengthening the power of the CMDA because it could claim the legitimacy of a democratically elected local government.
The organization's newspaper, *Izwi*, wrote that this was an historic agreement
because 'it is the first time that a framework has been established for co-opera-
tive governance between a Section 21 company [a non-profit organization] (the
CMDA), local government and provincial government' (*Izwi* 1997).

The CMDA has identified eight key dimensions to their project: housing;
transportation; social, educational and recreational facilities; infrastructure;
economic development; human skills development; land reform; and protection
of open spaces. According to CMDA's *Project Implementation Programme*,
none of these projects, with the exception of a show village in Chesterville, had
been completed by August 1997. But when I left in March 1997, the construction of houses in the Wiggins area of Cato Manor was well under way, and an
article in the *Mail & Guardian,* dated 31 August 1998, states that housing had
been provided for almost sixty thousand people in Cato Manor. However, on
further consideration it appears that most of these houses had been built on
vacant land, and that the area that is the subject of this study, Cato Crest, was
still considered one of 'the problem areas'. Where the organization could construct on previously empty land they did not have to negotiate with a community leadership. In those areas where squatters had settled, and the participatory
approach had to be put to the test, there had been severe problems.

Both the CMDA and the community leadership were formed in the complex
political situation in South Africa in the 1980s. The decade saw an escalation of
violence in the black townships, and KwaZulu/Natal was among the provinces
worst hit. The violence uprooted thousands of people and was part of the reason

1. This information is based on documents obtained from the CMDA web page. For details about
the various documents, see the list of references.

for the resettlement of Cato Crest. The CMDA grew out of a process whereby people sympathetic to the squatters tried to persuade the authorities to deliver housing and development instead of demolishing shacks. From its establishment it changed character, because the business of 'delivering development' puts certain constraints on the developer. It is impossible to plan without some sort of stability, order and boundaries around the entity that the plan concerns. When hundreds of people move into a shack settlement every week it undermines every attempt at constructing agreements and allocation policies. The CMDA, launched as it was in the transition period between apartheid and the first democratic elections, was also self-conscious about offering an alternative to the apartheid planning of the past. Inclusiveness and participation were central concepts here.

The same point can be made for the civic organizations. In Cato Crest, these were formed in response to events outside the area; first to resist demolition and when the situation stabilized, to demand services such as water supply. Makhathini (1992) predicted that Cato Manor would remain peaceful because the area lacked a material base for the emergence of warlordism. He was proven wrong; a leadership emerged that fought viciously over access to resources.

Formal Conceptions

Any present-day development project in South Africa, and especially in Cato Manor, takes place in the historical context of apartheid development (Nustad 1996). As Murray and Williams (1994) have argued, a top-down approach to development has been made impossible by the legacy of apartheid. To succeed, the development of Cato Manor had to demonstrate that it constituted a break with top-down approaches. The ANC was favouring a bottom-up approach to development in its *Reconstruction and Development Programme* (ANC 1994) and to have any chances of success, the development of Cato Manor had to be seen as a partnership between people living in the area and the developers.

The Cato Manor Development Association recognized that working in highly politicized settings like Cato Crest would be extremely problematic, and decided to postpone their involvement there. Instead they concentrated on the empty land in Cato Manor. But their hand was forced: because of the public outcry about land invasions, the CMDA had to start negotiations with the local leadership in Cato Crest earlier than they had wished. It turned out to be as difficult as they had anticipated. People involved in the community structures in Cato Crest were extremely distrustful of the CMDA. I was repeatedly told that the CMDA could not possibly be interested in promoting development out of fear that a developed Cato Crest would mean an end to their well-paid jobs.

Because the developers could not relate to the whole mass of people in Cato Crest, they had to construct a segment of it, the leadership, as representative of the rest. This formal understanding derives from Max Weber's notion of bureaucratic domination whereby an elected representative acts in accordance with the rules laid down and defined by his or her office. The assumption in Cato Crest, then, was that local leadership would act as representatives for the larger community. Instead, they acted more in accordance with the Weberian ideal type of traditional leaders.

Informal Responses

In this first period, the newly formed community organization successfully mobilized against outside attempts at expelling them. However, once the immediate threat was gone, another, and more disruptive, power mechanism seems to have underscored the actions of the local leadership. This mechanism is similar to what Bayart (1993) and others have termed neo-patrimonialism. In order to hold on to power as community representatives, the local leaders had to mobilize resources in some way, both to survive themselves, and to be able to build up a group of loyal followers.

The first such instance that members of the community structures recounted to me, and which drew the line between two antagonistic groups in the local leadership, occurred when the community organization managed to negotiate the erection of stem pipes for water supply. It was decided that the community organization would be responsible for collecting payment and that Cato Manor Residents Association would be the body formally responsible. This set-up resulted in allegations of mismanagement of funds, and the community organization was divided into two factions accusing each other of bad management and crimes.

This incident defined two groups among the local leadership who continued to fight for power throughout the period in which I followed the local political scene. One aspect is worth noting here. The water company was willing to erect standpipes and give credit to the population in Cato Crest because the members of the community organization were perceived as representative of the wider community. In other words, the space within which the informal economic activity of embezzlement took place was created by the formal abstraction of the water company. The company, if it was to extend its services to the community, needed a representative, responsible body with which to conduct business.

This example was relatively innocent, but the same mechanisms were involved later with much graver consequences. Events took a dramatic turn in mid-1993 when there was a huge influx of people into Cato Crest as a result of the pre-election violence in KwaZulu/Natal. In a few months, the population increased from a few hundreds to more than twenty thousand. As the settlement increased in size, it became the focus of targeted efforts at improvement. The Cato Manor Development Association was established and given the sole responsibility for coordinating development efforts in the area.

There was a mismatch between a formal understanding of the local leadership as representative of the local population, and the actual practice of the leadership. The factions in the leadership that were established right from the start continued to fight for control over the positions as community representatives in negotiations with outsiders. As a result, there were constant struggles over the positions of the community organizations and the establishment of rival organizations.

Why was it so important to gain access to these positions? The obvious answer is that positions meant access to resources. Whereas for the developer, a community organization represents a manageable manifestation of 'the community', for people living in the squatter settlement the organization represents a link to the world of government and NGO funding and equipment. Such positions become extremely valuable resources in themselves, resources that exist because of the way the development process is structured. This was best expressed by the first person I got to know in Cato Crest, who was assigned to me as an assistant by the community organization then in control. We were sharing a few beers, the situation was still very new to me, and I asked him why he had become involved in the community structures. 'People who do the projects do not like individuals', he said. When I asked him what he meant, he explained that if he, as a black person, wanted to do something for himself, he could not just go to the NGOs and ask for money or support. 'The people who do the projects' think of the black man as a group. In effect, membership of one of the community organizations was the only way to access beneficiary organizations.

Converting a position in a community organization to material gains and power took a variety of forms. One group of strategies was to allocate jobs given by the developers to dependants and followers; another to appropriate money and equipment from development organizations. A third very common strategy was the trading of registration numbers by people involved in the community organizations. Regardless of whether they were private developers, local or provincial authorities, or NGOs, the external agents involved in Cato Crest have been concerned with imposing some kind of order on the perceived chaos of the settlement. Making plans for the area necessitated that the planner had some control over those to be planned for. Two closely connected strategies of formalization were employed by the developers to achieve this. The first involved the transformation of persons into objects in the form of numbers. This was done through the allocation of registration numbers to the residents in the area, with the aim of establishing the size of the population. The second strategy entailed the extension of recognition of the right to stay, symbolized by the registration number, on condition that the recipients managed to keep others out. The idea, then, was that those given the right to stay would see it as in their interest to keep other people out. This strategy would then stabilize the situation and enable the planners to estimate the number of people to include in their plans. There were four different attempts at ordering Cato Crest in this way. Each time new shacks were built, and when the number system lost all resemblance to the reality on the ground, the developers devised new formulae.

These futile attempts at control underwent a transformation through their application. The numbers, in themselves, became commodities that obtained an exchange value. Ownership of a number not only gave freedom from police harassment, but also had an additional potential value. If the development of formal housing commenced, it guaranteed the number-holder a part in that process, and eventually a formal house. While the trading of registration numbers had taken place to a lesser degree when Cato Crest consisted of a handful of houses, trade became organized after the mass influx of 1993. As part of the agreement between the then active community organization and the provincial authorities, the organization was charged with controlling the influx of people into the area. The civic initiated a system of 'marshals', people who were to allocate registration numbers to those already settled and make sure that no one arrived after the cut-off date. This put the marshals in a position where they had, on the one hand, a valuable commodity to offer (the number which symbolized legality) and on the other hand a sanction; they had the power to inform demolition teams from the provincial authority that a shack had been erected after the cut-off date. The marshals were quick to exploit the opportunity opened up to them; they approached people building shacks and told them that they needed a registration number to stay. Prices for a number ranged from R 200 to R 500 (USD 37–95). The marshals could demand a relatively high price because they had the sanction of informing the provincial authority that the house was being built illegally and therefore had to be destroyed.

This, then, is an example of how social practices that are external to the formal understandings of the problematique undermine attempts at control. The practice of applying registration numbers that were supposed to serve as a basis for a development intervention was, from the point of view of the developers, corrupted. In its manifestation as a social practice, the allocation of numbers to residents in Cato Crest served to entrench another power structure, that of a faction of the local leadership.

THE TAXI WARS

The leadership dynamic in Cato Crest then, was driven by two mechanisms, one external to the community, another internal. The external concern was about the acquisition of resources. Cato Crest was a poor settlement, and almost all the resources available to the local leadership originated outside the area. More specifically, most resources originated in the meeting between local organizations and external aid and development agencies. But some resources originated in other areas than beneficiary organizations. It was in the struggle to achieve control over one of these, the minibus taxi industry, that the leadership struggle got out of control.

For many South Africans minibus taxis that operate out of the black residential areas are the main means of transportation. The industry has its background in the removal of black settlements to the urban fringe and has grown rapidly since deregulation in 1987 (Khosa 1990). This expanding sector has had a huge impact on the South African economy. It was estimated that in 1994 the industry provided four motor manufacturing companies with a turnover of about R 3 billion a year (USD 567 million), capital investments of R 3.5 billion (USD 661.5 million), and that it had created some three hundred thousand jobs (Khosa 1994:56).

At first the black taxi industry was seen as one of the success stories of the new liberal economic policy of the apartheid government. Former President P.W. Botha, commenting on the benefits of transport deregulation, spoke warmly about the 'astounding success of the black taxi industry' (Dugard

1996:17). But the industry was plagued by a violence that has had enormous consequences. The conflict between rival taxi organizations in the Cape between 1990 and 1993, for example, claimed more than sixty-six lives and caused R 3.6 million (USD 680.000) of property damage (Dugard 1996). Since 1987 more than twenty thousand people have been killed in violent conflicts in South Africa and many of those deaths have been attributed to taxi wars.

Between 1990 and 1994 the National Party Government set up a number of commissions to examine violence in South Africa. These commissions, of which seven dealt with taxi violence, are collectively known as the Goldstone Commission (Dugard 1996). The official explanation is that cut-throat competition is the cause of the violence. This is undoubtedly an important factor. Deregulation has led to an increase in the number of operators and to falling profits. Most of the conflicts seem to arise over rights to control certain routes (McCaul 1990). The organization of the industry has also changed; whereas before deregulation most taxis were driven by their owners, it is now most common for the driver to be employed by a taxi owner who owns more than one vehicle (Khosa 1994:62). Other factors have also contributed to the taxi wars. In addition to cut-throat competition, Dugard (1996) has pointed to factors such as internal rivalry in taxi associations, conflicts between drivers and owners, and police complacency.

In 1993, a taxi company commenced a service running between the city centre and Cato Crest. A community worker for the local provincial authorities, who is popular in the area because of the work that she has done, approached the taxi companies serving nearby townships and asked whether they would come and collect people in Cato Crest. They refused, saying that they did not want dirty squatters and prostitutes in their cars. A majority of the new arrivals were from Inanda, one of the areas that people fled to in the 1960s when Cato Manor was destroyed, and two of these owned taxis that they had operated for the Inanda Taxi Owners' Association (ITOA). They were willing to provide a route between Cato Crest and town, and they started a local association in co-operation with ITOA. These taxis ran the Inanda—town route in the morning, and then the extremely lucrative route between Cato Crest and town during the day. This route pays well because a return trip, Cato Crest—central city—Cato Crest, can be accomplished in twenty minutes. The fare is R 1.20 (20 cents) and a full taxi takes eighteen passengers. In the evening the taxis would run between town and Inanda again, leaving Cato Crest without transportation after six in the evening.

Also in 1993, ANC members who had been in exile came into Cato Crest and supplied military training to a group of about twenty-five to thirty young men. The soldiers were welcomed as they guaranteed the safety of Cato Crest residents. Towards the end of 1994, when the uMkhonto weSizwe (Spear of the Nation, the armed wing of the ANC, usually abbreviated to MK) and the old South African Defence Force were merged into the new South African National Defence Force, these youths went to an army training camp and were tested for admission. All but ten failed, amongst them the leader. They were given R 12,500

(USD 2,400) each and discharged. They came back to Cato Crest and by all accounts spent the money on drink and drugs.

The taxi war occurred when the MK tried to take over the taxi industry with the backing of a faction of the leadership. The ensuing conflict marked the end of the old leadership in Cato Crest. The MK was for a while successful in driving their opponents out and they instigated a regime of terror. They would go from shack to shack and demand money for protection, bullets and *intelezi* (a type of traditional medicine used in war). People who refused to pay, as well as people working for ITOA were killed. This sparked retaliations. For more than a month Cato Crest resembled a war-zone, with a police and military checkpoint at the entrance. The police were unable to halt the conflict and confined themselves to monitoring the situation. All in all fourteen people were killed. A group of residents finally managed to mobilize against the MK, and with the backing of ITOA finally drove the MK away. In the process, however, all the community structures were destroyed. For a long time there were no organized community politics going on in the area. Some of the people formerly active in the local leadership had been driven away by the MK, others were seriously discredited by their association with the group. When I left the area a few months after the taxi war, the group of residents that had successfully driven the MK away were attempting to set up a new development committee. There were indications, however, that a mechanism similar to that described above also marked the work of that group (see, Nustad 1999 for a detailed account).

CONCLUSIONS

The power struggle in Cato Crest took place in a framework constituted by the attempted development in Cato Crest. The labelling of these processes as 'informal' may lead to them being analysed separately from the formal attempt at development, as the conceptual negation of the formal. For the formal/informal dichotomy to be applicable to the analysis of the strategies of the leadership in Cato Crest, the processes described by the dichotomy need to be examined, not as a part of an informal political system, but in the interface of the formal and the informal. This is where Hart's original definition of informality is useful: for him, informality is a phenomenon that appears from a certain perspective, that of a formal understanding, and consequently, what is perceived as 'formal' determines the reference to informality.

My observations from Cato Crest provide evidence of three different constructions of the formal/informal dichotomy. These constructions of the formal/informal divide highlight the relational nature of the political processes in Cato Crest, and why it is necessary to include some conception of the formal to explain them. First, we saw the extension of the formal to something seen as informal. The developers attempted, but failed, to make local organizations in Cato Crest an extension of their own form of domination. The election of local community organizations that supposedly represented the people in Cato Crest was an attempt at imposing a bureaucratic form on the local politics in Cato Crest. The developers' intervention rested on an assumption that the form of bureaucratic organization and elected representation could be extended to Cato Crest.

Second, in its manifestation as a social practice, the relationship between developers and community organizations negated the formal. What was an attempt by the developers to extend their organization into Cato Crest had the consequence of negating any attempt at development. Resources were appropriated by the community leadership in Cato Crest and fuelled the local power struggle. The two constructions of the informal/formal dichotomy are here represented in the same relationship: the first as the ideal that the developers were striving for, the second in the practice of the community leadership. The two constructions therefore appear as two perspectives on the same relationship, the first from the point of view of the developers, the second from the point of view of the community leadership. When we look at this first nexus—the developers attempt at extending their formal structures to Cato Crest, and the community leadership's inversion of that attempt—one fact is immediately apparent. It is not possible to explain either of these strategies by focusing on the groups themselves. The strategy of building power through the control of development resources was made possible only because the community leadership in Cato Crest was placed in a relationship to a formal institution, which in turn saw the leadership as an extension of itself.

Third, The MK's regime of terror represents yet a different construction of the dualism: the regime they instigated, based on terror and extortion, was only indirectly linked to the developers' formal intervention. In that respect, it represented an alternative to the legal form of domination that the developers sought to establish. The regime of terror instigated by the MK soldiers is the informal activity most indirectly connected to the formal development. But again, they rose to power as hired guns in the struggle over representation between different factions in the community leadership. It was with the backing of one faction of the leadership that they first challenged the minibus taxi operation. Only subsequently, when that process spun out of control, did the MK become sufficiently strong to establish a local power base.

From the above it should be obvious that informality is in the eye of the beholder. One of the original merits of Hart's work was to point out that 'the informal' cannot be equated with the irregular, irrational, unpredictable, unstable and invisible. The informal denotes phenomena and processes that escape certain definitions of reality. The people whose strategies and acts are denoted as informal, would of course believe that they lived within social forms which help them to manage their lives.

Thus defined, the formal and the informal are two perspectives on the same issue, and both are defined by an attempt at control. But in the discussion of 'the informal', this relationality has been lost. Hart (1992) later criticized the concept that he had coined because of the uses it had been put to. He asks himself why the concept had been so readily taken up by development economists and supplies an answer: 'By stressing what it was not (not "good form", not amenable to the dominant form of rationality, beyond "management"), the concept appealed to the sensibilities of an intellectual class who could not grasp what the economic activities in question positively represented' (Hart 1992:217).

The concept seems to have suffered the same fate in South Africa. It gained in popularity in the mid-1980s when the apartheid regime set out to strengthen the informal sector as part of its reforms (Rogerson and Preston-Whyte 1991). In the first edited book on South Africa's informal economy, the editors begin by pointing out the fussiness of the concept. They nevertheless want to retain it as an analytical concept because 'it is difficult ... to eschew the use of the terminology in light of its massive popularity in planning and current policy circles in South Africa' (Rogerson and Preston-Whyte 1991:2). The thing to avoid, then, is a rigid definition of the 'informal' as a sector separate from the formal, and instead examine those social processes that are external to formal analyses.

Informal activities must be analysed in relation to a conception of the formal. The form imposed on Cato Crest was meant to stabilize the situation so as to open it up for the development intervention. But the model only captured a part of the dynamics of social life in Cato Crest, and the local leadership was able to turn this mismatch to their own advantage. The informal thus comes to denote that part of social life that escapes the definition of reality constructed by state and bureaucratic institutions. Further, and this is why I believe that retaining the dichotomy is useful, informal activities will necessarily be defined by the formal intervention.

In Cato Crest, informal political strategies replaced the developers' ideal of a participatory development process where the local community was connected to the developers by a representative community organization which would have been an extension of the developers' type of domination. These political strategies took a number of forms, from regimes of terror and extortion to inversions of the developers' intentions, and they all represented competing forms of domination. The formal/informal dichotomy reminds us, however, that all these forms were dependent on each other.

References

ANC 1994, *The Reconstruction and Development Programme.* Johannesburg: Umanyano Publications.

Bayart, Jean-François, 1993, *The State in Africa: The politics of the belly.* London: Longman.

CMDA Cato Manor Development Association, 1995a, *Annual report 1994*

—, 1995b, *Greater Cato Manor structure plan.*

—, 1994, *Business plan.*

The Cato Manor Development Association: Institutional Structure. Programme Management, http://www.cmda.org.za/cmda/history/methods/progress.html

Coovadia, C., 1991, "The role of the civic movement" in M. Swilling, R. Humphries, and K. Shubane (eds), *Apartheid city in transition.* Cape Town: Oxford University Press.

Dugard, Jackie, 1996, "Drive-On? An analysis of the deregulation of the South African taxi industry and the emergence of the subsequent 'taxi-wars'". MPhil dissertation, University of Cambridge.

Edwards, Ian, 1994, "Cato Manor: Cruel past, pivotal future", *Review of African Political Economy* (21)61, pp. 415–27.

Friedman, Steven, 1993, *The elusive 'community': The dynamics of negotiated urban development.* CPS Social Contract Series. No. 28, Johannesburg.

Friedman, Steven and Maxime Reitzes, 1996, "Democratization or bureaucratization?: Civil society, the public sphere and the state in post-apartheid South Africa", *Transformation* 29, pp. 55–73.

Hart, Keith, 1992, "Market and state after the cold war: The informal economy reconsidered" in Dilley, R. (ed), *Contesting markets: Analyses of ideology, discourse and practice.* Edinburgh: Edinburgh University Press.

—, 1973, "Informal income opportunities and urban employment in Ghana", *The Journal of Modern African Studies* (11)1, pp. 61–89.

Heymans, C., 1993, "Towards people's development? Civic associations and development in South Africa", *Urban Forum* (4)1, pp. 1–20.

Izwi, 1997, "Durban Metro takes over responsibility for Cato Manor development". December 1997.

Khosa, Meshack M., 1994, "Accumulation and labour relations in the taxi industry", *Transformation* 24, pp. 55–71.

—, 1990, "The black taxi revolution" in Nattrass, Nicoli and Elisabeth Ardington (eds), *The political economy of South Africa.* Cape Town: Oxford University Press.

Mail & Guardian, "Cato Manor on the fast track to growth", 31 August 1998.

Makhathini, Maurice 1992, "Squatting dynamics: A look from within Cato Manor". Paper presented to the 1992 ASSA conference, Pretoria, 28 June–1 July.

Makhathini, Maurice and T. Xaba, 1995, "A report on the socio-economic survey of the informal area of Cato Crest in Cato Manor". Unpublished.

Mayekiso, Mzwanele, 1995, "Bell Curve, South African style: Rewriting the civics movement", *Southern African Report*, March, pp. 29–33.

—, 1993, "'Institutions that themselves need to be watched over': A review of recent writings on the civic movement", *Urban Forum* (4)1, pp. 21–54.

McCaul, Colleen, 1990, *No easy ride: The rise and future of the black taxi industry.* Johannesburg: South African Institute of Race Relations.

Murray, Colin and Gavin Williams, 1994, "Land and freedom in South Africa", *Review of African Political Economy* (21)61, pp. 315–24.

Nustad, Knut G., 1999, *Community leadership and development administration in a Durban squatter settlement.* PhD thesis, University of Cambridge.

—, 1996, "The politics of 'development': Power and changing discourses in South Africa", *Cambridge Anthropology* (19)1, pp. 57–72.

Robinson, P.S., 1994, "Cato Manor: A legacy of South Africa's past or a model for reconstruction?" Paper presented to the Sixth International Planning History Conference at the University of Hong Kong, 21–24 June 1994.

Robinson, P.S. and C. Forster, 1996, "Cato Manor: Progress and obstacles facing South Africa's largest RDP project". Unpublished paper.

Rogerson, Christian and Eleanor Preston-Whyte, 1991, "South Africa's informal economy: Past, present, and future" in Preston-Whyte, Eleanor and Christian Rogerson (eds), *South Africa's informal economy.* Oxford: Oxford University Press.

Seekings, Jeremy, 1997, "Sanco: Strategic dilemmas in a democratic South Africa", *Transformation* (34), pp. 1–30.

—, 1992, "Civic organization in South African townships", *South African Review* 6, pp. 216–38.

Shore, Cris and Susan Wright, 1997, *Anthropology of policy: Critical perspectives on governance and power.* London: Routledge.

Shubane, K., 1994, "Civics have a future ongoing and vital role in development", *Finance Week*, 12–18 May, pp. 34–36.

Skar, Harald O., 1985, "Questioning three assumptions about the urban informal sector" in Skar, Harald O. (ed.), *Anthropological contributions to planned change and development*. Gothenburg studies in social anthropology 8. Gothenburg: University of Gothenburg.

Smit, Warren, 2001, "The changing role of community based organizations in South Africa in the 1990s, with emphasis on their role in development projects" in Tostensen, Arne, Inge Tvedten and Mariken Vaa (eds), *Associational life in African cities: Popular responses to the urban crisis*, pp 234–49. Uppsala: Nordiska Afrikainstitutet.

Swilling, M., 1993, "Civic associations in South Africa", *Urban Forum* (4)2, pp. 15–36.

Swilling, M., W. Cobbett and R. Hunter, 1991, "Finance, electricity costs, and the rent boycott" in Swilling, M., R. Humphries and K. Shubane (eds), *Apartheid city in transition*. Cape Town: Oxford University Press.

Tsenoli, L., 1994, "Interview with Lechesa Tsenoli: President of the South African National Civics Organization", *Development and Democracy* 8, pp. 31–35.

CHAPTER 4

Who Rules the Streets?
The Politics of Vending Space in Lusaka

Karen Tranberg Hansen

The official turn to "free market" economies in many African countries in the 1990s has altered the relations between states and informal economic activities described in much scholarship of the previous decades. These relationships are still taking shape, their precise nature depending on the specific situation and the cultural, political, and economic dynamics of their time and place. The need for contextualizing the meaning of "the market" forces us to examine market discourses both as webs of meaning and as empirical realities that are entangling the livelihoods of the people we study (Carrier 1998:8–9). Drawing on many years of work on informal economic activities in Lusaka, this chapter explores the meeting between the "free market" and ongoing informalization in Zambia. To do so, I draw on research I did during the summer of 1999 into controversies surrounding the 1997 opening of an "ultra modern" market in Lusaka, the New City Market, and the events that followed it, including a massive crackdown on street vendors across the country in 1999. Organized as a series of snapshots, the chapter begins with brief background remarks, moves on to the new market, and then turns to the street clearance and its aftermath.

By Christmas 1998, street vending in Lusaka, Zambia's capital with an estimated population of some two million, had achieved anarchic proportions. Main streets, alleyways, and shop corridors in the city centre, and many other spots besides, had turned into one huge outdoor shopping mall where thousands of street vendors were selling all manner of goods. The crowding in this the least capitalized and most labour intensive part of the economy caused traffic problems, posed public health dangers, and gave pickpockets and thieves a field day. Street vendors seemed to rule the streets. Walking about in the city centre had become sheer agony for shoppers and pedestrians alike. Several business houses and offices of international organizations relocated to outlying areas. Previous attempts by the Lusaka City Council (LCC) to remove vendors from the capital's main streets had at most a temporary effect. The street vendors always returned and nothing seemed to change.

With this lacklustre outcome of decades of failed street clearance efforts as a backdrop, it came as a great surprise to many Lusaka residents and long-term observers that street vendors did not return immediately following a vast removal effort by municipal councils, supported by police and paramilitary in all the cities and provincial towns between the end of April and June of 1999. Focusing on Lusaka's street vending scene, I explore the timing of this particular intervention and the relative truce that has followed it. I ask, what were the issues that mattered this time and made the aftermath of this intervention so different from most previous ones. I also briefly sketch developments in the tense relationship between street vendors and the state over the years that have passed since the most dramatic removal of vendors from Lusaka's main streets in 1999.

Government regulators and the news media talked about the crackdown on vendors as an issue of law and order or of sanitation and health. As I discuss below, lots of other issues were involved and they somehow converged at this particular time. Strikingly absent from most of the discussions were references to the "social" and "human dimension" of the removal of thousands of vendors from the streets. Issues such as these go to the core of the development predicament in a country like Zambia because they cast light on the vexed encounter, or more precisely the misfit, between the economic rhetoric of the "free market" and local efforts at making a living.

Informalization: Past and Present

Throughout history, markets and marketeers, traders, and vendors who pursue their work in public places in the developed and developing world have formed contested sites of interaction (Agnew 1986; Clark 1988; Cross 1998; Picavet 1989). From the earliest days of colonial Lusaka, African residents developed informal work and housing initiatives in efforts to provide the goods and services that colonial governance did not provide (Hansen 1997:34). Much like the colonial rulings that guided the location and type of economic activity Africans could pursue in the city, post-colonial regulations on markets, trade licensing, town and country planning, and public health restricted trading and small scale manufacture to established market places (Mulwila and Turner 1982). Over the years, highly profiled confrontations took place between traders and state agents in Lusaka as they did elsewhere (Clark 1994:372–401; Robertson 1997:130–145, 263–274; Tripp 1997:158–160). Although traders occasionally were chased off city streets, they usually returned. That is to say that small scale traders and marketeers throughout the city centre and the townships widely ignored the existing legal regulations.

The informalization process gained considerable momentum from the restrictive import and currency regime during most of President Kaunda's Second Republic (1972–91). Street vending was referred to as "black marketing" in the late 1970s and early 1980s, when shortages of basic commodities were a fact of everyday life (Fundanga 1981). Soap, detergent, candles, cooking oil, bread and sugar were among the items that were frequently in short supply in the legal retail outlets and therefore sold on the black market. When prices of several essential commodities were decontrolled and some subsidies phased out under pressure from the IMF in 1982, the term blackmarketing became used in a more inclusive sense, referring to any illegal marketing activity, among others, unlicensed vending in streets, yards, and homes (Hansen 1989). Some of those goods were obtained by "suitcase traders" travelling abroad to source them but on a much smaller scale and with a more limited variety of goods than today. Police occasionally undertook sweeps of black marketeers, confiscated their goods, and imposed fines or prison sentences on them. But most marketeers returned to the streets. In fact, the Second Republic could never have functioned without these informal activities because the command economy of the one-party state was unable to produce and distribute even basic necessities.

The shift toward a liberalized economic regime in the wake of multi-party elections in 1991 has had complicated effects. Privatization of major national assets is underway. Foreign investments in retail trade—with generous government tax rebates—have resulted in the establishment in Zambia's cities and towns of local branches of major South African companies involved in food provision, house wares, and apparel. There are Chinese investments at all levels of the economy from the former para-statal company Mulungushi Textiles in Kabwe, to steel production in Lusaka, and above all to retail of low-cost clothing produced in China and sold in Chinese operated shops. These enterprises hire low paid Zambian workers and repatriate their profits. At the same time as these new businesses began targeting customers across the board, street vendors and traders were selling all manner of goods to ordinary consumers. And the removal of trade barriers under the COMESA (Common Market for Eastern and Southern Africa) free trade deal in October 2000 has made Zambian products like cement, cooking oil, soap, and textiles expensive compared with COMESA imports, resulting in loss of domestic market share (EIU 2000:23). In popular representations of the formal economy, freeing the market has meant opening it up to external rather than local participation.

If life was hard for many during the long years of Kaunda's Second Republic, it has got harder for most Zambians during the Third Republic's liberalized economic regime. Retrenchment both in the public and the private sector has made more people depend for their living on self-reliance of the informal kind. The social and human costs of the IMF/World Bank's Structural Reform Programme (SAP) have been high. In terms of too many indicators—among them education, health, longevity, child mortality and nutrition, formal employment and wages—Zambians in the first half of the 1990s were worse off than they had been in the mid-1970s (GRZ and UN 1996).

The lack of formal economic development in the 1990s fuelled the rapid expansion of informal activities, micro-enterprises, and street vending across Zambia's cities and into the countryside. This growth was much more marked in retail trade than in small scale manufacture, and it was particularly visible and dynamic on the street vending scene. Because they contravene most existing regulations, such activities continue to be viewed as illegal. Exploiting the streets as an infrastructure, the vendors' expansion across public space kept on provoking interventions by municipal authorities. But these developments should not be considered as a mere replay of previously rehearsed battles. The Third Republic's political and economic liberalization combined with SAP are producing a state-informal economy relationship that is more antagonistic than ever. While control of public markets and vending has been a long-standing problem for the Zambian government, recent events are in fact rather different from previous ones. As I discuss shortly, continuous controversies before and after the opening in August 1997 of the New City Market in Lusaka give dramatic evidence of fundamental changes in the relationship between the government and the informal economy.

The "Office of the President" and the "Vendors' Desk"

Zambia's strained economic atmosphere and its tenuous political situation make intervention in marketing and street vending a complicated strategy. When in 1993 the LCC undertook one of many sweeps of street vendors—assisted by police and military, it clashed with the vendors and a riot ensued. President Chiluba, elected into office as the head of the Third Republic in 1991, intervened strongly on behalf of the street vendors, blaming the Council for not finding alternate places before forcing them off the streets. This decision was subsequently interpreted to mean that anyone could trade and erect a stand anywhere on the streets. And that is precisely what occurred: traders, and aspiring vendors, leaving designated markets within the city and the townships, descending on the city centre, and setting up stands they put together from wood, plastic sheeting, and cardboard. The term *tuntemba* came into use for these provisional structures, which from Bemba translates approximately as "area of operation". This term graphically captured what in fact the mass of traders were doing, staking claims on space for their own activities.

Because of President Chiluba's 1993 intervention, street vending as an activity became popularly known as the Office of the President. Extending this friendly atmosphere towards small scale business, the President in December 1996 established a Vendors' Desk at State House, staffed by a Deputy Minister, to attend to the concerns of vendors. Commenting on the high price for economic and political reforms paid by the people of Zambia who had brought him into office, the President said: "My government is promoting income generating activities in the informal sector. Now we have a street vendors desk at State House which caters for people in the informal sector" (*Post*, 7 August 1997).

The New City Market

Impressed by open-air markets he saw during his first official trip to Israel in 1994, President Chiluba returned to Zambia speaking enthusiastically about plans for Israeli built public markets (*Post*, 2 May 1995). The "ultra modern" market that in turn was commissioned to be developed on the site of a section of the Old Soweto Market was already controversial before its opening (*Chronicle*, 4–7 July 1997). There were questions about the source of the market's funding as conventional tender procedures seem not to have been followed (*Sunday Times of Zambia*, 7 December 1997).[1] Israeli consultants supervised the

---

1. The market was not financed by Israel (*Post*, 2 May 1995). According to one report, some funding was rumoured to come from undisclosed government budget lines and some from the European Union. The prefabricated structures were imported from Israel (*Times of Zambia*, 3 July 1996). When the Auditor General's Office queried the expenditures, it revealed irregularities in the handling of finances, record keeping, and contract allocation (*Sunday Times of Zambia*, 7 December 1997).

construction which was carried out by personnel from the Zambian Army and the National Service (*Zamba Daily Mail*, 4 January 1996). Before the development of the new market infrastructure within the space of the Old Soweto Market could even begin, many vendors had to be relocated in order to make room for the construction. The vendors did not vacate the old market until after several demonstrations at the City Council where they were promised stands in the new market. Construction began in 1995 and was completed in 1997. When it opened in August 1997, the New City Market was the first, and so far only, market in Zambia to be managed by a private management company rather than the municipal council.[1]

Because the construction of the new market took longer than expected, many vendors left the market area, setting up *tuntembas* in the streets. Although many vendors initially had fought to be allotted market stands, they began an exodus within the first days of the opening of the new market. And those who operated from within the new market complained of the high fees charged by the management company and of competition for customers from the vendors who had moved out on the streets.

Ever since the new market's opening, there were conflicts between inside and outside vendors, police, and the City Council. On the night of the opening, *tuntembas* on the outskirts of the market and in nearby streets were burned—according to reliable sources, by the City Council (*Post*, 11 August 1997). Vendors demonstrated at the Civic Centre[2] and State House, but to no avail (*Post*, 13 August 1997). The Council invoked a rule to the effect that no vending was allowed within a 200 meter distance from the new market. Vendors kept shunning the new market, leaving their stands for the streets. In the first months after the market's opening, the occupancy rate hovered around 35 per cent (*Post*, 12 December 1997). A year later, it had dropped to 25 per cent (*Financial Mail*, 3–9 December 1998). In April 1999, the occupancy rate stood at 10 per cent, that is, some 400 registered traders to approximately 4,000 permanent stands (*Times of Zambia*, 22 April 1999). The press roundly described the new market as a "white elephant".

The Crackdown on Street Vendors

In the pre-dawn hours of 28 April 1999, council workers, police and paramilitary in riot gear razed the temporary market structures in Lusaka's city centre, extending the demolition the following night and weeks all across the city, into the townships and residential areas (*Times of Zambia*, 29, 30 April and 3 May 1999). In the city centre alone, more than 2,000 street vendors were reported to have been removed from the streets (*Sunday Times of Zambia*, 2 May 1999). In June, similar operations took place on the Copperbelt and in the towns along

---

1. In debates leading up to the development of the new market and during the years of its construction, it was always referred to as the New Soweto Market. On the day he officially opened it, president Chiluba introduced the name, the New City Market. By 2002, the LCC was in charge of managing the market.
2. This is the local name for the Lusaka Town Hall.

the line-of-rail (*Times of Zambia*, 5 June 1999; *Zambia Daily Mail*, 10 June 1999).

Representatives of the various Municipal Councils insisted that vendors everywhere were given advance notice so that they could salvage materials from their *tuntembas* prior to the demolition. Although they were aware of the LCC's plan, many vendors in Lusaka expressed their disbelief, or opposition, to the implementation. We are "under" the Vendors' Desk at State House, not the LCC, they claimed (*Zambia Daily Mail*, 23 April 1999). Steven Daka, a 23 year old paint vendor, told a news reporter that he never expected such decisive action. No one really took council warnings seriously, he said, since previous threats had not usually been backed by deeds. He and many other vendors expressed their anger, directing their frustration against the Vendors' Desk deputy minister whom they felt had let them down (*Sunday Times of Zambia*, 2 May 1999).

On the morning of 28 April, "It was a very unnerving experience to be greeted by the sight of countless numbers of demolished stalls [that were] previously a hive of activity", Steven Daka told a journalist. Moses Chishimba, a 23 year old "barbecue" vendor who ran a roadside tea-making, meat-roasting, and potato chips frying business, had come to work as usual at 6 am to set up his food operation. Although he was "greeted by the sight of demolished stalls..., somehow, he just couldn't bring himself to accept that a similar fate had befallen him... Yet he was just in time to see a LCC bulldozer making short work of his wood and polythene sheet stall... He could not believe his eyes as his stall, from which he had raised the money to build a two-roomed structure in Kanyama township, was loaded among several dozen others, onto council tippers" (*Sunday Times of Zambia*, 2 May 1999).

Prior to, and after, the demolition, the LCC encouraged vendors to return to designated markets in the townships, apply for stands in the new City Market or set themselves up at Chibolya, a site west of the light industrial area that in 1997 had already been slated for a market to accommodate some 2,000 traders. Its development had been slow and by 1999 it was in fact not completed (*Zambia Daily Mail*, 12 June 1997). And vendors complained that Chibolya was too far away to walk from the city centre for its new market to attract customers. The stalls at the New City Market did fill up, and the interior built-up sections of Lusaka's long established markets, Kamwala, Old Soweto, and the City Centre Market were soon unbelievably crowded. Six months after the street clearance, the number of traders in those markets had trebled (*Times of Zambia*, 24 October 1999). The open-air section, Kambilombilo, between the new City Market and Old Soweto Market under a line of high power electric pylons also filled up immediately. By March 2000, more than 3,000 people were selling their merchandise under the power lines (*Times of Zambia*, 14 March 2000). And some returned to designated markets in the townships. Police and paramilitary kept a visible presence in the city centre. While vendors have attempted to return to trading in public in a variety of disguises, among them car boot sales, sales from containers, and doing business during morning and afternoon rush hours, Lusaka's main streets for a while remained almost clear of the mass of street vendors that was a common sight throughout the 1990s.

Public reactions to the removal of street vendors were almost unequivocally positive. Everyone agreed that street vending had grown out of hand. Something had to be done. Across the country, the crackdown had taken place with hardly any incidents of violence and rioting. In Lusaka, the City Council and its first woman mayor took the main praise for the action. The deputy minister in charge of the Vendors' Desk in State House insisted that vendors should comply with the LCC and conduct their business from designated markets (*Zambia Daily Mail*, 24 April 1999). But Steven Daka, the paint vendor whom I quoted earlier, asked: "What is the use of having our own minister if he can't protect our interests?" Daka argued "since there are no more [street] vendors, he should also be declared redundant" (*Sunday Times of Zambia*, 2 May 1999). The President, who on so many previous occasions had intervened to overturn LCC attempts to implement municipal authority rulings, kept out of the fray, letting his Vendors' Desk deputy minister take the flak.[1] Two weeks later, the President was reported as saying that the LCC crackdown on street vendors had State House blessing. With no explanation of his sudden change of mind, he referred to the working out of measures to ensure that vendors conducted their businesses "in a well managed area" (*Post*, 14 May 1999).

The War against the *Tuntembas* and Its Timing

When the dramatic removal of street vendors took place in Lusaka, the New City Market had been open, and nearly empty, for almost two years. In addition, there were lots of vacant stands in the 40 designated city markets as there were in the 54 designated township markets. What prompted the removal at this particular time rather than, say, one year earlier? The demolition exercise must have been costly, involving paramilitary, police, and LCC workers who actively and forcefully continued to harass potential street vendors for several weeks after the demolition. In the wake of the street clearance, police and paramilitary maintained a visible presence in Lusaka's streets for quite a while.

What made all of this happen? While it is evident that the President must have given the green light to the removal, the LCC itself had changed. Since early 1999 Lusaka had a new mayor, who was bent on cleaning up the capital, and a cohort of new council members less connected though bribery and favours with business and special interest groups in the city. They appeared to be more pro-active on the civic front than previous council members. Invoking existing regulations on the location of trade and concerns with public health to remove the vendors from the streets, they also instituted new by-laws to prevent their return.

The removal of the vendors was said to create a conducive environment and promote better health for all in Lusaka and to enhance the security both of vendors and the urban population in general. I suggest that environmental and

---

1. References to "political interference" from the highest level of the government were frequently made in news media discussions and such references were part of the official statements the public relations spokesman of the LCC made both to the press and in individual conversations. Daniel M'Soka, LCC public relations officer, personal communication, 4 August, 1999.

health concerns coupled with law and order issues precipitated the specific timing of the removal but that the underlying reasons were of a political and economic nature. Last but not least, few commentators took the vendors' side and
the social and human costs the removal represented were not seriously reckoned
with.

The City Council and the Vendors' Desk deputy minister argued that the
move to designated markets would situate vendors in an enabling work environment with necessary amenities (water and sanitation) that would enhance their
security. But the amenities were not ready at the new market site at Chibolya
and they had never been sufficient in the established markets at Kamwala and
Old Soweto that now experienced oppressive overcrowding.

The move to designated markets had regulatory effects that attracted little
attention in the news. Placing vendors in designated markets made supervision
and discipline more straightforward than when they operated temporarily, on a
shifting basis, in different street locations. What is more, it would be possible to
make vendors pay trade licenses and market fees, thus enhancing council reve-
nue collection. Vendors had not paid such fees when operating on the streets,
and the freedom from fee payment was in fact one reason why many had left
established markets for the streets. Most of them were small operators, and
small scale vendors and marketeers complain that fees in designated markets
would deplete their capital. They would also lose the network of customers they
had established on the streets. "Going to the market [e.g., the New City Mar-
ket]," said Steven Daka, "is like going from town to the village, it means having
to start afresh all over again and that is not easy". Daka had grown up on the
Copperbelt and he was worried about what to do (*Sunday Times of Zambia*,
2 May 1999).

The public health issue constituted a strong concern. The crowding of vendors in Lusaka's city centre area that had grown to anarchic proportions
through the 1990s took place in a city whose basic infrastructure was lacking in
too many respects, including water, sanitation, electricity, refuse removal, fire
protection, and transportation. Lusaka's garbage piles had grown into moun-
tains. Every rainy season for many years had sadly witnessed the return of chol-
era. There is no doubt that issues of health and sanitation helped to tip the
political scales in favour of demolition. These issues were bound to adversely
strike the thousands of international specialists who were expected to participate in an international conference on HIV/AIDS and STDs (sexually transmit-
ted diseases) in Lusaka in September 1999.

Unlike in the 1970s and 1980s when international development policy
prioritized rural areas, in the 1990s major international organizations bent on
improving local infrastructure, resources, and the environment, began to involve themselves on the urban policy scene. In the late 1990s, the European
Union was the largest single founder (rather than lender) of Zambia's external
development support, in a variety of sectors.[1] Part of this support was an urban
markets upgrading programme financed from the European Development Fund.

1. Keith Reid, EU liaison to the Zambian ministry, personal communication, 9 August, 1999.

In Lusaka, this program targeted Chilenje (upgrading), Lilanda (new market), and Nyumba Yanga (new market). The project plans included market developments on the Copperbelt as well. Clearly, the departure of vendors from local markets was embarrassing for the implementation of this program. How would it make sense to plan or upgrade markets when no vendors were operating?

But above all, in my judgement, issues that were closely linked with economic liberalization efforts, with introducing "free market" practices, were at the heart of the exercise to remove vendors from public spaces. A modern shopping mall, financed by British and South African capital, had been under construction for a couple of years and opened in October 1999. Manda Hill, the name of this new mall, is located outside the city centre in a transitional zone between medium to upper-income residential areas, the parliament, and a small scale industrial area. Not far from Manda Hill, another upscale mall, the Arcades, has been planned. Additional mall developments were proposed on Cha Cha Cha road in the heart of the city where for decades the bustling City Centre Market had been located.

How could the government open up the market to potential investors when anarchy and lawlessness reigned on the streets? To be sure, the country's investment climate was not attractive when goods produced by local firms and potential investors did not sell well in formal shops because of a strong black market and the easy availability of counterfeit products from Southeast Asia. In fact between 1997 and 1998, several long-established branches of international firms that had manufactured locally pulled out. They included Dunlop Tyres that quit operating in Zambia entirely, and Colgate-Palmolive, Johnson & Johnson, and Reckit & Coleman that moved their operations to Zimbabwe, using the Zambian market only for distribution. The local textile and garment industry had already shrunk as its poor quality and expensive products were unable to compete with imported textiles and garments, including second hand clothing.

In the end, the street vending issue had acquired a political complexion that concealed the social nature of the vending phenomenon, masking its human implications. People in Zambia took to selling in the streets because wage labour jobs were few and far between; even if you held a conventional job, the purchasing power of your wage was less in 1999 than it had been twenty-five years earlier. Except for a few lone voices, hardly anyone expressed concerns about the effects of the crackdown on the future livelihoods of vendors. In a letter to the editor of one of the dailies, Chama Mulalami from Lusaka expressed his disappointment and indignation against insensitive press articles celebrating "the vendors' demise". Vendors were "poor souls", he said, "making a living in these hard times" (*Times of Zambia*, 26 May 1999, p. 5). And the executive director of an NGO coordinating committee, Grace Kanyanga, criticized the LCC for not considering the consequences suffered by women. Women vendors she said, lost their investments because of the street clearance. She called on state and local authorities to strengthen income generating activities for women "because they were more responsible in feeding their families than men who wasted income on selfish activities" (*Times of Zambia*, 21 June 1999).

Vending as a Way of Life: The Social and Human Dimension

And what of the vendors themselves? The news media introduced their experiences and reactions largely as apt illustrations, much in the manner that I have done here. More detailed information about the world of small scale trade is available from a 1995 survey commissioned by the LCC of some 450 street vendors in the city centre and the area around Kamwala Market. This survey was part of a comprehensive study of street vending commissioned by a government established inter-ministerial committee of relevant ministries, the LCC, and NGOs.[1] The findings from this unpublished survey (LCC 1995), a newspaper report (*Post*, October 1997), and my own observations from brief interviews with 100 traders in two designated markets in Lusaka three months after the removal of the vendors in 1999 differ in significant respects from descriptions presented in studies of the informal economy in Lusaka in the late 1970s and early 1980s, including my own (Bardouille 1981; Hansen 1980, 1982, 1989; Jules-Rosette 1979). While none of these recent findings are representative in any statistical sense and need to be interpreted with caution, they do hint at new interrelationships and patterns that invite much closer scrutiny.

The 1995 LCC survey suggested that Lusaka had approximately 7,000 street vendors, some 3,000 of whom operated in the city centre. With each vendor taking up around one square meter, some 3,000 square metres of city centre space was occupied by vendors who were constructing two to five *tuntembas* per day (*Post*, October 1997). A 1997 estimate sets the number of vendors in Lusaka, excluding the townships, at 12,000 (*Zambia Daily Mail*, 24 February 1997). At this rate of growth, it is not surprising that a threshold of intolerability was being reached around Christmas 1998 as I indicated at the outset.

The majority of the vendors came from low-income residential areas that all have poor access to health and education facilities. A small proportion came from medium to high-income areas (*Post*, October 1997). Almost half of all these vendors had left established markets in order to set up their own operations on city centre streets.

Most of the vendors had basic education or more. Only 5 per cent had never attended school, 45.7 per cent had grade 7 education, close to 40 per cent had left school after grade 9 or 10, and a little less than 10 per cent had completed grade 12 (LCC 1995). That is to say, street vending in Lusaka in the mid-1990s was definitely not an occupation for persons who had never gone to school, but rather a refuge for school leavers who had not found formal jobs.

---

1. I read this unpublished report in the LCC research office thanks to MaCloud Nyirenda, research officer, on 5 August, 1999. The report contains several documents prepared by a number of participants in the study; many pages were lacking and the report is not sequentially paginated. The following ministries and NGOs participated in the study: the Office of the President; Ministry of Home Affairs; Ministry of Information; Ministry of Environment and Natural Resources; Ministry of Health; Ministry of Community Development and Social Welfare (Youth Department); Ministry of Youth, Sport, and Child Development; Ministry of Housing; Lusaka City Council (LCC), LCC epidemics control, and LCC legal department; University of Zambia, School of Medicine, and Institute for African Studies; Environmental Council of Zambia; ZARD (Zambia Association for Research and Development).

More than half of the vendors sold groceries, vegetables, fruit, meat and candy; a little less than one third sold new and second hand clothing apparel, and shoes. The rest sold a variety of other things. More than half purchased their commodities from Lusaka based wholesalers, and almost a quarter got their supplies from local retail shops. Less than 10 per cent of the vendors obtained their goods from neighbouring countries, a proportion that suggests that at this level of the economy, suitcase trade may be taking place on a more limited scale than is usually assumed (LCC 1995).

Two observations make this survey very different from those of the past. First, the majority of street vendors were male: close to 90 per cent male compared to 10 per cent female (LCC 1995); and second, the majority were young people: three quarters of the vendors were in the 20 to 30 age category, which in this part of Africa is considered to be youth (*Post*, October 1997). While the LCC survey does not address marital status, my own observations from research in city centre and township markets since 1992 as well as from the work I discuss below from 1999 suggest that the majority of these young men were not married. Many earn so little that they are unable to establish their own households. In short, today's age and gender profile differs from that of the late 1970s and early 1980s when the overwhelming majority of small scale traders in city and township markets as well as in streets and yards were middle-aged women who contributed to household support.

Because I was interested in the aftermath of the removal of the street vendors, I conducted two brief surveys in 1999. One set of interviews was done in the New City Market and the other in the peri-urban township, Kaunda Square, Stage 1. In choosing the latter location, I wanted to explore whether former street vendors were returning to township markets. In each market, I interviewed a sample of vendors in trades that loosely approximated the different categories of trade commonly practiced in Lusaka. When engaging vendors in conversation my concerns were with their work histories, personal backgrounds, and household contexts. I was particularly anxious to learn how they explained the events that had taken place on Lusaka's market and street vending scene.

In the New City Market, twenty of the 53 vendors I interviewed had operated from designated stands within the market since its opening in August 1997. When business had been slow inside the new market, they had also sold their goods in the outside section, Kambilombilo, in the Old Soweto market; or they had traded illegally, on the streets. And close to one third, namely 19 vendors, had obtained stands inside the new market after their *tuntembas* on the streets were destroyed. The rest, some 16 vendors, had moved into the market sometime during the two preceding years. The majority of the long-established vendors operated in the most profitable trading categories, second hand clothing sales and tailoring, while the majority of those who had entered the market after the removal worked in trades that account for more than half of the entire trading sector in this market: drinks and food, groceries, tapes, and hardware. The profit margin in this sector is small and vendors depend on a very fast turnover to make money.

Thirteen of the vendors who had obtained stands in the new market after their removal in 1995 to yield space for its construction were young men, most of them selling groceries, hardware, and tapes. While they liked the improved security and cleanliness in the new market, they all complained of lack of business and loss of profit since their relocation. We have to pay a market fee here every day, they explained, but we don't always make money. They said that some of their colleagues had already left the new market to operate from Kambilombilo at Old Soweto, others were making occasional forays with selected merchandise into the city streets, while some said that they would give the new market a few more months to see if and how business was going to develop.

The sample of 50 vendors interviewed in the designated market at Kaunda Square, Stage 1, a peri-urban township planned as a site-and-service scheme in the early 1970s, was a proportional cross-section of the same trade categories as in the New City Market. After the crackdown in the city centre, the LCC had turned toward the townships and residential areas removing all street and outside vendors who since the early 1990s had everywhere left their designated market stands in large numbers to trade in the open air.

By the end of July 1999, the market at Kaunda Square, Stage 1, had expanded in the number of vendors it accommodated but not in space. The place was crowded and disorienting. Previously established space divisions between different trades had become blurred as prepared food vendors were cooking and serving meals next to second hand clothes vendors. The vendors who had remained within this market for years were now joined by vendors relocated from the township's open-air markets and a smaller number who had come back to this market after operating in the Old Soweto Market and on the streets.

My observations in both these markets three months after the vendors were removed from the city centre streets suggest that only a fraction had secured stands in designated markets. Inevitably, the question arises of where all the vendors had gone? Many of the vendors with whom I spoke said that they were "confused". They had heard rumours about plans for a demolition of their *tuntembas* but did not know the date. Their confusion reflected the implication they had drawn about freedom in the Third Republic's new political culture. Indeed, an environment had been created in which street vendors believed that their activities were sanctioned by the head of state. It is not a surprise that the massive crackdown confused them.

While attempting to control the environment within which vendors operated, the government has not proposed any consistent or substantive policy to improve the opportunities for the thousands of people, the majority of them young men, whose livelihoods were destroyed in this massive demolition. From the point of view of the vast majority of people in Zambia, "vending" and "marketing" are understood, not as economic categories, but as personal livelihoods. Indeed, many street vendors had made money; some of those who had been displaced to the New City Market told me that they built their own homes from earnings they made selling goods from their *tuntembas* and that they were "going broke" in the new market.

What marketing represents at this socio-economic level is first and foremost household provisioning. The earnings first go into the pot, *mapoto,* and next they contribute to reproducing the enterprise. Many enterprises never expand because marketing serves household provisioning. Above all, the organising of marketing hinges on the socio-cultural dynamics within households. These dynamics do not operate according to the textbook principles that are assumed to structure the "free market" but instead they embed economic practices in the socio-cultural relations of households. These relations shape the reality on the ground and are physically evident in who is an "owner" or a "worker", and who, by gender and age, operates in what trades and which product lines. After the crackdown, the least well capitalized of all these vendors: young men who are unable to establish their own households, and middle-aged women burdened by household headship, faced more difficulties than they had ever encountered before.

Upholding the Truce

There have been intermittent reports of vendors defying council police, returning to main streets at rush hour to target customers and of youth selling fruits, vegetables, and household items at traffic light intersections (*Zambia Daily Mail*, 14 November 1999; *Times of Zambia*, 18 February 2000). Still, as I noted at the outset, it came as a great surprise to many Lusaka residents and long-term observers of local developments that the vendors had not returned at once to the streets of Lusaka's city centre.

To keep vendors off the streets, the LCC insisted on enforcing existing local authority regulations and enacted a set of rules referred to as a "nuisance act" originally proposed in 1992. Among other things, the nuisance act prohibits the sale of produce in any public place other than a designated market and it also prohibits the purchase of goods from street vendors. A new magistrates court was to be established at the Civic Centre to deal with cases contravening local authority regulations (*Zambia Daily Mail*, 16 March 2000). While the planning of the "nuisance court" was underway, the LCC swept across the urban landscape to "keep Lusaka clean." The mayor's fervent action has earned her the name, the "iron lady". The list is too long for more than brief mentions.

In September 1999, the vendors in Lusaka's City Centre Market in the heart of the city, learned that their market was to be demolished to provide space for the development of a high-cost shopping complex (*Zambia Daily Mail*, 28 September 1999). In early November, the mayor announced that trading under the high voltage power lines at Old Soweto's Kambilombilo Market would be prohibited because of "dangers involved during the rainy season" (*Post*, 1 November 1999). We recall that this particular market had absorbed a very large portion of the overflow after the street clearance exercise in early May. Toward the end of November, police undertook a sweep of street vendors, street kids, and currency dealers (*Sunday Mail*, 21 November 1999).

Just before Christmas and at the beginning of 2000, the LCC undertook two high-profiled actions. One was the demolition of buildings containing shops and warehouses outside Kamwala Market allegedly because they did not meet building standards (*Zambia Daily Mail*, 11 December 1999). The Indian traders whose buildings were reduced to rubble complained that members of the former city council had allotted the plots to them (*Times of Zambia*, 14 December 1999). The second action took place at the beginning of January 2000, when the LCC evicted "foreign" marketeers from all designated markets. According to LCC investigators, one half of the space of the major markets was taken up by foreigners (*Times of Zambia*, 5 January 2000). Foreigners with valid trading licenses and immigration documents were told to relocate to a special market building opened in a warehouse in 1999 to accommodate foreigners and transborder traders. With its 1000 stands, the COMESA flea market, as this new market was called, was already crowded (*Times of Zambia*, 3 February 2000). Illegal foreigners were to be deported. Several were arrested. This action did raise some concern about the effects it might have on the survival efforts of the thousands of refugees that Zambia hosts and about "retaliation from abroad" for Zambian traders working in other countries (*Zambia Daily Mail*, 10 February 2000).

High-handed in its efforts to control Lusaka's trading environment, the LCC applied the same yardstick to all, lumping together many different types of activities. Because vendors have different needs, depending on age and gender, and because distinct trading and vending activities have different space requirements, there have been many casualties of the clean-up. The removal exercise around Kamwala Market, for instance, included all the "corridor" tailors who ran their businesses outside established shops in several streets in the second class trading area behind the market. The tailors did not constitute a health hazard or cause traffic problems nor did they pose particular problems of security. In fact, they added a very colourful aspect to some rather drab looking streets. On a cold July morning in 1999 at the New City Market, I ran into Enock Chipondo, a tailor in his sixties, whose tailoring career on a corridor stand behind Kamwala Market I have followed since 1992. He despaired when he tried to give me directions to find him inside the Kamwala Market next to some tobacco vendors. No one will see me there, he complained, customers won't know where to look. The Kamwala crackdown also included the vendors of live goats who had operated behind the Indian stores for years from a location known by everyone, Indian and African alike, who needed a goat for special occasions. The new location the LCC proposed was too far removed from the city centre for customers to reach the goat vendors on foot.

Where Have All the Vendors Gone?

Recent and ongoing market and mall developments in Lusaka have not reduced the economic attraction of the streets to which many vendors kept returning. Some have constructed mobile stands or displays they can easily dismantle. Since 1999, only one of the EU funded new markets in Lusaka that I described earlier has been completed. This is the market in Nyumba Yango, a middle-income residential area where no market existed before. The construction of market structures in Chilenje and Libala almost reached completion. Parts of already existing markets were demolished to yield space for this construction and hundreds of vendors lost their stands. In 2002, the unfinished market structures stood in ruins, testifying to a breach between the LCC and the building contractor (*Zambia Daily Mail*, 29 November 2002). The LCC lacks funds for market developments and looks elsewhere for financing. At Lusaka's oldest market, Kamwala, hundreds of vendors were forced away as a Chinese funded market redevelopment began. The project is a private investment by a firm, China Hainan, through a contract that allows it to run the market for 65 years in order to recover the capital investment (*Zambia Daily Mail*, 11 August 2001). During the construction phase, the initial plan for a single storey market complex with over 400 stalls and 12 shops was revised to 101 shops of different sizes (*Sunday Mail*, 12 January 2003). Most of these shops were allotted to Chinese and local businesses that were able to pay the high rentals. It is not surprising that problems arose as vendors displaced by this development were unable to acquire stalls (*Sunday Times*, 2 February 2003).

Many vendors uprooted by market and mall developments are retreating into the Old Soweto Market. Because the built-up core of the market is severely congested, vendors continue to operate under the electric power lines in spite of the LCC's repeated warnings that the market is a health hazard and must be demolished (e.g., *Sunday Times of Zambia*, 1 December 2002). Within the market different groups of marketeers quarrel over the collection of illegal market fees in a process that is pitting marketeers associations, the LCC, and the ruling political party against one another (*Zambia Daily Mail*, 9 February 2001).

Unlike president Chiluba, Levy Mwanawasa who succeeded him at the end of 2001 has not taken any stand on the vendors' issue. Lusaka's new mayor, colonel John Kabengo, often refers rhetorically to the LCC's five-year strategic plan to rid the city of street vendors and make it clean and green (*Zambia Daily Mail*, 26 July 2001). However, he was tardy at implementing any action against vendors. Slowly but surely the vendors returned to Lusaka's streets although they did not take them over in the manner they did in the period 1993–99 with the blessing of the Office of the President. While since 1999 the LCC has removed vendors from specifically targeted locations in Lusaka now and again, a major action to clear vendors from the streets did not take place until August 2002 in a joint effort by the Zambia police, paramilitary, and LCC police (*Zambia Daily Mail*, 26 August 2002). In the wake of this action, paramilitary personnel and trucks with police at the ready were stationed in heavily trafficed parts of Lusaka for quite a while.

The "war" between street vendors and the local authority in Lusaka has been continuing on and off since the 1970s. Each major effort by the LCC and the state police to join forces to remove vendors from the streets is followed by a lull during which vendors devise new ways of selling their goods on the streets. The "nuisance court" to deal with violators of the market by-laws that was planned after the crackdown on vendors in 1999 did not in fact start operating until February 2003 (*Sunday Mail*, 20 April 2003). New market and mall constructions are either not completed, such as the case of the markets at Chibolya,

Chilenje, and Libala, or stalled, such as the Arcades mall. With a local authority that is poorly organized and lacks financial means to construct markets from which vendors can operate on a fee paying basis, it is no surprise that vendors in Lusaka keep returning to the streets in order to make a living.

Conclusion

Because local authority regulations on markets and vending had been ignored for many years, the crackdown on street vendors in 1999 took many by surprise. Why was this action staged at that particular time and what took place subsequently? In this chapter I explored issues concerning sanitation and health, and law and order, that no doubt helped precipitate this action. Even then, I suggested that the overriding issue was a Zambian version of "free market" policy that was bent on opening up the economy for investments. Its implementation required in fact not freedom but institutional control (Carrier 1998:13). That is to say that the issues that pitted marketeers, street vendors, enforcers of market rules, and state actors against one another in the crackdown on vending in public in 1999, and its aftermath, are to do with the variable meanings of a "free market" and the significance of vending as a way of life in Zambia today.

In the time of SAP in Zambia, markets and vending activities in public have absorbed growing numbers of people due to employment retrenchment in both the public and private sector. But "the market" that the head of state and policy reformers are talking about has increasingly become detached from its social bonds (Thrift 1998:161) as concerns about fiscal and economic reforms have sidelined distributional issues and questions about opportunities and life chances for the general population. Although the scope of informalization has widened as more and more people are trying to make a living without being wage employed, the relationship of vendors to their state has become more hostile than before. For at the same time as the Zambian government is opening up "the market" to foreign investment, it has accentuated regulations that contain and control opportunities for informal activities on the home front.

The crackdown and its aftermath lumped small scale economic activities together without regard to the many levels of differentiation both among marketeers and vendors and among their activities. But considering absolute numbers, growth rates, and divisions by gender and age of street vendors at the time of the crackdown, this world of informal economic activity was both quantitatively and qualitatively different from the small scale marketing and trade of the 1970s and 1980s. These differences have important implications for policy that the government has not spelled out. I have suggested in passing that the structures of difference that are most likely to have consequences for future economic opportunity in Lusaka continue to be based on gender and that they will be increasingly shaped by age. Which is to say that youth is a particularly salient category to figure into policy if we are to enhance urban household reproduction efforts for tomorrow. The call is not for an iron fist of control actions to be applied across the economic board, but a policy that is flexible enough to reckon with the distinct needs of some of the many diverse branches of activity conducted on the streets.

Acknowledgements

This chapter is a product of long-term research in Zambia and draws specifically on work I conducted in Lusaka during the summer of 1999 with support from Northwestern University's University Research Grant Committee and its Centre for International and Comparative Studies. During my time in Zambia, I was a research affiliate of the Institute for Economic and Social Research at the University of Zambia. Norah Rice and Chris Simuyemba worked along with me on a variety of research tasks. The chapter also draws on observations from subsequent research in Lusaka on a project concerning urban youth.

References

Agnew, Jean-Christophe, 1986, *Worlds Apart: The Market and the Theater in Anglo-American Thought*. Cambridge: Cambridge University Press.

Bardouille, Raj, 1981, "The Sexual Division of Labour in the Urban Informal Sector: Case Studies of Some Townships in Lusaka", *African Social Research* 32:29–54.

Carrier, James G., 1998, "Introduction" in Carrier, James G. and Daniel Miller (eds), *Virtualism: A New Political Economy*, pp. 13–24. New York: Berg.

Clark, Gracia, 1994, *Onions Are My Husband: Survival and Accumulation by West African Market Women*. Chicago: University of Chicago Press.

—, (ed.), 1988, *Traders versus the State: Anthropological Approaches to Unofficial Economies*. Boulder: Westview Press.

Cross, John C., 1998, *Informal Politics: Street Vendors and the State in Mexico City*. Stanford: Stanford University Press.

EIU (Economist Intelligence Unit), 2000, *Country Report. Zambia*. 1st Quarter 2000. London: EIU.

Fundanga, Caleb, 1981, "Shortages of Essential Commodities and the Urban Poor in Lusaka" in International Labour Office (ed.), *Zambia: Basic Needs in an Economy under Pressure*. Technical Paper No. 11, pp. 151–60. Addis Ababa: Jobs and Skills Programme for Africa.

GRZ and UN (Government of the Republic of Zambia and the United Nations System in Zambia), 1996, *Prospects for Sustainable Human Development in Zambia: More Chances for Our People*. Lusaka: Pilcher.

Hansen, Karen Tranberg, 1997, *Keeping House in Lusaka*. New York: Columbia University Press.

—, 1989, "The Black Market and Women Traders in Lusaka, Zambia" in Parpart, Jane I. and Kathleen A. Staudt (eds), *Women and the State in Africa*, pp. 143–60. Boulder: Lynne Rienner Publishers.

—, 1982, "Planning Productive Work for Married Women in a Low-Income Settlement in Lusaka: The Case for a Small-Scale Handicrafts Industry", *African Social Research* 33:211–23.

—, 1980, "The Urban Informal Sector as a Development Issue: Poor Women and Work in Lusaka, Zambia", *Urban Anthropology* 9:199–225.

Jules-Rosette, Bennetta, 1975, "Alternative Urban Adaptations: Zambian Cottage Industries as Sources of Social and Economic Innovations", *Human Organization* 18(3):389–408.

LCC (Lusaka City Council), 1995, "Report of the Technical Sub-Committee of the Inter-Ministerial Committee on Street Vending". Unpublished report filed at LCC research unit.

Mulwila, John and Kaye Turner, 1982, "Small-Scale Industrial Development and the Law", *African Social Research* 33:151–74.

Picavet, Ruud, 1989, "The Love-Hate Relationship between Government and the Informal Sector: The Case of Street-Vending in Peru" in van Gelder, Paul and Joep Bijlmer (eds), *About Fringes, Margins and Lucky Dips: The Informal Sector in Third-World Countries*, pp. 181–208. Amsterdam: Free University Press.

Roberston, Claire C., 1997, *Trouble Showed the Way: Women, Men, and Trade in the Nairobi Area, 1890–1990*. Bloomington: Indiana University Press.

Sklair, Leslie, 1998, "The Transnational Capitalist Class" in Carrier, James G. and Daniel Miller (eds), *Virtualism: A New Political Economy*, pp. 135–59. New York: Berg.

Thrift, Nigel, 1998, "Virtual Capitalism: The Globalization of Reflexive Business Knowledge" in Carrier, James G. and Daniel Miller (eds), *Virtualism: A New Political Economy*, pp. 161–215. New York: Berg.

Tripp, Aili Mari, 1997, *Changing the Rules: The Politics of Liberalization and the Urban Informal Economy in Tanzania*. Berkeley: University of California Press.

Zambian Newspapers

Chronicle
"New Soweto Market too far for buyers", 4–7 July, 1997.

Financial Mail
"Stalls still go begging at new market", 3–9 November 1998, p. 2.

Post
"Markets were to be ready by October 1994"; and Editorial Comment, "Constructing false markets", 2 May 1995, p. 1 and 6.
"Chiluba justifies SAP", 7 August 1997, p. 1 and 2.
"Lusaka council sets *tuntemba* ablaze", 11 August 1997, p. 1 and 3.
"Burnt *tuntemba* owners protest", 13 August 1997, p. 1, and 6–7.
Guest Columnist, Sibalwa Mwaanga, "Street vending", October 1997.
"Only 35% of New Soweto Market is occupied", 12 December 1997.
"Chiluba blessed vendors' removal", 14 May 1999, p. 3.
"Mayor Nava explains removal of marketeers", 1 November 1999, p. 1.

Sunday Mail
"Police swoop on Lusaka vendors, street kids", 21 November 1999, p. 1.
"Crisis looms over new Kamwmala market", 12 January 2003, p. 8.
"Vendors face wrath of the law", 20 April 2003, p. 8.

Sunday Times of Zambia
"A parliamentary committee's report unveils can of corruption", 7 December 1997.
"Stalls razing leaves Lusaka vendors in shock", 2 May 1999, p. 9.
"Illegal Soweto market to be demolished, warns minister", 1 December 2002, p. 2.
"Marketeers, LCC showdown looms", 2 February 2003.

Times of Zambia
"New Soweto Market takes shape", 3 July 1996.
"Lusaka vendors ejected", 22 April 1999.
"Vendors bow out", 29 April 1999, p. 1.
"Kamwala stalls razed", 30 April 1999, p. 1.
"Vendors crackdown spreads to the townships", 3 May 1999, p. 1.
"Lusaka City Council being run by remote control?" 23 May 1999, p. 6.

Letter to the editor, "Final triumph over vendors: Don't gloat over hapless souls yet",
    26 May 1999, p. 5.
"UNIP admits backing vendors." 5 June 1999, p. 3.
"Kalulushi vendors given 30-day ultimatum." 21 June 1999, p. 3.
"Lusaka's cleanest 'Uhuru' without street vendors." 24 October 1999, p. 7.
"Lusaka's Kamwala 'ruins'." 14 December 1999, p. 5.
"Lusaka Council to evict foreign marketeers." 5 January 2000.
"200 traders arrested." 3 February 2000.
"Hawkers still a nuisance." 18 February 2000, p. 7.
"Council orders Old Soweto market traders to vacate." 14 March 2000.
"Police, Lusaka council sweep away vendors." 26 August 2002, p. 3.
"Market stalls temporary—mayor." 17 April 2003.

Zambia Daily Mail
"Delays to erect Soweto Market worry vendors." 4 January 1996.
"Vendors desk stirs to life at State House." 24 February 1997.
"'War' erupts between vendors desk and Lusaka Council." 12 June 1997.
"Lusaka vendors await word from State House." 23 April 1999, p. 1.
"State orders street vendors to move out." 24 April 1999.
"Mufulira vendors given ultimatum." 10 June 1999, p. 2.
"Lusaka marketeers reject to be shifted." 28 September 1999.
"Vendors trickling into the streets." 14 November 1999, p. 1.
"Demolition squad strikes again." 11 December 1999.
"Lusaka starts to sieve aliens from council markets." 10 February 2000, p. 7.
"Vendors Court gazetted." 16 March 2000, p. 4.
2001, "Soweto market posing danger to traders and customers." 9 February 2001.
"Vendors re-emerge on Lusaka streets." 26 July 2001, p. 7.
Editorial "Comment" on Chaina Hainan contract. 11 August 2001, p. 4.
"Lusaka vendors swept off the streets." 26 August 2002, p. 2.
"Government revokes contract to construct markets." 29 November 2002.

SECTION II
ECONOMY, WORK, AND LIVELIHOODS

The political and economic contexts in which the research discussed in this section's chapters was conducted differ from those of the early 1970s when the term the informal sector was first coined. Since then, Structural Adjustment Programmes advocated by the World Bank and the International Monetary Fund have aimed to reshape Africa's faltering economies as has the more recent introduction of 'free market' policies in many former centrally planned economies. Many Africans today are freer but poorer than they have been in decades. And income inequalities are more marked than ever before. These macro-level processes are giving rise to critical questions concerning the effects of ongoing economic and spatial transformations in cities across the African continent.

How are we to understand the massive growth of urban informalization across class in turn-of-the-century Africa? As the chapters in this section demonstrate, if informal activities provide an economic safety net, they do so differently, depending on type and level of activity, the resources brought to bear on their operation, and the local context that shapes the participation of actors. Whether a growth potential in fact exists requires understanding of the nature both of the activities in question and of the social relations that structure them.

Ilda Lourenço-Lindell uses her longitudinal research in Bissau to qualify the positive view of informal activities by donor agencies and NGOs who advocate a micro-enterprise model as a solution to overall economic decline. She identifies two strategies in the domain of trade: one for accumulation and one for survival. A hierarchical political culture of patron-client relationships was taken so much for granted in Guinea-Bissau that its operational principles became pervasive. In the time of structural adjustment the merchant class enriched itself through preferential access to adjustment loans and imports, establishing lucrative businesses that straddled the formal/informal divide. By contrast, a growing number of small scale traders, largely in foodstuffs, many of them women who operated from peripherally located and often spontaneously developed markets, struggled for daily survival. She concludes that celebratory approaches to the informal economy must be tempered by a recognition of the heterogeneity and change of informal economic activities as well as of the exploitative conditions under which many of these activities are carried out.

Barbara Kazimbaya-Senkwe's chapter on home-based enterprises (HBEs) in Kitwe on the Copperbelt of Zambia provides additional insights into the heterogeneity of informal economic activities. They are not solely performed by individuals from low-income groups. The actors in her preliminary study were disillusioned formal sector employees, some of them retrenched from the public sector, others were persons who had deliberately left their formal jobs for self-employment and higher earnings, and still others held on to their formal jobs at the same time as they engaged in economic sideline activities from home. Most of these home based enterprises (HBEs) were in service and trade, only a few were in manufacturing (mat making, carpentry, tailoring, battery making). More men than women were the proprietors of these enterprises. Household members, including women, young adults and children, often contributed labour.

HBEs testify to the productive nature of housing by combining the economic use of housing space, family labour, and time. Profitability depends on type of activity and types of amenities available in the residential area, particularly electricity and water supply. Such services are not regularly available in low-income areas. The operation of these enterprises raise several legal issues as most of them take place in settings zoned for residential use. They also raise environmental issues.

The relative success of HBEs in this study is due, not to the availability of micro-credit arrangements or bank loans but for the most part to assistance with start-up capital from other household members. Many of Kazimbaya-Senkwe's respondents did not know where to obtain credit. Those who knew considered the credit amounts to be too small to be of any use and the short repayment schedules to be too demanding. Hardly anyone had collateral to secure a bank loan.

Amin Kamete's chapter on home industries in Harare also highlights the limited degree to which operators of small scale enterprises had received credit from any of the local and external NGOs who advocate credit support. What are called home industries in Harare differs from HBEs by their location in high-density areas in designated 'industrial estates' zoned for small scale economic activities in manufacturing and commerce.

The home industries Kamete examined included carpenters, brick-makers, spray painters, welders, tailors and hairdressers. While some of these activities violated rules regarding taxes, labour and wages, they have a reputation for illegal activity which according to Kamete is wrong. They are popular with customers because they provide commodities and services that are needed at affordable prices. They also provide skills training and employment to the young. And they make use of both family and non-family labour. Situated on the frontier between the formal and the informal city, these activities have both forward and backward linkages, and many of them add value to their products. But this is not understood by local authorities who tend to view them as less business oriented than their formal sector counterparts.

Like Kazimbaya-Senkwe, Kamete highlights that hardly any of his respondents had obtained micro-finance, and that most of them relied on family, personal savings, or retrenchment packages for their start-up capital. The chapters offer hardly any evidence of direct NGO support such as credit and training programmes. Kazimbaya-Senkwe also notes how formal sector skills in some cases had to be unlearned and new skills acquired as a result of a personal, rather than an institutionally supported, quest. Such observations are striking, given the popularity of credit provision and skills training in program and policy statements in the development industry. Improving this state of affairs requires more than self-help by small scale entrepreneurs and intermittent support by NGOs. It also invites government action on many fronts to reshape the institutional structures that continue to reproduce livelihoods in the interstices of the economy.

CHAPTER 5

Trade and the Politics of Informalization in Bissau, Guinea-Bissau

Ilda Lourenço-Lindell

Informal activities in African cities have experienced a rapid expansion in recent decades. Policies of structural adjustment and a marginal position in the global economy have changed the conditions under which African urban dwellers make a living. In the face of poor availability of wage jobs and declining real wages, urbanites increasingly rely on informal ways of income earning. Thus, while African cities have long been characterized by the presence of an "informal sector", they are now experiencing new waves of "informalization". In this context, understanding the dynamics of informal economies seems to be of relevance. This chapter attempts to make a longitudinal analysis of social processes of informalization in Bissau, the capital of Guinea-Bissau. It aims to show that the production of informality is a more complex process than is often assumed, as it may involve a variety of groups and interests. Further, it uncovers how various groups in Bissau are faring differently in the context of the current extensive informalization.

The literature where state-society relations and informal economic activities cross paths is one useful entry point into understanding processes of informalization. One position within this literature has been that much informal activity in Africa can be traced to a societal "disengagement" from the state and formal market channels (Rothchild and Chazan 1988; Azarya and Chazan, 1987). Unfavourable state laws and policies, poor performance and declining opportunities for political participation prompt urban residents to develop alternative solutions such as circumventing official channels and regulations and withholding production, in order to reduce dependence on and gain autonomy from those channels. It is often argued that such rather unorganized popular responses may have far-reaching consequences, in terms of undermining the credibility, the outreach and revenues of the state. In this line of reasoning, economic informalization in a context of structural adjustment is seen as bearing the seeds of the liberation of society, and informal activities are portrayed as in opposition to and autonomous from state power and as inherently democratic. This celebratory view of informal activities has inspired a great number of studies of urban informal economies (for example, Tripp 1989 and 1997). These assumptions have been strengthened by other influential texts such as Hyden (1990) and de Soto (1989), and appropriated by the anti-state agenda of donor agencies.

The basic assumptions on which the above understanding is based have however been challenged. Firstly, some have emphasized the inseparability and symbiotic interactions between the informal activities, the state and the formal economy, and how the expansion of informality usually involves a large degree of political networking (for example, Bangura and Gibbon 1992; Roitman 1990; Lemarchand 1991; Macharia 1997). Actors may seek to have one foot in each sphere and may neither need nor wish to disengage from the state. The implications are that informal actors are not necessarily autonomous from the state and that the growth of informal activities does not necessarily signal their liberation or the increasing irrelevance of the state in the economy. Secondly, some have highlighted the role of externally induced structural adjustment policies imposing economic liberalization and restrictions in the extent of state regulation and intervention (Bangura and Gibbon 1992; Sjögren 1998; Grey-Johnson 1992). International institutions have prompted African countries to join the global drive towards economic deregulation and given high priority to turning the "informal sector" into an engine for economic growth and into a major provider of services. As Grey-Johnson summarizes it: "The emerging policy thus seems to be one of shrinking government responsibility in providing economic and social protection to the African people and let them (...) fend for themselves" (1992:79). Or as Peattie (1987:856) explains in relation to housing policy, "what appeared in the 1960s as an emancipatory movement has been translated into a language of privatization".

Structural approaches have also been concerned with understanding contemporary informalization processes. They have come to focus on the role of global economic restructuring in fostering a proliferation of informal activities across the globe, what has been termed the "informalization approach". This perspective highlights the ways in which capital is using informal or unregulated ways of operating as part of flexible production practices, and its strategies to reduce costs and protect profits, often with the complicity of the state (Castells and Portes 1989:13, 30; Portes and Schauffler 1993:49; Sassen-Koob 1989; Sassen 2000:118; Meagher 1995). From this point of view, an increase in informal activity in the current phase of late capitalism is not interpreted as the liberation of small informal actors but rather seen as the worsening of their working conditions and a downgrading of labour.

In this chapter, I will probe the value of the above approaches for understanding the expansion of informality in post-independence Bissau. Pervasive informality in Bissau, I will argue, is a process resulting from the interplay of a variety of actors and pressures, whose complexity is better grasped by combining elements of different perspectives that might seem *a priori* incompatible. On the one hand, some components of the disengagement perspective lend credit to the struggles and achievements of popular groups. On the other hand, the informalization perspective gives us the tools to understand current changes and developments in informal economies, including the role of the state and international actors. In Bissau, the politics of informalization has involved instances of both engagement and disengagement.

The shifting character of the informal economy and its relations with formal institutions necessitates a definition of informality that is not too narrow or rigid. Here, the informal economy is generally understood to consist of economic activities that evade one or several aspects of existing legislation pertaining to those activities (but not necessarily unregulated or independent from the state). However, the boundaries delimiting this field are permeable, they encompass a considerable grey zone and are trespassed by categories of actors who operate in both formal and informal spheres. The emphasis here is less on the distinction between formal and informal and more on the relations between the two.

The analysis focuses on the food trade sector, which illustrates well the social processes of informalization and is the arena where major struggles between the rich and the poor unfold in Bissau. Trade has been an historically important activity in the city and its importance has probably increased in the last couple of decades. On the one hand, in spite of an extremely peripheral position in the global economy, growing volumes of international commodities are channelled through the city. On the other hand, increasing numbers of Bissauans rely on trade activities for survival. Indeed, the range of options for income generating activities is narrow. The industrial sector is very small and declining, along with a shrinking public sector. Bissau is a small capital city, with a population estimated at something over 300,000 inhabitants. Beyond the old colonial centre, the urban landscape is dominated by unplanned settlements, including many unplanned market places. The largest of these market places was reported to gather about 3,000 traders in the late 1990s (Monteiro 2001).

The analysis is based on both available literature on the Guinean process of adjustment and my own fieldwork conducted in 1992, 1995 and 1999, when I studied household food strategies, informal livelihoods and social networks among disadvantaged groups in Bissau (Lourenço-Lindell 2002). A survey of 453 households was conducted in two neighbourhoods in Bissau, covering close to 10 per cent of their populations. The survey included information on the trading activities of household members who headed small trading enterprises. In addition, qualitative interviews were conducted with the heads of about sixty trading enterprises. The majority of these were small traders selected on the basis of the household survey but a handful were engaged in wholesale and import-export enterprises. Government officials connected to market activities were also interviewed.

INFORMALITY IN THE PRE-ADJUSTMENT ERA

Guinea-Bissau gained independence in 1974 after eleven years of war with Portugal, the colonial power. During this period, the liberation party PAIGC (Partido Africano para a Independencia da Guiné e Cabo Verde) succeeded in mobilising a large segment of the population, in establishing alternative systems of distribution of goods and services and in instituting local government structures that functioned more or less democratically. At independence, people's political engagement was high. The single party proclaimed itself as the leading force in society and declared a socialist orientation towards development. The state assumed a leading role in the economy. Among other things, it largely monopolized external trade and established a network of some 230 commercial outlets throughout the country, the People's Stores. Their function was to collect agricultural produce from peasants and supply consumer and producer goods, at prices fixed by the state (Galli and Jones 1987).

Only a few years after independence, disappointment started mounting (Rudebeck 1988). The state, increasingly centralized and repressive, alienated itself from the masses. The political elite became insulated from popular influence. Mass organizations were controlled by the Party and did not allow for participation in top-level decisions (Galli and Jones 1987). The government distanced itself from initial social goals and failed to improve the conditions of the population (Galli 1990; Rudebeck 1990). In fact, government policies turned the terms of trade against producers. In the sphere of distribution, the People's Stores were insufficient in their coverage of the territory. They functioned inefficiently and irregularly and shortages in consumer goods were frequent. The party rapidly lost its political and economic credibility.

The responses of Guineans to these worsening conditions are described in a number of texts, sometimes in a "disengagement" vein (Galli and Jones 1987; Galli 1990; Bigman 1993; Handem 1987). Succinctly, "producers became increasingly unwilling to cooperate and sacrifice to maintain the state", Galli and Jones argue (1987:108). Some emigrated to Senegal and Gambia to grow cash crops there instead. There was a tendency for peasants to cut back on sales of rice, the main staple. Sales of export crops to official outlets also declined sharply, as producers sold their goods at higher prices through clandestine networks. Acting in the interstices of the state's commercial network, the Dyulas, a group of professional itinerant traders that has been active in West Africa for centuries, continued to move goods across borders and to be a major source of supply for many villages. They offered an alternative to official channels, which paid disadvantageous prices and had frequent supply disruptions. This reportedly intensified smuggling of rice and cash crops across borders.

The far-reaching effects of these popular responses are also discussed by the same authors. Diversion of crops from official channels and the large scale of smuggling deprived the government of taxes but also of export products and thus of foreign exchange. The government losses were estimated at US$14 million in 1983 (Galli and Jones 1987:114). This decline in domestic revenues eventually contributed to an increase in state dependence on external assistance for importing food and covering the budget deficit, which resulted in a growing external debt.

The disengagement argument often focuses attention on resistance by rural producers. The above analyses on Guinea-Bissau also give little attention to what was happening in urban areas, while rural people were supposedly disengaging. The city of Bissau is mainly portrayed as a consumer of a large share of the national resources, the beneficiary of state policies and an enclave increasingly distanced from the rural masses. The little that has been written allows, however, for some reflections on the problems that urban residents were facing during this period and how they were responding.

Continuing a trend already clear in the colonial time, supply of basic goods such as food to the city was largely dependent on international sources, aid and externally financed imports, as the government seems to have been unable to buy enough rice from domestic producers (Bigman 1993). Given the trade deficit and the lack of foreign exchange, the government cut down on imports of basic items. This situation resulted in chronic shortages and empty stores in Bissau, where rice shortages were acute in the 1970s and early 1980s (Bigman 1993; Funk 1991). Ration slips were required to buy imported goods in state stores and a large amount of time was spent queuing to acquire them. The urban population often had to resort to the parallel market with its speculative prices. But urban groups were positioned differently to cope with or even benefit from the scarcities, and were not all affected in the same way.

According to the same authors, government employees had priority to food rations. Access to basic items was thus facilitated by having a public job or contacts with the party and party organizations. Two groups in particular seem to have benefited from chronic food scarcities and the related deepening external dependence for food. These were high rank state officials controlling the flow of imports and the employees in state stores. Bigman (1993:115) refers to "a certain amount of corruption and nepotism" among the latter. Galli and Jones (1987:115) say that shortages were partly due to "increasingly widespread corruption which pilfered supplies and skimmed off profits". State officials took part in large scale smuggling and hoarding of goods and made "them scarce in order to charge exorbitant prices on the black market" (Galli and Jones 1987:69). Fernandes (1994) also asserts that basic goods could rarely be found in official stores but circulated through "clientelist networks", originating among state employees and nationalized enterprises. While the latter gradually decayed, he argues, private fortunes accumulated by using informal channels of circulation. These groups thus derived great power from their privileged access to goods in an environment of scarcity as well as from their manipulation of the interface between official and parallel distribution systems.

The majority of the population in the city had no protection against this kind of exploitation by state officials. Some people were in a position to cultivate a relationship with them or with a friend or relative holding a public job. But a large number were recent migrants lacking both access to public work and state contacts, as Bigman (1993) states. This large group had to find ways to survive outside the wage and state marketing systems (see, Funk 1991 and Handem 1987). Petty trading, especially by women, grew as a way of survival.

The state's attitude to this increasing informal economy was negative. It fought the Dyulas as they were powerful competitors and directly inflicted losses on the state's coffers. Making strategic use of a socialist morality, the state denounced Dyulas as being immoral elements in society. At times, Dyula traders were put in jail for long periods without a trial, accused of hoarding and speculation (Galli and Jones 1987). The government also antagonized other groups trying to make a living in petty trade. According to Bigman (1993) women who travelled to rural areas to buy produce to sell in the city had to pass intranational checkpoints set up by the government to control contraband. In Bissau the police harassed sellers in the market places, confiscating produce. Even these petty traders were accused of hoarding goods and became the scapegoats for the food shortages (Funk 1991).

Both Funk (1991) and Galli and Jones (1987) report that antagonism towards the state and its agents grew. State officials were seen as responsible for the shortages and as guilty of corruption. Political channels were however unavailable for expressing discontent. So when a factional division turned into a military coup in 1980, conditions were ripe for widespread popular support for the new regime. The coup became known as "the rice coup". Some party cadres deeply involved in irregular practices were exposed and purged. However, the change in regime did not put an end to these practices nor did it bring much change in the level of repression or the material conditions of the masses.

Informal systems of distribution on the other hand were gradually taking more and more space while the performance of state institutions weakened. The fact that the government forced journalists to lie about the date of arrival of the next shipment of rice (Galli and Jones 1987) indicates its vulnerability in the face of alternative economic agents. In spite of harassment, Dyulas prospered and petty traders resisted and increased in numbers. These multiple individual responses were having a collective impact. Thus, elements of disengagement were at work during the pre-liberalization era in the sense that producers and traders were creating a space of autonomy from state channels. Indeed, Guinea-Bissau and its capital seem to be as good an example of disengagement as those chosen by proponents of the disengagement approach. The similarities with for example Ghana and Guinea (Azarya and Chazan 1987) or Dar es Salaam (Tripp 1997) are many.

But a disengagement account does not provide a complete picture of the process of informalization in Guinea-Bissau. Firstly, as discussed above, parallel to popular responses that were antagonistic to state policies, there was one small group composed partly of state officials who operated in both the formal and the informal economy and thrived on the manipulation of the two. Secondly, the possibility of informal traders attaining a degree of autonomy from state channels and the formal economy probably varied for different groups among them. While those dealing in imported goods were probably directly or indirectly dependent on state officials for supply, those selling local produce may have enjoyed a greater degree of autonomy. Similarly, the possibility of straddling the formal and the informal realms, which may constitute a valuable resource for survival and/or accumulation, seems not to have been open to everyone. Further research is needed to clarify these issues in the pre-adjustment era.

Thirdly, the relations *between* informal actors need to be addressed. This issue is left blank in the literature on Guinea-Bissau as attention is focused on the contradiction state-society. For example, the relations between Dyulas and rural producers may not have been all that symbiotic. Galli and Jones (1987) state that Dyulas offered better prices to producers than official outlets but also charged high prices for consumer goods and that peasants were annoyed by this but could not change the situation as they could not rely on the irregular official market. Although the parallel economy in this period in Guinea-Bissau seems to support the disengagement thesis, it is likely that at least one part of those involved in it, i.e. rural producers, would not consider themselves as happily "disengaged". Their supposed disengagement from the state may have meant a forced engagement in other relations of exploitation, such as potentially those with Dyulas.

Finally, one should also point out that people's avoidance of state institutions and policies was nothing new or unique to the post-independence state, as it only continued well established responses from colonial times. In addition, it also involved pre-colonial regional patterns of exchange, as represented by the Dyula traders' networks. This would justify a deeper analysis of how such ancient forms of relations are reworked in a context of disengagement.

THE INFORMAL BOOM IN THE ADJUSTMENT ERA

In a situation of deep dependence on external assistance, the government of Guinea-Bissau negotiated with international financial institutions a first programme of economic stabilization in 1983 and a structural adjustment programme in 1986. As in other countries undergoing adjustment programmes, the Guinean government was urged to liberalize trade, to deregulate and to decriminalize the "informal sector", which instead was to be regarded as a dynamic and competitive sector of the economy (Padovani and Delgado 1993). Under the pressure of donors, there was a major change in official policy and discourse towards informal actors. International institutions advocating these policies were, in this sense, themselves contributing to the expansion of an informal economy. While the state bureaucracy was reluctant to give up its monopoly over trade as this was one of its major sources of power and wealth, the adjustment program would bring new economic opportunities into sight for this group, facilitating its compliance.

The liberalization of domestic and external trade resulted in a more regular and diversified supply of imported goods and in a great increase in commercial activity in the city. This expanding activity has taken mainly an informal character: on the one hand, a part of the operations of larger private trade firms is poorly regulated by the state; on the other hand, there has been a proliferation of petty traders who are denied protection by the state. So I will proceed by looking closer into each of these two sub-spheres within the informal trade sector: that which derives from the accumulation strategies of capitalist merchants and that which results from the strategies for survival of disadvantaged groups.

Informalization for Accumulation

Structural adjustment policies have imposed heavy costs on the majority of Bissauans. But a minority has benefited greatly, as it was in a position to rapidly seize new economic opportunities emerging in the context of adjustment. There is a consensus among observers of the adjustment process in Guinea-Bissau about who this minority is and the means by which it attained a position of dominance in the informal trade sector (see, Galli 1990; Imbali and Cardoso

1996; Cardoso 1994; Gomes 1993; Cardoso and Imbali 1993; Handem 1987; Fernandes 1994). Firstly, from the early 1980s, exports of a new cash crop, cashew nuts, experienced a dramatic increase. Import-export firms have made considerable profits by bartering imported rice for cashew nuts with small producers and by speculating on rice prices in the city. Secondly, a large amount of adjustment credits were made available to importers in order to support the balance of payments and sustain the flow of imports of basic goods (Galli 1990; Gomes 1993). These credits were amassed by the state marketing agency (which continued to be involved in external trade for some years), by high rank government officials acting as private importers, and by the new "independent" private merchants.

A high level of default on loan repayment ensued, which several have interpreted as being possible due to an intimate relation between importers-exporters and the government. Firstly, those supposedly independent from the state were reported to be able to count on its protection and privileged access to adjustment credits (Cardoso 1994; Galli 1990). Secondly, the overlapping of trade and public functions set in motion a type of liberalization adapted to the interests of traders-officials (Gomes 1993; Galli 1990). Fernandes (1994) argues that liberalization in Guinea-Bissau turned formerly clandestine private accumulation by bureaucrats into a legitimate one and the state bureaucratic class into a commercial bureaucracy. Thus, one can hardly say that the transition from a state monopoly of the economy with state bureaucrats in privileged positions in a liberalized and informal economy led to a significant decrease in their influence over the economy.

More significantly, this small group that enjoyed the protection of and access to the state and the resources controlled by it came to occupy dominant positions in informal trade, especially in those sub-sectors directly linked with international trade. Indeed, just like former parastatal agents, they seem to have partly derived this position from their ability to operate in both the informal and formal spheres. With their privileged access to formal institutions such as bank credits and the state apparatus, importers have been able to exert significant influence over the whole chain of distribution of imported goods, determining prices and access to informal credit. Concerning the latter, Monteiro (2001), in a study of the largest market place in the city, discovered that importers dominate the informal financial market in Bissau. Large numbers of traders are seemingly hindered from direct access to bank loans and depend on informal credit suppliers. Through my own interviews with some six wholesale and import-export enterprises and key informants I became aware of the hierarchical business networks linking patrons and middlemen in the cashew-rice business (on this, see also Crowley 1993 and la Mettrie 1992). Middlemen who succeed in reaching an informal contract with a patron, i.e. a contract sanctioned by social rather than legal codes, often on the basis of shared cultural norms, kinship or acquaintance, gain access to credit and to a niche in the growth sector of the Guinean economy. But they also enter a situation of dependency and acquire a subordinate position which greatly decreases their autonomy of action and ultimately works for the benefit of the patron. These vertical networks tend to be exclusivist and tightly drawn and tend to frustrate the efforts of others to penetrate them. In this way, they contribute to a visible ethnic and gender segmentation in the urban market.

Merchants in Guinea-Bissau are able to draw on a large supply of informal labour. At the production end, the cashew harvest is carried out by seasonal workers, including large numbers of Bissauan women, who work on small farms under conditions unregulated by the state. In town, big merchants make extensive use of casual labour. They hire large groups of men for short periods, to load and unload the ships and trucks, as and when they are needed. As workers themselves have explained to me, they are paid by the day or by task. When the task is completed and payment is made, there are no further obligations between the parties. These short-term, often unwritten agreements mean for the workers that they cannot expect compensation from either employer or the state for periods without work or for accidents on the job. These agreements thus free the employer from any lasting responsibilities towards labour.

In addition to the large numbers of cashew pickers and casual workers, merchants have increasingly made use of informal outlets for retailing their commodities. Gomes (1993) maintains that many merchants imported goods with adjustment loans and then resold the merchandise in the parallel market, allowing them to collect "astronomic profits" by taking advantage of the differences in exchange rates between the parallel and the official markets. Monteiro (2001) echoes common local perceptions when he states that many informal businesses at the largest market place in Bissau are owned by "invisible" owners who work in the central and local government. In my fieldwork I interviewed some twenty retailers of imported rice who were supplied by wholesale stores. I found that merchants had penetrated peripheral spontaneous market places in the city and subordinated a myriad of small retailers, either through exploitative price practices or credit agreements. For the smallest kind of retailers, often elderly women and young girls, incomes oscillated between very low and nil. Drawn into these international commodity circuits, rice retailers became the lowest link of a vertical network facilitating accumulation at the top (Lourenço-Lindell 2002).

The emerging picture is one of an informalization process favouring merchants as the informal strategies of well-to-do operators facilitate accumulation while the current form of economic liberalization is not conducive to a regulatory environment that protects the self-employed and informal labour.

In sum, in the context of economic liberalization, accumulation by big merchants operating in international commodity markets is facilitated by their use of informal strategies. At the same time, many unprotected small retailers and casual workers directly linked to those merchants are left on the threshold of survival.

Informalization for Survival

The informalization of Bissau's economy is also manifested in an increased reliance by popular groups on informal activities for survival, in the context of the austerity related to adjustment policies, and of a small and declining state regulated wage sector. The household survey elicited data on how household members generated cash incomes. Trade was by far the most common source of income, with 66 per cent of all registered and processed income activities. Retail trade of food items, including prepared food, drinks and charcoal was the most widespread. All other income activities were much less common. They included brick making, taxi driving, domestic service, dressmaking, car repairs and work at the port. Households also engaged in various forms of food production, including farming and fishing, for their own consumption or for sale. The larger share of the households (57 per cent) had no written contracts for their work, no regular income or paid sick leave, thus conforming to the most common attributes of "informal work". Only a minority (9 per cent) depended exclusively on regulated wage work while one third relied on a mixture of work situations. The general picture is that the urban households rely heavily on informal trade in goods and services.

Within the food trade category, the most common items being sold were vegetables, fruits and locally produced cashew wine. Most traders got their merchandise from other traders or producers or through their own production and a smaller share from wholesalers. Virtually all food trade enterprises (a total of 527 enterprises) were retail enterprises and the majority were one-person enterprises. Food trade shows a gender and ethnic based specialization, with women from coastal ethnic groups and men from the Eastern groups dominating numerically.

Given the lack of alternatives, small scale trade was the source of income most readily available to large segments of the urban population. Unsurprisingly, there has been a true explosion in the number of small scale traders and a mushrooming of market places in the city, as reported by different officials interviewed and other studies. Most of these market places are of a spontaneous kind, i.e. they consist mainly of precarious structures built by the traders themselves. Most of them offer mainly low cost items, as they cater for poor neighbourhoods. In fact, while spontaneous markets and commercial activity proliferate in the periphery of the city, the old commercial centre in the city core has decayed. Several modern retail outlets selling mainly high cost imported goods have closed down and the Central Market, which once supplied the entire city, is now called "the cooperants' market", which reflects its narrow clientele of aid workers and other expatriates. The locus of commercial activity has clearly shifted to the periphery of the planned city and much of it operates according to informal rules rather than the laws of the state.

These trends require a nuanced interpretation. On the one hand, they reflect the creativeness of small actors and the impressive collective impact of their individual responses. Small informal traders have drastically changed the face of the city in a way clearly beyond the control of the government. In this sense, a number of them may have conquered for themselves a space of relative autonomy. On the other hand, while the efforts of popular groups are impressive, the trends also reflect a darker reality. Firstly, the rise in demand for retail outlets offering low cost items signals an impoverishment of a large share of the population. Secondly, the growth of informal trade and the informal economy in general can be partly attributed to the burdens that have been placed on the urban population by adjustment related austerity, in the form of retrenchments, frozen and delayed salaries and high inflation (see, Handem 1987; Galli 1990; Cardoso 1994; Imbali and Cardoso 1996; Duarte and Gomes 1996). Low rank public workers were forced to seek refuge in informal activities to supplement declining real incomes or to mitigate the effects of redundancy. For better positioned civil servants, their public contacts and access to public equipment and financial assets have been said to have helped them to become owners of vehicles for collective transport, of repair shops and other informal enterprises (see Duarte and Gomes 1996; Handem 1987). The majority of the urban population, usually not in a position to straddle the two spheres or lacking access to employment or connections in the public sector, has had to multiply its income generating activities in the informal economy.

Some have managed to establish viable businesses. But many traders live hand to mouth. In almost 80 per cent of the 527 food trade enterprises registered during my household survey, respondents said they were not able to make any savings and a large share spent most of their incomes on food. My interviews with some sixty traders, many of whom were women, also revealed many cases in which respondents declared decreased scale of operation and longer working hours in an attempt to attain former levels of consumption (Lourenço-Lindell 2002). Their incomes were being crushed between higher costs of operation and a lower purchasing power among their customers, increased competition among an expanding number of small retailers, or, as in the case of rice retailers, exploitation by suppliers. A large share reported that they were frequently unable to recover their small working capital by the end of the day or that they were often forced to spend it on food and other necessities. Sustaining their trading activities was dependent upon assistance from husbands, relatives, credit from suppliers and participation in savings clubs.

Thus, an important share of food traders seemed increasingly marginalized from the accelerated economic growth that has reportedly been taking place in the country. While not much can be said here about the other sectors of the Bissauan informal economy, these findings ressemble those of other studies on trends in informal economies in African cities (Lugalla 1997; Meagher and Yunusa 1996). Neo-liberal assumptions about the potential of informal work for providing sufficient incomes for the working poor in a context of adjustment, have not come true for many of the respondents in this study.

In the context of economic liberalization, the practices of the local government towards these small informal traders are enlightening. Despite a supposedly positive policy towards informal actors, municipal agents have in practice remained essentially hostile to them. Some of the interviewed officials expressed a negative attitude towards spontaneous market places. Municipal collectors operate in all market places including those erected by the sellers themselves. These markets do not offer any kind of municipal services, but nevertheless charge daily fees that are higher than officially stipulated and are discriminatory for small retailers. When business lags sellers often have to pay repeated fees for the same merchandise, further depleting their meagre income (Lourenço-Lindell

1995). Relations between sellers and collectors are therefore strained. The relations between local government in general and trader associations in the largest market place of Bissau, Bandim, have been characterized by Monteiro (2001) as antagonistic; traders complain about the oppressiveness and arbitrariness of public agents as well as their lack of accountability. Thus a major contradiction between a section of the informal economy and public institutions remains, albeit seemingly in a less pervasive way than during the state monopoly period when public agents determined prices and levels of supply. One way of verifying the popular perception that officials from local and central government are involved in informal ventures would be to identify who is being harassed and who maintains good relations with the municipal agents.

Considering the above trends, it is not surprising that contradictions only increased during the adjustment period within the informal economy and in Bissauan society in general. These contradictions were laid bare in the aftermath of an armed conflict in 1998–99.

CONCLUSIONS

In tracing the evolution of informal trade in Bissau in the last two decades, one finds that a combination of processes has been at work; processes which are often analysed separately. During the period of state monopoly over trade, private illegal traders increased in numbers in response to the failures and unfavourable practices of state agencies. They were both escaping government control and posing serious competition to state channels of trade. In this sense, they could be said to be disengaging from the state. In the mid-1980s international financial institutions urged the state to liberalize the economy and to decriminalize informal activity. In this way they themselves became important actors in the process of informalization. In a liberalized economic environment, informal trade activities grew in Bissau as a result of both popular efforts for survival and strategies of accumulation. Import-export firms have made extensive use of informal strategies which assist them in keeping a foot in the international commodity market. Meanwhile, the majority of the urban population, hit by adjustment austerity, often multiply their survival activities in petty trade, the economic sphere available to them.

Concerning the relations between the public/formal institutions and informal actors, both elements of opposition and symbiosis could be identified, in the 1974–83 period and from 1983 onwards. Insisting either on a total disengagement from the state or on a complete integration between formal and informal does not take us very far in understanding the politics of informalization. Some informal actors may have antagonistic relations with the formal sphere and struggle for autonomy from it while others maintain alliances with it. There seems to exist a selective permeability between formal and informal realms, where opportunities for straddling may not be equally open for all. In Bissau's trade economy, a restricted group enjoyed a privileged relationship with the state and seemed to be particularly well positioned to manipulate the formal-informal interface and built their fortunes in this way. The precariousness of their position surfaced however at moments of political upheaval, as in 1980 and in 1998–99.

Some small trade enterprises have been able to expand or find a viable niche in the context of economic liberalization in Bissau. But a large share of the food traders have seen their conditions deteriorate. While data on other sub-sectors of the economy are not available, these findings about small scale food traders in Bissau suggest they have not been "empowered" by the current wave of informalization, as is often assumed in the neo-liberal literature. Rather, small traders continue to struggle on a variety of fronts, including against big merchants and a persistently hostile local government. A pertinent issue for further research would be the ways they organize in order to struggle against the deterioration of conditions and rights in the informal economy.

References

Azarya, V. and N. Chazan, 1987, "Disengagement from the state in Africa: Reflections on the experience of Ghana and Guinea", *Comparative Studies in Society and History* 29, pp. 106–31.

Bangura, Y. and P. Gibbon, 1992, "Adjustment, authoritarianism and democracy in sub-Saharan Africa: An introduction to some conceptual and empirical issues" in Gibbon, P., Y. Bangura and A. Ofstad (eds), *Authoritarianism, democracy and adjustment: The politics of economic reform in Africa*, pp. 7–38. Uppsala: Scandinavian Institute of African Studies.

Bigman, L., 1993, *History and hunger in West Africa: Food production and entitlement in Guinea-Bissau and Cape Verde*. London: Greenwood Press.

Cardoso, C., 1994, "A transição democrática na Guiné-Bissau: um parto difícil", *Soronda* 27, pp. 5–30.

Cardoso, C. and F. Imbali, 1993, "As questões institucionais e o programa de ajustamento estrutural na Guiné-Bissau" in Imbali 1993, pp. 19–79.

Castells, M. and A. Portes, 1989, "World Underneath: The Origins, Dynamics, and Effects of the Informal Economy" in Portes, Castells and Benton 1989, pp. 93–139.

Crowley, E., 1993, "Guinea-Bissau's informal economy and its contributions to economic growth". The Hague: USAID (unpublished).

Duarte, A. and A. Gomes, 1996, "O sector informal" in Monteiro 1996, pp. 97–115.

Fernandes, R., 1994, "Processo democrático na Guiné-Bissau", *Soronda* 17, pp. 31–43.

Funk, U., 1991, "Labor, economic power and gender: Coping with food shortage in Guinea-Bissau" in Downs, R., D. Kerner and S. Reyna (eds), *The political economy of African famine*. Philadelphia: Gordon and Breach Science Publishers.

Galli, R., 1990, "Liberalization is not enough: Structural adjustment and peasants in Guinea-Bissau", *Review of African Political Economy* 49, pp. 52–68.

Galli, R. and J. Jones, 1987, *Guinea-Bissau: Politics, economics and society.* London: Frances Pinter.

Gomes, P., 1993, "O financiamento externo e a liberalizacao comercial durante o PAE" in Imbali 1993, pp. 111–50.

Grey-Johnson, C., 1992, "The African informal sector at the crossroads: Emerging policy options", *Africa Development* 17:1, pp. 65–91.

Handem, D., 1987, "A Guiné-Bissau a adaptar-se à crise", *Soronda* 3, pp. 77–100.

Hyden, G., 1990, "Creating an enabling environment" in World Bank, *The long-term perspective of Sub-Saharan Africa*, pp. 73–80. Washington: The World Bank.

Imbali, F. (coord.), 1993, *Os efeitos sócio-económicos do programa de ajustamento estrutural na Guiné-Bissa*. Bissau: INEP.

Imbali, F. and C. Cardoso, 1996, "A familia" in Monteiro 1996, pp. 203–39.

La Mettrie, D., 1992, "Rapport Technique diagnostic sur le commerce de cereales en Guinee Bissau". Rome: FAO (unpublished).

Lemarchand, R., 1991, "The political economy of informal economies", *Africa Insight* 21:4, pp. 214–21.

Lourenço-Lindell, Ilda, 2002, *Walking the tight rope: Informal livelihoods and social networks in a West African city*. Stockholm studies in human geography, 9. Stockholm: Almqvist and Wiksell International.

—, 1995, "The informal food economy in a peripheral urban district: The case of Bandim district, Bissau", *Habitat International* 19:2, pp. 195–208.

Lugalla, J., 1997, "Development, change and poverty in the informal sector during the era of structural adjustment in Tanzania", *Canadian Journal of African Studies* 31:3, pp. 424–516.

Macharia, K., 1997, *Social and political dynamics of the informal economy in African cities: Nairobi and Harare*. Lanham, New York, Oxford: University Press of America.

Meagher, K., 1995, "Crisis, informalization and the urban informal sector in Sub-Saharan Africa", *Development and Change* 26:2, pp. 259–84.

Meagher, K. and M.-B. Yunusa, 1996, *Passing the buck: Structural adjustment and the Nigerian urban informal sector*. UNRISD: Discussion Paper 75.

Monteiro, A. (coord.), 1996, *O programa de ajustamento estrutural na Guiné-Bissau: análise dos efeitos sócio-económicos*. Bissau: INEP.

Monteiro, H. (ed.), 2001, "Bandim: subsídos para uma política de apoio ao pequeno negócio", *Colecção Lala Kema* No. 2. Bissau: INEP.

Padovani, F. and A.M. Delgado, 1993, "O sector informal e o ajustamento na Guiné-Bissau" in Imbali 1993, pp. 151–62.

Peattie, L., 1987, "An idea in good currency and how it grew: the informal sector", *World Development* 15:7, pp. 851–60.

Portes, A., M. Castells and L. Benton (eds), 1989, *The informal economy: studies in advanced and less developed countries*. London: The John Hopkins Press Ltd.

Portes, A. and R. Schauffler, 1993, "Competing perspectives on the Latin American informal sector", *Population and Development Review* 19:1, pp. 33–60.

Roitman, J., 1990, "The politics of informal markets in Sub-Saharan Africa", *The Journal of Modern African Studies* 28:4, pp. 671–96.

Rothchild, D. and N. Chazan (eds), 1988, *The precarious balance. State and society in Africa*. Boulder: Westview Press.

Rudebeck, L., 1990, "Ajustamento estrutural numa aldeia oeste-africana" in *Nas encruzilhadas: alianVas politicas e ajustamento estrutural*. Uppsala University: AKUT.

Sassen-Koob, S., 1989, "New York City's informal economy" in Portes, Castells and Benton 1993.

Sassen, S., 2000, *Cities in a world economy*. London: Pine Forge Press.

Sjögren, A., 1998, *Civil society and governance in Africa—an outline of the debates*. Cities, Governance and Civil Society in Africa/Working Paper No. 1. Uppsala: Nordiska Afrikainstitutet.

Soto, H. de, 1989, *The other path*. New York: Harper and Row.

Tripp, A., 1997, *Changing the rules: The politics of liberalization and the urban informal economy in Tanzania*. Berkeley and Los Angeles: University of California Press.

—, 1989, "Women and the changing urban household economy in Tanzania", *The Journal of Modern African Studies* 27:4, pp. 601–23.

CHAPTER 6

Home Based Enterprises in a Period of Economic Restructuring in Zambia

Barbara Mwila Kazimbaya-Senkwe

Q.: Suppose a person today gave you a new job, a full time well paying job; would you leave this shoe repair to go and work for them?

A.: No. I have chosen not to work for anyone. And in addition, even in Zambia Consolidated Copper Mines (ZCCM), I would thank God if I was pruned today, the way my friends are. They think that they are unlucky, but no, they are lucky, because now they can work for themselves. I am old. So if I am offered a job just like the way I work for ZCCM, it is slavery. It is better for me to do my business full time since God has given me sons, I can use them, we make one company.

The above is an extract from a recorded interview with a mine employee in Kitwe who works in his spare time repairing and making shoes, from home. His sentiments were echoed by almost all eleven respondents in a pilot study of home based enterprises in Zambia's Copperbelt Province. There is a widespread disillusion with formal sector employment in the wake of massive job losses due to public sector restructuring and inadequate incomes in formal employment. Faced with bleak opportunities of ever getting formal employment and lacking access to a social welfare system, many people have resorted to self-employment in the informal economy. For some, informal work is also undertaken as a means of supplementing their meagre incomes earned in the formal economy.

This chapter explores the productive nature of housing by focusing on the role of home based enterprises in sustaining the livelihoods of households. The frequent use of the home for economic activities must be seen in the context of an increasingly harsh macro-economic environment. Over the past two decades, Zambia has experienced a severe economic crisis, which has led to high rates of urban poverty. This has been partly the result of a drastic decline in formal employment opportunities mostly due to the poor performance of large state enterprises the bulk of which have since the 1990s been either liquidated or privatized. Increasing proportions of the urban population are no longer directly or indirectly to rely on formal employment or housing. Cities on the Copperbelt which were established to serve the copper mines have been particularly badly affected.

At the national level formal employment declined from 30 per cent of the labour force in 1980 to less than 10 per cent in 1990. Muneku (2001) reports that formal employment has been declining at an average annual rate of 2 per cent. Between 1992 and 1995 a total of 77,300 formal jobs were lost, while informal sector employment increased from about 1.8 million in 1986 to 2.3 million in 1993. It must be noted that whilst loss of formal sector jobs affects mostly males, women however are less likely to get a formal job in the first place and therefore predominate in the informal sector. In 1993 they represented 53 per cent of the 2.3 million employed there. Further decline in formal employment is expected as more people lose jobs through the continuing privatization and restructuring of public enterprises, government departments and the newly privatized copper mines.

Alongside this shift in the labour market there has been the accelerated growth of poverty. Urban poverty has escalated; the percentage of urban households living below the poverty line increased from 4 to just under 50 between 1975 and 1991 (World Bank 1994:24). Substantial declines in urban real incomes have occurred. Incomes in the formal sector have often fallen fastest, forcing even those who are in formal employment to seek supplementary incomes within the informal sector.

HOME BASED ENTERPRISES AS A SUBJECT OF STUDY

Hays–Mitchell (1993) has argued that the distinction between reproduction (domestic activities) and production (economic activities) is not clearly drawn in developing country households. Despite this, in many countries including Zambia, planning and land use regulations are designed to promote the separation of these two activities. In Zambia for instance, Hansen (1975:791) describes how, in the early 1970s, even in the low-income neighbourhoods, the use of the home for economic functions was illegal and how people made every effort to hide these activities from the authorities. Despite the desire by authorities to separate the two, home based enterprises (HBEs) continue to proliferate in many cities. In Zambia, home based enterprises date back to the colonial period when residents of the 'African compounds' would engage in such activities as beer brewing, trading or carpentry (see for instance Kay 1967; Hansen 1975, 1982, 1997: and Heisler 1974). The Central Statistical Office (1997) reported that at least 50 per cent of all informal sector workers in Zambia operate from home.

This chapter draws on the work by Lipton (1980:190–91) who describes small scale informal activities as "family mode of production enterprises" (FMPEs) whose key characteristic is the control of the major factors of production (i.e. money, time, space and labour) by the family. Because they are owned by the family, these resources are fungible, i.e. they can be converted swiftly, conveniently and without loss from one use to another.[1] The flexibility of housing space means that even those without access to serviced industrial/commercial land can afford to engage in economic activities. The fungibility of time means that even those who are unable to work full time, such as women and children,

1. It must be noted that although Lipton's work is in reference to FMPEs in rural areas, the fact that HBEs in the urban areas have similar characteristics in terms of utilization of their own resources, means that his idea of 'fungibility' can justifiably be extended to the urban context. His assertion that the rural FMPE is more fungible than the urban one is however a subject clearly worth pursuing in future research.

and those who are formally employed but have some spare time or require extra income can also engage in informal income generating activities.

Their "extended fungibility" in Lipton's terminology, makes home based enterprises an ideal strategy for making a living and having access to shelter (see Kellett and Tipple 1997). As Moser and Holland (1997:50) have argued "Housing can be an important asset that cushions households against severe poverty particularly during times of economic adversity". Because the informal sector survives on family resources, the home and the HBE constitute an important entry point for new informal sector entrants.

A lot of work on home based enterprises has focused on low-income neighbourhoods. However HBEs are not restricted to low-income groups. Strassman (1986) for example presents an analysis of HBEs in four different housing categories in Lima, Peru. Similarly in a study of 172 households in Kitwe, Kazimbaya-Senkwe and Mwale (2001) found that 55 per cent of households in peri-urban squatter areas, 50 per cent in low cost housing areas, 30 per cent in medium cost, and 34 per cent in high cost areas had an HBE. The spread of HBEs in all housing categories can be taken to suggest either the dearth or unattractiveness of formal employment, a laxity or failure of planning authorities to enforce land use regulations or the spreading of poverty across all social groups. Olufemi (2000) reports a similar situation in Nigeria where HBEs have spread from low-income to high-income neighbourhoods. An analysis of HBEs therefore presents an opportunity to follow both livelihoods and land use trends through the eyes of those directly affected.

THE COPPERBELT PROVINCE: AN OVERVIEW

The Copperbelt Province is the second most urbanized province in Zambia, after Lusaka. Of the province's population 86 per cent reside in 7 urban districts and the remaining 14 per cent in 3 rural districts. The 7 urban districts constitute the economic and industrial heart of Zambia, housing the 7 major copper mines which were owned by the government through the Zambia Consolidated Copper Mines (ZCCM) until March 2000, when they were privatized. Copper accounts for over 80 per cent of the total export earnings of the country. In 1989, the province had over 355 manufacturing industries ranging from heavy duty engineering to textiles and banking, the bulk of them operating as suppliers to the mines (NCDP 1989:612). The province like the rest of the country has been going through a period of economic decline in the last couple of decades. The last 10 years have witnessed significant decline in the formal economy. At the same time, the country has tried to address some of the structural problems in the economy through a World Bank/IMF supported Structural Adjustment Programme (SAP). Part of the SAP measures have been the liberalization of the economy, which has left many industries exposed to outside competition. This has resulted in the closure of companies that cannot compete and others have rationalized in order to stay afloat.

It must be noted that in comparison to the national figures, the Copperbelt Province still has a significant number of people working in the formal sector.

For example, in a study of 722 households on the Copperbelt, Malama and Kazimbaya-Senkwe (2001) found that at least 55 per cent of household heads were employed in the formal sector, 36 per cent were employed in the informal sector and the remaining 9 per cent were either in full time agriculture, retired or had no source of income. The new owners of the copper mines have however indicated that a significant number of the labour force have to be laid off. At the same time, the government plan for the public service is to reduce the number of civil servants from 115,000 in 2000 to about 10,000–12,000 by 2010 (World Bank 2000). A significant number of these job losses will be on the Copperbelt which houses the second largest number of government departments in the country. However the rate of job creation in the formal sector is very low. For instance a recent study of 207 retrenched miners on the Copperbelt found that only 15 per cent had been able to regain formal employment (see Malama and Meleki 2002). With little discussion and no concrete action about redeployment of these retrenchees informal activities are bound to increase.

A PILOT STUDY OF HOME BASED ENTERPRISES IN KITWE

Kitwe is the second largest city on the Copperbelt and the third largest city in Zambia. The city has a geographical area of approximately 447km^2, with a population of about 400.000 people and an annual growth rate of 1.1 per cent (CSO 2001:9). The town evolved as a copper mining town in the early 1930s, and like 5 of the other copper mining towns is made up of two townships, one administered by the mining company and the other by the Kitwe City Council, hereafter referred to as Mine and Council Township respectively.[1] The study by Malama and Kazimbaya-Senkwe (2001) referred to above found that only 43 per cent of household heads in Kitwe were formally employed. 50 per cent were in full time informal work while the remaining, either, worked in agriculture, were retired or had no income.

Both the council and mine townships' residential areas have developed on the basis of the income level of residents, namely low, middle and high income. The Mine Township also has one housing estate with 'substandard dwellings'. The Council Township also has two middle-income areas which have been developed as site and service schemes. A total of over 30 squatter settlements are scattered around the city. Home based enterprises (HBEs) are present in all neighbourhoods.

Inspired by the work undertaken by Kellett and Tipple (1997) in India and by Kellett et al. (2000) in Ipusukilo Compound in Kitwe in 1999, a pilot study was drawn up in order to explore how home based enterprises were established, how the home was adapted to house these economic activities as well as the challenges and opportunities presented by working from home. Particular em-

---

1. In all except one of the 7 Copperbelt towns, the mining companies settled there first and developed their own urban areas equipped with all necessary urban services for their employees. The Municipal Councils emerged later and also developed complete urban areas to service those not employed by the mines. See Kay 1967 and Heisler 1974 for presentations on the evolution of Copperbelt towns including the dual administrative system.

phasis was placed on describing how workplace and residential activities and spaces were integrated. The study used in-depth conversational interviews which were recorded on tape and supplemented by notes, physical observation and a follow-up questionnaire, relying on construction of case histories as the central means of data collection and analysis. A research assistant conducted the interviews in January 2000, for 2 weeks. Due to the preliminary nature of the study, the first two available houses with evident home based enterprises were picked in each neighbourhood although a deliberate effort was made to pick two different types of HBEs in each neighbourhood. A total of 12 respondents (2 from each of 6 neighbourhoods) were targeted, but only 11 interviews were transcribed and analysed, as one respondent did not have time to complete the interview. The interviews were conducted either in the vernacular (Bemba) or English depending on the ability of the respondent to converse in English.

The study had three main aims: the first was to define variables that would be used to explain the causes, nature and extent of mixed use in residential areas including the similarities and differences of these between different neighbourhoods. The second was to explore the data collected in order to establish appropriate methods of questioning, data gathering and analysis, and the third to define a set of research questions to be tested in a larger survey, which would provide inputs for policy.

The Case Study Townships

The neighbourhoods chosen were Ipusukilo, Buchi, Chamboli, Ndeke Village, Nkana West and Riverside representing four neighbourhood types: Ipusukilo is a squatter settlement with over 16,000[1] inhabitants occupying self built houses on undefined plots and with no access to publicly provided urban services such as water and electricity. Buchi with 9,600 people and Chamboli with over 23,000 inhabitants, are both low-medium income neighbourhoods with houses built by the Kitwe City Council (KCC) and the mining company respectively. The average plot size in these neighbourhoods is about 300m² and house size of about 120m². All houses in Chamboli have a connection to water and electricity whilst most houses in Buchi had until 2001 access only to communal standpoints and up to now still have no electricity. Ndeke Village with a population of just over 8,400 is a medium cost neighbourhood initially planned to house KCC workers but later allocated to private individuals who built their own houses according to council approved plans. Average plot size is about 600m² and house size of about 240m². Main service lines for water and electricity have been provided but each individual household has to arrange to get connected. Nkana West with population of 5,190 and Riverside with 12,000 inhabitants are both high cost neighbourhoods built by the mines and KCC respectively with average plot sizes of 1,500m² and house sizes of 375m². Most of the new houses in both townships are however self built. These houses have connections to all public services.

---

1. All the population figures have been calculated from the 2001 Preliminary Census Report and the GRZ (1993) KWSP report.

Households from very high-income areas and from substandard settlements were not included in the pilot study. In terms of employment levels in the six neighbourhoods, Malama and Kazimbaya-Senkwe (2001) found that in high cost areas like Riverside only about 20 per cent of household heads were engaged in the informal economy while the rest were formally employed. The figures for informal employment in medium cost areas like Ndeke Village was about 50 per cent and that for low cost areas like Buchi was over 57 per cent. In the Mine Townships, a study of about 430 households found that 66 per cent were still in mine employment, 14 per cent were retrenched and the rest were either in government or private employment (see World Bank 2000). The study also found that 34 per cent of the retrenched miners were re-employed in the informal sector and only 5 per cent had another job with regular income.

As yet no study has been done in Kitwe or the Copperbelt to show how the different HBE activities are typified in the different house categories or in specific neighbourhoods. However, data obtained by Kazimbaya-Senkwe and Mwale (2001) indicated that in peri-urban, low cost and medium cost areas, trading was the major activity, followed by carpentry, tailoring and chicken rearing. Chicken rearing was the major activity in high cost areas, followed by tailoring and trading. High cost areas like Riverside had a much wider range of activities, 8 types for 28 respondents, as opposed to peri-urban areas, where the 12 respondents were engaged in only two types of activities.

Range of Economic Activities

A wide range of economic activities is undertaken in homes. From the sample of 11 respondents, a total of 8 different activities were identified (Table 1).

All these activities except reed mat making, battery acid manufacture and shoe making were also identified in the Kazimbaya-Senkwe and Mwale study. These activities all fall neatly into the three categories of informal sector activity outlined by Bardouille (1991:24) namely petty trading or retailing, petty manufacturing and repair, and services. In several cases, there was more than one enterprise operating on the premises. The female tailor for instance was also operating a hair saloon; the male tailor in Ipusukilo was also running a bar and renting out rooms; the mat-maker was also selling some vegetables and the male trader was also running a barber-shop. Interestingly, none of those respondents engaged in manufacturing jobs (i.e. the carpenters and the acid manufacturer) were running other businesses. This finding raises important questions about the relative productivity, as well as the time and capital requirements of different types of HBEs.

Seven of the enterprises had begun operations in the 1990s, the remaining four dated from the 1980s. Two important issues emerge from this finding. Firstly, home based enterprises do not appear to be transient or stop-gap measures, but have been the main lifeline for some households particularly those in the older generation (see also Bardouille 1991:28). This notwithstanding, the idea of working from home appears to have increased in the 1990s, linking the HBEs to both the decline in the national economy and the related growth of the informal sector.

Table 1. Type of HBE by Neighbourhood Type and Sex of Respondent

Residential Neighbourhood	Description of Neighbourhood	Home Based Enterprises Studied	Sex of Respondent
Ipusukilo	Squatter Settlement: Recognised by Council for Upgrading	Reed Mat Making Reed Mat Making	Female Male
Chamboli	Low/ Middle-Income Mine Estate	Carpentry Shoe Making / Repair	Male Male
Buchi	Low-Medium-Income Council Estate	Battery Acid Manufacturing	Male
Ndeke Village	Medium-Income Site and Service Scheme	Tailoring/Hair Dressing Nursery School	Female Female
Nkana West	High-Income Mine Estate	Nursery School Trading	Female Male
Riverside	High/Very High-Income Council Estate	Carpentry Trading	Male Female

Most of the HBEs studied were not registered with any formal institution. The exceptions were the nursery schools, the battery acid manufacturer and the female tailor who were registered with the Registrar of Companies. If legality is the main determining factor, they should not be considered as informal sector activities. However these activities exhibit other characteristics of informal enterprises in Zambia, such as the small size of the establishment (1–5 persons), and workers working for their own account.

The battery acid maker required a yearly licence from the copper mines to allow him to purchase acid from them. The one HBE which seemed to have a link with the local Council, was the young male trader who did not have a licence but somehow paid a 'personal levy' twice weekly to the council. It is difficult from the preliminary results to explain why this is so. Nonetheless, it suggests acceptance of HBEs by different organizations, which may cause confusion if the different organizations do not agree on the status of the HBE. For instance does possession of a Certificate of Incorporation legitimate the use of the house for HBEs? It also raises the issue of equity between those whose HBEs are approved by authorities and therefore subject to taxes and other regulations and those that are not. It is worth noting that apart from the female trader in Ndeke Village and the tailor in Ipusukilo who indicated being harassed by the Kitwe City Council, none of the other respondents mentioned harassment as a particular problem. In effect, laxity on the part of the planning authority might have contributed to the spread of home based enterprises particularly in formal housing areas.

Who Are Involved In Home Based Enterprises?

Home based enterprises are operated by both men and women. In this survey however, 7 of the 11 respondents were male. Other studies have shown that more women are generally engaged in trading activities, but in this study we deliberately sought to include a variety of enterprises. Which ones are easily accessible to women and the gender specificity of various enterprises would need a quantitative survey. In this survey, the nursery schools were operated by women while activities such as carpentry, battery acid manufacture and shoemaking were operated by men. Tailoring and trading were not gender specific.

Studies undertaken by ILO/SATEP (1982), Milimo and Fisseha (1986) and the CSO (1988) found that the average age of informal sector employees in Zambia was above 30 years, but not below 20 or above 45. In this survey, 4 of the 11 respondents were in their early 20s, the youngest being 20, 3 were in their 40s, while the eldest was 55. Another interesting result was that the 4 oldest respondents were engaged in manufacturing. They also had the oldest enterprises.

Seven had attended formal school. Their education levels were however fairly low. The most educated were the nursery school teachers. To run a home based nursery school seems to require some form of tertiary education. These schools are recognized by the local authorities and are thus subject to formal regulations and inspections. All the others had learned their new skills 'on the job' with 3 of them abandoning formally acquired skills. The shoemaker for instance was a trained welder, the carpenter in Chamboli was an electrician, and the male tailor was a marketing clerk. This result does not suggest that formal training is useless but rather indicates its limited usability outside the formal sector, necessitating informal retraining for new entrants to the informal sector. This preliminary conclusion must of course be verified in a larger scale survey.

An important question in the survey was the role of spouses in the HBEs. Eight of the respondents were married. Only one, the shoemaker, indicated that his spouse was directly involved. She had been instrumental in setting up the business, having taught him how to use the sewing machine. At the time of the survey she was running her own tailoring business but was also responsible for selling the shoes her husband made at the local markets. The wife of the carpenter was a full time housewife but occasionally assisted him with purchasing materials. In all but one of the other 6 cases, the spouses got incomes from other sources, and provided both financial and moral support to their spouses' HBEs. The exception was the husband of the female tailor in Ndeke who was not employed and who was not even involved with the HBE. This finding shows that presently both men and women are contributing to household income. The results also indicate that women still bear responsibility for traditional household chores.

Whilst all the HBE operators were adults, children were in almost all cases involved in one way or the other with the HBE except where they were very young. The shoemaker for instance did not employ any outsider, but relied on his children both to make and sell shoes. Similarly the female tailor worked with her son in tailoring whilst one of her daughters was in charge of the hair saloon. The male trader was assisted by his school-going brothers and sisters. In this way the children learn important life skills which they would not learn in formal school. It also raises a question of the impact of economic hardship on school performance particularly for girls who traditionally are also expected to assist with household chores.

All respondents valued formal education highly and all of them ensured that their school-going children remained in school. Whilst the children were expected to assist with the business, the HBE was not seen as their future employment opportunity. In many instances, the respondents valued the usefulness of passing on their skills to their children as a means of ensuring survival. The question of how children divide their time between assisting with household chores, home based enterprises and school-work is an important one. From another angle, one could also ask whether HBEs have the potential to contribute to the development of better parent-child relationships due to constant interaction.

The HBE operators also relied on informal support networks involving friends and business partners. During the interview with the mat-maker for instance, it soon became clear that she did not work alone but was part of a group of four women, some of whom joined in the interview later. These women had a system whereby at any given time, the whole group made and sold mats for only one group member. The mat women also assisted each other in times of need including paying bills for any member who was unwell. In addition, the women collected the reeds from the river as a group, with some playing the role of watch-women against crocodiles. Mat making was conducted from the house of the oldest woman from whom all the others had learnt their skills.

Similarly, the male tailor worked with his father-in-law and the two were in the process of expanding his tailoring shop to cater for a bar. They also had plans to employ a bar tender, who would sleep in an annex to the bar without paying rent but who would also not be paid for acting as night watch-man. The carpenter in Chamboli was assisted by his neighbours to ensure that the items he displayed by the roadside were not stolen or tampered with by children. And the female trader had a neighbour who looked after her shop while she herself went to church on Sundays.

Seven of the respondents owned the houses from which they were operating. The others were the nursery teacher in Ndeke Village who was renting the house for both domestic and business purposes; the carpenter in Riverside lived in another part of Kitwe but was renting the house in Riverside which he was using as a carpentry workshop; and the nursery teacher in Nkana West and the male trader who were operating from their parents' homes. Given that traditionally houses have been rented out for domestic purposes, it would be worth investigating whether this finding denotes a shift in perceptions of what legally and socially constitutes housing. In addition, it would be interesting to find out whether the traditional view of housing as a domestic sphere limits or prevents those households who are renting from developing HBEs and what alternative survival strategies they use.

Why Are People Involved in Home Based Enterprises?

Respondents offered three reasons for why they were involved with HBEs: the need for employment and income, the type of enterprise they were involved in, and the advantage of working from home.

The Need for Employment and Income

Respondents could be divided into five groups namely:

(i) those who had never been employed in the formal sector and had always relied on the informal sector for their economic survival (i.e. the female tailor, female trader and the female mat makers;

(ii) those who had been employed in the formal sector and then were severed through either retirement or retrenchment (i.e. the carpenter, the battery acid maker, the male tailor, the nursery teacher in Nkana West);

(iii) those that had been employed but severed themselves from the formal sector through resignation (i.e. the nursery teacher in Ndeke Village and the carpenter in Riverside);

(iv) those who were still employed but in need of an extra income (the shoemaker who was still working for ZCCM); and

(v) those who whilst being looked after by their parents still found it necessary to earn their own income. This last group included the male trader who had completed school a year earlier and was waiting to go to college, and the nursery teacher in Nkana West.

Here are both workers for whom the informal sector is seen as an employer of last resort because they have been displaced or are unable to find jobs in the formal sector and workers who by choice separate themselves from the formal sector because of its inadequacies. We see also the failure of the formal sector to provide for its workers when they retire. The carpenter in Chamboli for instance only got K12,000,000 (US$3,243) as his retirement package after 35 years of employment. The cases of the shoemaker and the male trader also indicate the failure of the formal sector to provide adequate incomes, requiring supplements from the informal one.

It is perhaps not surprising then that apart from the young male trader, who was fresh out of school, none of the others were keen on formal sector employment. When asked whether they would accept a well paying formal job, all respondents indicated that they were better off working for themselves and would only accept a formal job if the pay was very high. Even the shoemaker had handed in his application to the mines for voluntary retrenchment so that he could concentrate on shoe making. The nursery teacher in Nkana West had been called for interviews at a 'formal' school but she decided it was not worth the trouble. This indicates a high level of disillusionment with the formal sector, as its enterprises are not able to meet the income needs of its workers.

The HBE operators in Kitwe were able to make substantial amounts of money. Table 2 shows the approximate incomes raised by each HBE. Most respondents were not able to give an accurate breakdown of their expenditure and revenues. The figures are therefore not profits but total earnings.

Table 2. Approximate Monthly Incomes by HBE and Neighbourhood

HBE	Neighbourhood	Approx. Monthly Income ('000 Kwacha)
Tailoring/Saloon	Ndeke Village	800
Nursery School	Ndeke Village	600
Nursery School	Nkana West	300
Grocery Shop/Barber	Nkana West	1,900
Carpentry/Electrical	Chamboli	800
Shoemaking/Repair	Chamboli	900
Liquor Trading	Riverside	144
Carpentry	Riverside	**
Acid making	Buchi	**
Tailor	Ipusukilo	**
Mat making	Ipusukilo	210

** Figure not given. (K3,700=US$1)

Although it was difficult to gauge the actual profit from HBEs, it was clear that the incomes from the HBEs compare favourably with wages for formal sector employees, particularly those in the public service. For instance, the average monthly income in the civil service in 1999 was K186,577.33 (US$64.73) (see World Bank 2000:76). The incomes from the HBEs also seem to compare well with the 'Food Basket' monitored monthly by the CCJP[1] which in 2000 was about K300,000. An important issue which fsor lack of information could not be explored here but which would be critical in any larger survey would be to compare the trends of incomes in the HBEs with those in the formal sector and possibly those in other non-home based informal activities. According to the respondents, the manufacturing sector is a better investment in the long term but the service sector is better in terms of providing income for daily sustenance. This was the reason for instance that the female tailor decided to open the saloon to run concurrently with the tailoring business.

Type of Enterprise

Why did the respondents choose particular types of enterprises? Answers to this question included perceived profitability due to either low capital outlays or effective demand. Others chose their enterprises because they either possessed the necessary skills or the equipment required. Others again were just interested in the particular occupation. This was the case with the female tailor who said:

1. The Catholic Commission for Justice and Peace (CCJP) monitors the food basket which measures the amount of money a family of 6 needs to meet their basic subsistence. The food basket is generally accepted as a proxy poverty datum line.

"It attracted me because many times I always wanted to make my own things and then I noticed that I was developing a keen interest. This is what led me to buy the machines and employ people".

Of course all these reasons were supported by other considerations but they were to a large extent the primary ones for choosing the particular type of enterprise. The suitability of the home for the intended economic purposes did not seem to be a consideration for any of the respondents. This supports Lipton's argument (1980) about the flexibility of the house and households to respond to changing situations. Households adapt the house to provide their economic sustenance in the most practical ways available to them. But as they do so, they too adapt to the new environments created by these new uses. It is only through such adaptation for example that the acid maker, carpenters and shoemaker can ensure that their activities do not pose immediate danger to their household members. Kellett and Tipple (1997) in their work in India also showed how households adapted living space to accommodate economic activities by physically separating the home into working and living spaces. This adaptation in some way also explains why none of the respondents considered the mixed use of the house as a problem except in terms of competition for space and limited markets due to location away from main traffic centres.

Advantages of Working from Home

Why did people choose to work from the home? In all cases, one of the main reasons why respondents were operating from home was because it was rent-free. The shoemaker and the female tailor had both moved from designated formal places because they could no longer afford to pay rent. The acid maker had tried to get a place in a designated area but was unable to meet the rental obligations. It is important to point out here that while rent was an important determinant for locating at home, the data also seemed to indicate two opposing views on the use of the home. When asked whether it was better to operate from home or from a designated place, those involved in manufacturing activities e.g. the carpenters, tailors, the acid manufacturer, and the shoemaker perceived the use of the home as necessary for starting the business but not as a permanent work place. On the other hand, those offering services such as the nursery schools, hair saloons and to some extent the traders, saw their enterprises as being locally orientated. They were within easy access of their clients. For instance, the nursery teacher in Ndeke Village when asked whether she planned to move to a designated place once her business was fully established said: "No. No. Okay we've got a plot somewhere we are building a house and we are thinking of even putting the classroom outside".

This may be an example of land being a limiting factor in the productivity of informal activities, supporting ILO/SATEP's (1982) argument about the need for relevant authorities in Zambia to make affordable sites available as a means of promoting small scale enterprises. There are questions as well about HBEs that have matured and moved out of the residential areas. On the other hand the home based service enterprises challenge the planners to rethink their current concept of centralising economic activities particularly those providing basic daily services like hair dressing. At yet another level, the service based HBEs also raise interesting questions about how residents define domestic space and concepts of privacy related to this space.

Other factors cited elsewhere such as ease of extending working hours into the night, and ease of combining two jobs at no extra cost, were also cited. One other important factor cited was availability of utility services such as water and electricity which in the case of the acid manufacturer and the shoemaker, had contributed to moving their enterprises from the markets where they had been operating initially.

DIFFICULTIES OF STARTING HOME BASED ENTERPRISES

Studies by House et al. 1993:1210, Humphrey 1992:15, Cordera and Gonzalez 1991:29, Glewwe and Hall 1992:26, and Hays-Mitchell 1993 have indicated that the informal sector is not easy to enter. The ILO/SATEP (1982) study identified similar problems in Zambia. Napier and Mothwa (2000), Olufemi (2000), Titus (2000), Gough (2000) and Kamete (2000), have also identified very similar problems with informal activities generally and HBEs specifically in South Africa, Nigeria, Tanzania, Ghana and Zimbabwe respectively. This study also seems to support this view, even if informal enterprises do not have to comply with prescribed rules, regulations or standards and do not have to meet specified production targets in order to remain operational. Nonetheless new entrants must deal with a whole set of difficulties and must continuously struggle to stay within the informal sector.

Limited Access to Start-Up Capital

One of the main problems was resource mobilization. For all respondents, initial capital outlay was obtained from personal savings, friends or relatives. The young male trader for instance raised his initial capital by doing odd jobs during his free time from school. The male tailor started with no capital outlay but relied on an ancient Singer Simanco 94779 sewing machine which he inherited from his grandfather. The nursery teacher in Nkana West obtained money from her father to start the school.

This lack of start up capital somehow explains why the HBE is seen as "the core of the informal sector". For indeed without the home there would be no money for rent, and by implication, no informal sector activity. It also explains why these activities are small scale familial concerns. None of the respondents had bothered to get a loan because they either did not see the need for it or they were afraid of the risks or did not know where to obtain one. Informal sector employees in Zambia rarely obtain financial assistance from the banks because they lack collateral (see Bardouille 1991). Some soft loans for small- scale businesses are currently available in Zambia, e.g. those offered by the Christian Enterprise Trust of Zambia (CETZAM). However none of the 11 respondents wanted these loans because they were either too small (US$50 for the first loan) or demanded weekly repayments and some form of collateral. This view that US$50 is too small raises interesting questions about micro-finance and small scale informal businesses, not least the potential differences in perception of what constitutes a 'small business' between the creditors and the borrowers.

Limited Skills

The second problem with entering the informal sector is related to acquiring skills, which in this study seemed to be a matter of self-determination, self-discipline and no little cost to the operators. They had either had to employ trained people to teach them or simply 'learn on the job'. The lack of skills and capital means that development of HBEs takes a lot of time and is undertaken through progressive improvements as and when funds allow. There also seems to be a lot of experimentation in the initial stages of an enterprise until people get to some fairly stable level.

Most work on the informal sector assumes that the proprietors pass on skills to the younger generation and indeed some do. However, this study demonstrated the repeated incidence of proprietors seeking skills from their employees who in some cases may be much younger. In follow-up research, it would therefore be worthwhile to explore the possibility of a two-way flow of skills, i.e. across generations and possibly across the formal and informal divide.

The Home as a Work Place

Because of the easy availability of land in Zambia and the benign climate, most HBE activities were conducted outside the house. Except for in the cases of the nursery schools and the female tailor, the house seemed to be used for storage rather than for production. This is not surprising given that in most residential neighbourhoods in Zambia each house has a significant parcel of free land around it. In this study, even the respondents living in low cost housing had more than 200m^2 of free land on their plots. Many proprietors built 'work-shops' either attached to or separated from the main house. The carpenter in Chamboli, the male trader, the male tailor and the shoemaker all had erected sheds outside the main house from which they operated their HBEs. Only the female tailor had added a room to the main house to cater for her tailoring and hair saloon. HBEs in Kitwe seem to enable participating households to consolidate their housing through either extension of the existing house or construction of new out-buildings. It is interesting to note that in her study of HBEs in Ghana, Gough (2000) found very similar results, i.e. the bulk were undertaken outside either in specially built sheds or in the open. Olumefi (2000) found that in Nigeria women used either the house itself, or out-buildings such as the garage and the servants quarters for their HBEs. At the same time, Untari et al. (2000) found that HBEs in Indonesia were operated from either inside the house, small sheds attached to the house, out in the open yard or in some cases on plots of land away from the house due to lack of space. Kellett and Tipple (1997) on the other hand found HBEs in India that were completely restricted to the house because of complete lack of alternative outside space.

The conspicuous absence of the nursery schools from the list of those who built external work spaces or extensions might be explained by the large capital investment required to construct a classroom block which must be made of approved building materials. In addition, not very many parents would want to send their children to a school made of 'cheap' materials such as timber or mud bricks. On the other hand, it seems quite acceptable for a small barber shop or local shop, popularly known as 'kantemba', or indeed a local carpentry workshop to be built with either timber or mud bricks.

The use of external space also limited the activities of some HBE operators. For instance the mat makers had to stop making mats during the rainy season because they had nowhere to store either the reeds or the mats. It must be noted though that the seasonality of the mat making was also influenced by the high water levels in the river during the rainy season which made it difficult for the women to both cross the river and to see the crocodiles which were a constant threat. It is also important to note that the mat makers were located in the peri-urban area and therefore had less access to land and storage facilities compared to their colleagues in the other areas.

Household Space and Working Space

Use of external space may explain why having the enterprise based at home does not seem to bother the occupants. Activities such as hammering and chiselling take place outside the home during the day when everybody is busy with their own work, and so do not interfere with daily household activities. Most respondents seemed to indicate that the inconvenience caused by the HBE was bearable as long as it only affected the immediate (nuclear) household members. Even in cases where the sitting rooms had been completely taken over by HBE activity, this was seen as inconvenient only when the household had outside visitors.

It must be noted however that only the proprietors of the HBEs were interviewed. The views of the other household members on this matter may therefore be very different. Although mixed use of the plot was not seen as a problem, most respondents indicated a need for household privacy. There was therefore a sense of distinction between 'HBE space invaded by outsiders' (clients) and 'household space'. For instance, the male trader would not allow his clients to use the household toilet and he was in the process of trying to build one for them outside. Similarly the teacher in Ndeke Village had two toilets in the house, each painted a different colour to differentiate between the school toilet and the household toilet. Both teachers also stated that they would want to continue operating from home but that the school functions should be separated from the domestic functions. It appears therefore that there are some interesting perceptions on what constitutes home space and work space and that whilst HBEs are accepted, there are limits to the level of outside intrusion that is acceptable.

Home Based Enterprises and Infrastructure

Large plots have been helpful to the HBEs. But the state of plots has also created problems for some HBEs, because the city council has become increasingly unable to maintain or expand physical infrastructure such as water, roads and sewerage. People operating HBEs in Ndeke Village for instance suffered erratic water supply. They therefore had to keep water in drums all the time or in dire situations they had to pay some boys to bring water for them from the nearest mine townships. Electricity supply disruptions were also very frequent. Despite this, the operators got regular bills based on fixed charges from both the council and the Electricity Corporation.

The operators in Riverside and Buchi suffered utility disruptions, but the frequency was not as high as in Ndeke Village. Those in Ipusukilo had no access to potable water or electricity. This inhibited investment in electrical equipment, forcing the operators to rely on manual tools. As the tailor in Ipusukilo said when asked how he managed to work without electricity:

> Yes, yes that's a very big problem I always face when it comes to working at night. Then I use candles, there's not enough light. So sometimes I have to work in the day only. It's like that.

The operators in Chamboli and Nkana West had a constant supply of water, electricity and indeed all other utility services provided by the mining company at a nominal fee. In the case of the carpenter in Chamboli he was not paying anything for all the utilities because he was no longer employed by the mines, which were therefore not able to deduct the Municipal Charge from his salary.[1]

Poorly equipped residential neighbourhoods may thus adversely affect the already disadvantaged, even if they try to get themselves out of their poverty trap. Residents in higher income areas are not only more likely to have a higher financial base for starting their HBE but they also have more land and better access to utilities. In addition, HBEs located in areas with physical infrastructure are manufacturing their goods or services using utility services charged at domestic tariffs. This may give them a competitive advantage but it has equity implications for the unconnected poor, and economic implications for the utility companies.

CONCLUSIONS AND RECOMMENDATIONS

This chapter has shown that the house is not necessarily just a dwelling place, but may also be a factory floor as well as a storeroom. And in cases where goods produced are not taken to the market, the house also plays a commercial function. It is also a retail outlet for goods produced elsewhere and offers a base for a range of services. Apart from the obvious benefits of not paying rent and tax, households engaged in HBEs maximize all possible income sources by undertaking a variety of activities. Basing their activity in the home enables participants simultaneously to perform both domestic as well as economic functions. This is

---

1. All five towns on the Copperbelt with a Mine and Council Township, have two water supply systems one run by the mines and the other by the city council. The mine system has always been the reliable system subsidized by the mines. Currently the miners are subsidized by the government through a World Bank Loan Facility that is managing municipal services in the mine township. The municipal charge is a fixed nominal amount deducted from every miner as a contribution for utility services.

of great significance to women who do not have to worry about child minding. Business can be conducted any time of the day at no extra cost. Because their activities are located in residential neighbourhoods, HBE participants are able to use non-monetary exchange neighbourhood networks which would be relatively difficult to establish in specially designated business areas due to competition. In times of extreme difficulties such networks might provide community members with a support system to fall back on. Activities conducted from the house foster free skills training for willing young people, equipping them with basic working skills, which they might not otherwise learn from the formal school. The minimal income raised from the HBE also enables children to go to formal school. In this way the HBE prepares the young people for future prospects both within and outside the formal sector.

HBEs are fundamental to the struggle against poverty. Most of them are encumbered with a myriad of operational constraints and are therefore not very lucrative but offer only a basis for survival for the households concerned. Formalising these activities by locating them in designated land use zones might attract new and unmanageable costs such as rent, transport and in some cases tax, all of which would diminish the viability of the business. A home is therefore critical for the operations of these enterprises and the survival of the households. As the HBE progresses and brings in extra income, the household is then able to invest in housing improvement both through expansion of the house or separation of economic from domestic functions.

The fact that most operators lack access to financial support re-emphasizes the importance of the house in the survival of those involved in HBEs. Unless they can get funds to reinvest in their businesses, their activities are not likely to expand. But as long as they remain in the informal sector and have no tangible collateral, their chances of getting loans are very limited. The importance of secure land tenure as well as improvements in housing quality can therefore not be over-emphasized.

There are obvious distinctions across gender, generations, income groups and neighbourhoods. For instance physical infrastructure was more readily available in some neighbourhoods compared to others. Men, women and youth seemed to have different areas of interest and opportunity in so far as choosing the type of HBE was concerned. Thus advantages and constraints of operating economic activities from home will vary from one group to another. Last but not least, it is important to seriously examine the social aspects of HBEs, in particular the potential of HBEs to contribute to developments in gender and generational relations at household level. These relationships no doubt have a bearing on the development of the HBE to the extent that they represent a re-arrangement of household structure to enable HBE activities.

Whilst this study has focused on the economic aspect of HBEs their physical implications must in no way be underplayed. There is no doubt that development of HBEs has led to a change in the landscape of many residential areas. The continued development of sheds for workshops and retail outlets will give a different outlook from that envisaged by the planners. A question then is whether this trend should be stopped or simply regulated. Whatever decision is taken must be based on a clear understanding of the economic reality of the people who live there and perhaps a rethinking of concepts of land use zoning and plot usage.

This study has shown that housing is indeed fundamental to the fight against poverty. If this argument is accepted, should we then discard all planning and land use regulations in order to assist the HBEs? Or should we perhaps treat the phenomenon as a transitional phase in city development? There are of course no straightforward answers to these questions. But one thing which is obvious is that there is a need to broaden the conceptual categories of home use to include income generating activities as valid and normal within the domestic environment (Kellett et al. 2000). Home based enterprises challenge us to re-evaluate our definition of what is acceptable within the home. Strict land use controls can no longer be taken as the norm without jeopardising the lives of hundreds of city residents. What we need is a better, research–based understanding of HBEs and to identify the areas where planning can play a role both to assist their development and also to mitigate their negative impacts.

There will of course be variation of needs and problems between different social groups and between neighbourhoods. For informal areas for instance a priority concern might be provision of infrastructure services, whilst for formal areas priority concerns might be with mitigating negative environmental effects. For the youth and women priority might be access to start-up capital and maybe a place to work from, while for the men it could be skills training and markets for their goods.

Whatever the problem and however they are dealt with, it is clear from this study that HBEs have become an important part of the urban landscape from both their physical as well as economic aspects. With the levels of formal job losses forecast in the public sector, it can only be assumed that there will be more not fewer such enterprises in the foreseeable future. More importantly, the HBEs have 'thrived' regardless of planning regulations designed to prevent their growth. It is therefore fair to conclude that if urban planners want to be relevant to the urban development agenda, then they should rethink their fixation with master planning ideas which hitherto has limited their role in the development of the informal sector. They must adopt approaches in which solutions do not come from master planning text books but rather are developed with the people concerned, using planning tools that respect the economic reality of the city and the voices of other stakeholders. The essence of planning after all should be about people and not buildings. Only in this way can planning make a positive contribution to enhancing people's lives and be made relevant to the economic and social context of today's developing city.

Acknowledgements

This study was part of the Newcastle University–Copperbelt University exchange programme funded by the British Council. The author wishes to thank the research assistant Kamenda Mataa for collecting data, Dr Thomas Kweku Taylor of Copperbelt University, Mr Nkole Senkwe and Mr Ohene Sarfor for their encouragement and support.

References

Bardouille R., 1991, *An Annotated Bibliography of Research on the Urban Informal Sector in Zambia: Suggestions for Future Research and Support*. Lusaka: FINNIDA.

Central Statistical Office, 2001, *2000 Census of Population and Housing: Preliminary Report*. Lusaka: CSO.

—, 1997, *Informal Sector Activities in Zambia. Report on HBS 1993–1996*. Lusaka: GRZ.

—, 1988, *Labour Force Survey 1986*. Lusaka: CSO. Unpublished.

Cordera, Campos R. and Tiburcio E. Gonzalez, 1991, "Crisis and Transition in the Mexican Economy" in Gonzalez, M. and A. Escobar (eds), *Social Responses to Mexico's Economic Crisis of the 1980s*, pp. 19–56. San Diego, La Jolla: Center for US-Mexican Studies, University of California.

Glewwe, P. and G. Hall, 1992, *Poverty and Inequality during Unorthodox Adjustment: The Case of Peru, 1985–90*. Living Standards Measurement Study Working Paper No. 86. The World Bank.

Gough, Katherine, 2000, "Regulating Home Based Enterprises: Formal and Informal Mechanisms of Control in Urban Ghana". Paper presented at the Conference on "The Formal and the Informal City – What Happens at the Interface?", Copenhagen, 15–18 June 2000.

Government of the Republic of Zambia (GRZ), 1993, *Rehabilitation and New Sources Development Study for Kitwe Water Supply Project (KWSP) Report on Phase 1 Works*. Vol. 2. Annexure 2, Demography, Settlements, Water Demand and Balance.

—, 1989, *Fourth National Development Plan*. Lusaka: National Commission for Development Planning.

Hansen, Karen Tranberg, 1997, *Keeping House in Lusaka*. New York: Columbia University Press.

—, 1982, "Planning Productive Work for Married Women in a Low-Income Settlement in Lusaka: The Case for a Small Scale Handicrafts Industry", *African Social Research*, June 1982, pp. 211–23.

—, 1975, *Married Women and Work: Explorations from an Urban Case Study*, pp. 777–99. African Social Research, 20, December 1975.

Hays-Mitchell, M., 1993, "The Ties that Bind. Informal and Formal Sector Linkages in Street Vending: The Case of Peru's Ambulantes", *Environment and Planning A25*, pp. 1025–1102.

Heisler, H., 1974, *Urbanization and the Government of Migration: The Inter-relation of Urban and Rural Life in Zambia*. London: C. Hurst and Co. Publishers.

House, W.J., G.K. Ikiara and D. McCormick, 1993, "Urban Self Employment in Kenya: Panacea or Viable Strategy?", *World Development 21*, pp. 1205–1224.

Humphrey, J., 1992, *Are the Unemployed Part of the Urban Poverty Problem?* IDS mimeograph.

ILO/SATEP, 1982, *The Urban Informal Sector in Zambia: A Program of Action*. Lusaka.

Kamete, Amin Y., "Home Industries, the Formal Sector and Urban Governance: Grappling with the Interface in Harare, Zimbabwe". Paper presented at the Conference on "The Formal and the Informal City – What Happens at the Interface?", Copenhagen, 15–18 June 2000. (Revised version in this volume).

Kay, George, 1967, *A Social Geography of Zambia: A Survey of Population Patterns in a Developing Country*. London: University of London Press.

Kazimbaya-Senkwe, Barbara M., 2001, "Land Use Conversions in Zambia's Urban Residential Neighbourhoods: Defining the Issues", *Construction News, Journal for the National Council for Construction in Zambia*, July/August 2001, Issue No. 5, pp. 18–19.

Kazimbaya-Senkwe, Barbara M. and Alexander Mwale 2001, *Solid Waste Characterization Study for the City of Kitwe: Phase 1*. Consultancy Report for the SINPA-Zambia Project, Support to the Implementation of National (Habitat) Plans of Action-Zambia, Kitwe.

Kellett, P. and A.G. Tipple, 1997, "The Home as Workplace: A Study of Income-Generating Activities within the Domestic Setting". Paper presented at the International Symposium on "Culture and Space in Home Environments: Critical Evaluations and New Paradigms", Istanbul, Istanbul Technical University and IAPS, June 1997.

Kellett, P., B.M. Kazimbaya-Senkwe and S. Speak, 2000, "Creating and Sustaining Livelihoods in Ipusukilo: A Pilot Study of Home Based Enterprise and Poverty Alleviation in Zambia". Paper presented to the CARDO International Conference on "Housing, Work and Development: The Role of Home Based Enterprises", Newcastle upon-Tyne, 26–28 April 2000.

Lipton, M., 1980, "Family, Fungibility and Formality: Rural Advantages of Informal Non-Farm Enterprises versus the Urban Informal State" in Samir Amin (ed.), *Human Resources, Employment and Development*. Volume 5, Developing Countries, Proceedings of the Sixth World Congress of the International Economic Association, Mexico City, 1980. London: MacMillan.

Malama, Albert and Barbara M. Kazimbaya-Senkwe, 2001, *Consumer Assessment Survey for Water and Sanitation in Council Townships: Phase 1: The Copperbelt Province*. Consultancy Report for the Government of the Republic of Zambia, Kitwe.

Malama, Albert and Douglas Meleki, 2002, *Participatory Analysis of Experiences and Livelihood Options of the Zambian Copper Mine Retrenchees*. Consultancy Report for the Government of the Republic of Zambia, Kitwe.

McGee, T.G., 1976, "The Persistence of the Proto Proletariat: Occupational Structures and Planning for the Future of Third World Cities", *Progress in Geography 9*, pp. 3–38.

Milimo, John T. and Yacob Fisseha, 1986, *Rural Small Scale Enterprises in Zambia: Results of a 1985 Country Wide Survey*. Lusaka, Rural Development Studies Bureau and Michigan State University, International Development Working Paper. No. 28.

Moser, C., 1987, "Women, Human Settlements and Housing: A Conceptual Framework for Analysis and Policy-making" in C. Moser and L. Peake (eds), *Women, Human Settlements and Housing*, pp. 12–32. London: Tavistock.

Moser, Caroline and Jeremy Holland, 1997, *Household Responses to Poverty and Vulnerability Vol. 4: Confronting Crisis in Chawama*. Lusaka and Washington DC: World Bank.

Muneku Austin, 2001, "The Informal Sector in Zambia: An Exploratory Study" in Herrick, Mpuku and Austin Muneku (eds), *The Impact of Structural Adjustment Programmes on the Zambian Economy: A Trade Union Perspective*, pp. 81–94. Kitwe: Congress of Trade Unions.

Napier, Mark and A. Mothwa, 2000, *Push and Pull Factors in the Initiation and Maintenance of Home Work in two Pretoria Settlements: the Myths and Realities of South African Home based Enterprises*, pp. 253–69. Proceeding of the CARDO International Conference on "Housing Work and Development: The Role of Home Based Enterprises", Newcastle Upon-Tyne, 26–28 April 2000.

National Commission for Development Planning (NCDP), 1989, *Fourth National Development Plan*. Lusaka. GRZ.

Olufemi, O.A., 2000, *Home based Work of professional Women in Nigeria and South Africa: Its implications for Development Planning and Policy*, pp. 286–301. Proceeding of the CARDO International Conference on "Housing Work and Development: The Role of Home Based Enterprises", Newcastle Upon-Tyne, 26–28 April 2000.

Sethuraman S.V. (ed.), 1981, *The Urban Informal Sector in Developing Countries: Employment, Poverty and Environment*. Geneva: ILO.

Strassman, Paul, 1986, "Types of Neighbourhood and Home-Based Enterprises: Evidence from Lima Peru", *Urban Studies* 23, pp. 485–500.

Titus, Colman, 2000, "Kiosk Business in Moshi Municipality, Tanzania: From Informal to Formal Municipal Economy". Paper presented at the Conference on "The Formal and the Informal City-What Happens at the Interface?", Copenhagen, 15–18 June 2000.

Untari, R. et al., 2000, *Clustering of Home based Enterprises (HBEs) in Semarang, Indonesia and its Environmental Impact, pp.* 363–72. Proceeding of the CARDO International Conference on "Housing Work and Development: The Role of Home Based Enterprises", Newcastle Upon-Tyne, 26–28 April 2000.

World Bank, 2000, *Public Service Capacity Building Project in Support of the First Phase of the Public Service Capacity Building Program.* Project Appraisal Document on a Proposed Credit to the Republic of Zambia. Report No. 19239 ZA. Capacity Building Unit. Africa Region. February 22, 2000.

—, 1994, *Zambia Poverty Assessment.* HRD. Washington DC: Southern Africa Department.

CHAPTER 7

Home Industries and the Formal City in Harare, Zimbabwe

Amin Y. Kamete

In urban Zimbabwe, the term 'home industries' refers to a particular type of enterprise situated at the very frontier between the formal and the informal city. Based on a study concluded in 2000, this chapter is about home industries in a high-density area of Harare. The discussion identifies some crucial issues in the relationship between the formal and the informal city as typified by the situation of the home industries. They have, since independence, established themselves as zones of viable enterprises in terms of production, trade and commerce. Home industries attract all sorts of clients from their respective urban centres and the rural hinterland. They also have complicated institutional and individual alliances in all the urban areas of Zimbabwe. While their role in and contribution to the urban socio-economic well-being is understood and appreciated in some quarters, these industries have also gained a reputation for being places of all sorts of illegalities and vices. Not surprisingly, local authorities as well as financial institutions view them as socio-political rather than economic entities.

Home industries in Zimbabwe are not synonymous with home-based enterprises (HBEs). The latter are economic activities that take place in or around the housing unit (see UNCHS/ILO 1995), while the Zimbabwean home industries are located in officially designated 'industrial estates' areas set aside for the informal sector units (MLGRUD 1996; cf. Mhone 1995). In urban planning terms, a home industry refers to a site legally zoned for small scale urban informal economic activities. In organizational terms, home industries are small enterprises located in these designated zones. Such zones are usually located in high-density, low-income residential areas, close to or within shopping centres. They are an expression of government's heavily politicized and currently racialized policy of indigenization, where the ideal is to help the hitherto marginalized black population to be economically empowered by participating in mainstream economic activities and owning a sizeable part of the means of production (DSEI 1997; Kamete 1997).

Home industries are home to a variety of commercial and industrial enterprises. Among the industrial activities are welding, carpentry, building materials manufacturing and automobile engineering and rebuilding. The commercial activities include trading in furniture, motor vehicle parts, domestic appliances and other scarce and/or expensive commodities. The goods and services at home industries are always considerably cheaper than elsewhere in the urban economy. This understandably raises eyebrows about the legality and/or authenticity of the service or product in question.

Home industries straddle the dividing line between the legal and the illegal city. While recognized, sanctioned and even promoted by the rulers at both local and central government levels, home industries frequently get into trouble with institutions of urban management and with commercial and industrial enterprises in the formal sector. As sources of affordable and essential goods and services home industries provide a valuable service to the urban residents as well as private and public institutions including those in the industrial, trading and commercial sectors. They also create employment and strengthen income generation opportunities for retrenched, semi-skilled, enterprising and low paid urban residents (MLGRUD 1996).

These enterprises have extensive backward and forward linkages, extending beyond the petty commodity production sector into households, industry, trade, commerce and public sector agencies (cf. Burgess 1985). However, even the staunchest sympathizers, suppliers and clients of home industries view them with suspicion. Home industries are commonly perceived as zones of infractions and all imaginable vices like theft, cheating, corruption, bribery and exploitation. They are rumoured to be havens for theft syndicates, especially those dealing in household appliances, hardware equipment and vehicle parts. They are also perceived as breeding grounds for dishonesty. It is commonly prescribed that one has to always painstakingly check and verify the cleanness of any transaction that is taking place there to avoid being duped or conned (*The Herald* 1998). Finally, according to city planners and managers, they are known to break every operative rule and regulation regarding property, labour, tax, planning, public health and environmental sanitation (MLGRUD 1996; Kamete 1999). These are the standard arguments used when the authorities embark on their 'clean-up' campaigns designed to restore 'order' to the urban centres (*Daily News* 2001).

These industries are thus widely stigmatized. Be that as it may, they also have demonstrated an ability to attract individual and institutional clients of all types because of two basic attributes. The first one is the provision of scarce, essential and popular commodities; especially spare parts for vehicles, machinery and other equipment. The second attraction is affordability; an advantage that is further enhanced by the possibility of successfully bargaining for an even lower price.

INFORMAL ECONOMIC ACTIVITIES IN HARARE

The informal sector in urban Zimbabwe has been growing primarily because of the inability of the formal sector to create employment at a rate that satisfies increasing demand (Mhone 1995:2). While the national annual growth in the labour force is currently at 300,000, the formal sector in Zimbabwe can only create about 20,000 new jobs per year (see Kamete 1997:6). A 1991 survey estimated that 845,000 micro and small scale enterprises in Zimbabwe employed about 1.6 million people or 27 per cent of the national labour force

(Gemini 1991:1). Due to the upsurge in retrenchments and the closing down of established industries, this figure has increased and by 2002, over 50 per cent of the national labour force was estimated to be in the informal sector (Gemini 1991:1; Kumbawa 2002).

Informal sector activities in Harare are littered throughout the urban land-scape. In spatial terms, these activities take place in several strategic locations, such as along busy streets, on shop fronts, at public transport terminals, at designated sites, and at intersections (MLGRUD 1996: 6; Mhone 1995). Table 1 summarizes these activities.

Table 1. Spatial and Operational Features of the Small Scale Informal Sector in Harare

CLASS	LOCATIONAL FEATURES	COMMON ACTIVITIES
Home-based enterprises	In and around the housing unit	Selling of foodstuffs; small household goods; repairs; services
Home industries	Designated sites within residential areas	Manufacturing; repairs; welding; trading; engineering works; services
Street vending	Along busy streets, on pavements, at intersections	Sale of confectionery; cigarettes; vegetables; fruits; books; clothing items
Shop-front vending	Near or at the entrance of busy super-markets	Sale of plastic bags; confectionery; cigarettes; vegetables; fruits; books
Bus-stop vending	At public transport termini. Sometimes structures are provided but still some vendors operate outside the structures	Sale of confectionery; cosmetics; ciga-rettes; vegetables; fruits; books; clothing items
People's markets	Designated areas usually near bus-stops or shopping centres in the middle and high-income areas	Making and sale of crafts; sale of con-fectionery; cigarettes; vegetables; fruits; books; clothing items
Flea markets	Designated sites within the Central Business District and suburban shop-ping centres	Selling of mixed consumer goods; clothes; appliances and accessories; clothes
Roadside stalls	Along busy distributors or national roads leading out of the city	Selling of curios; building materials and accessories; crafts; maize; fruits; vege-tables; sculptures; carving
Designated vend-ing sites	On sites within the Central Business District identified by planners Not necessarily provided for in local plans or town planning schemes	Confectionery; cigarettes; vegetables; fruits; books; clothing items

Source: Research findings, 2000

By far the most common activity in all sites is the selling of various consumer products. The sites of these activities range from the legally designated market places called people's markets and flea markets, to the contested and illegal in the streets and in front of shops. Street vendors regularly engage in battles with the city authorities who frequently arrest them, confiscate their wares and fine them for violating town planning, public health, property, sanitation and trading laws.

HOME INDUSTRIES

This chapter reports the results of a study carried out in Harare between the years 1999 and 2000. It was born out of the observed enduring love-hate relationship between home industries on one hand and the urban planning and management system and the formal economy on the other. The aim of the study was to explore the dialectic between the informal city, as represented by home industries, and the formal city, as represented by large established enterprises and the urban planning and management system. The nature and composition of home industries is examined and their operational characteristics are analysed. Issues of urban governance in the relationship between home industries, the formal economy and the urban planning and management system are also raised.

The study focused on four zones of home industries in the high-density residential area of Warren Park. Situated about five kilometres to the south of the city centre, Warren Park is a typical high-density residential area most of whose residents are in the low-income bracket. Ten units were randomly selected for further scrutiny. These are units whose owners were willing to be involved in extensive interviews. Information was gathered from home industry operators, the local authority, non-governmental organizations, and the formal private sector. A semi-structured questionnaire was administered to the operators. Information from the rest of the respondents was obtained by means of structured interviews. In addition, information was also gleaned from secondary sources such as the media, administrative records from central and local government, academic and professional publications as well as legal instruments and policy documents.

Most of the home industries in Zimbabwe appeared after independence when the euphoria of co-operatives, socialism and self-reliance gripped the nation. However, it should be noted that although the term 'home industries' was popularized after independence, the activities had their origin before independence. The difference between the activities in colonial times and those after independence is that the latter are formally sanctioned by both central and local government and are officially recognized by the urban planning and management system. Before independence, activities in the sites that have been turned into home industries were to all intents and purposes illegal. It was only through 'benign neglect' by the tough colonial urban planning and management system that they were allowed to continue.

The Nature and Composition of Home Industries

Table 2 summarizes the nature and composition of home industries at the four sites studied. The sites have a total of 153 enterprises. About 40 per cent are in manufacturing. Activities under this category include metal welding, producing building materials and making furniture, carts and various farming implements. Service provision, which constitutes over 27 per cent of the total, is the second most popular activity. Among the services offered are hairdressing, arc welding, tinkering and car-washing. Repairs constitute just over 12 per cent of the total activities at the four centres. The repairs are undertaken on such items as motor vehicles, household appliances, furniture and various tools.

Table 2. Home Industries in Warren Park, Harare, by location and type of activity

SITE	NUMBER OF UNITS BY THE TYPE OF ACTIVITY				
	Manufacturing	Buying and selling	Service provision	Repairs	Total
Warren Park I Shopping Centre	15	2	3	1	12
Warren Park Light Industry	13	5	6	2	26
Warren Park Heavy Industry	20	16	19	10	65
Warren Park D	12	10	13	6	41
TOTAL	60	33	41	19	153
Percentage of all units	39.2	21.6	26.8	12.4	100.0

Source: Survey, 1999–2000.

The levels of equipment are generally low. The units in Warren Park fall into three broad types: a) enclosures with planning permission and some infrastructure, b) enclosures with planning permission but little or no infrastructure, c) open spaces, legally occupied but without any equipment.

It is at the heavy industrial site that most units are located. This site takes up over 42 per cent of the enterprises. Warren Park Shopping Centre has the least number of industries (14 per cent). This may be because most people there prefer to operate outside the designated industrial site, which in any case is also very small.

The picture shown above seems to deviate from popular perceptions that regard home industries as areas of buying and selling, some kind of informal wholesale activity. The profile is just like any other industrial site with diversity rather than uniformity. This is a very important fact considering that even official perceptions regard these zones as the home of the notorious 'briefcase business people', whose role in the economy is akin to that of an opportunistic parasite (cf. *The Herald* 1998). 'Briefcase business people' are mostly men who have no business specialization or fixed business premises. They move around soliciting for any business deals especially those involving buying and selling.

The Workings of Home Industries

We shall now have a closer look at the ten cases selected for closer scrutiny. In three of them, the business had started as a result of retrenchments. Of the remaining seven cases one was 'inherited' from a parent, one was a 'conversion' from another line of business, while another one had started as a family venture. One is an 'original' in the sense that it is the owner's first ever business. Of the remaining three units, two (scrap metal collection and hairdressing), were initiated by employees in the formal sector while one started off as a home-based enterprise. This picture suggests that home industries cannot be regarded as being solely a response to the current economic problems hitting the country.

Table 3. Financing of Business in Warren Park Home Industries

BUSINESS UNIT	INITIAL CAPITALS		WORKING CAPITALS		LABOUR	
	Source	Amount (Z$)[a]	Source	Average amount (Z$ per month)	Source	Number
1. Welding	Father	20,000	Profits	15,000	Family	5
2. Carpentry	Package[b]	20,000	Profits	30,000	Market[c]	2
3. Tailoring	Father	2,000	Profits	27,000	Market	3
4. Brick-moulding	Savings and Zambuko[d]	10,000	Profits	30,000	Market	4
5. Carpentry	Father	20,000	Profits	15,000	Family	5
6. Scrap-metal dealing	Savings	10,000	Profits	100,000	Market and Family	6
7. Block builder	Package	15,000	Profits	45,000	Market	7
8. Spray-painter	Savings	30,000	Profits	60,000	Family and Market	7
9. Hairdresser	Package	10,000	Profits	25,000	Market	5
10. Hairdresser	Savings	7,000	Profits	20,000	Market	4
TOTAL		144,000		367,000		48

[a] At the time of writing US$1 was equivalent to about Z$55 at the controlled official rate.
[b] This refers to the retrenchment package.
[c] This refers to the labour market.
[d] A local NGO that provides micro-finance.

Source: Survey, 1999–2000.

Table 3 shows the financing of the business ventures and their human resources aspects. The most popular method of accessing initial capital is the use of personal savings. This method was used by four of the ten entrepreneurs. In three cases fathers provided the initial capital. The three retrenchees used their retrenchment packages. One of the four respondents who used their own savings also received a small loan from Zambuko, a local non-governmental organization that specializes in micro-finance.

In total the ten units used Z$144,000 as initial capital. This equals US$2,618, as in early 2000, US$1 was equivalent to about Z$55 at the official rate. On average the initial investment is Z$14,400 for each unit. The median is slightly lower at Z$12,500. In half the cases the initial capital was Z$10,000 or less. Only one case had a Z$30,000 start-up capital. All the entrepreneurs interviewed stated that their working capital is financed wholly from their business profits. The average working capital for the year was Z$36,700. The median was lower at Z$28,500. Seven units had a monthly working capital base of over Z$20,000. Of the remaining three cases, two registered a working capital base of Z$15,000 each. In comparison, the minimum wage was then about Z$3,000 while the poverty line was fixed at Z$8,000 (CCZ 2001). Some workers especially domestic workers and security guards earned wages below the minimum wage in the industrial sector.

The ten industrial units employ a combined total of 48 people, an average of about 5 per unit. Six of the units get labour entirely from outside the family circle. Only one unit employs people from outside Warren Park. Two units rely wholly on family labour, with the remaining two using a mixture of family and non-family labour.

Table 4. Raw Materials, Transport and Storage in Home Industries in Warren Park

| BUSINESS UNIT | RAW MATERIAL PROCUREMENT | | | TRANSPORT AND STORAGE | | |
	Source	Terms	Average amount (Z$ per month)	Transport	Storage	Value adding
1. Welding	Formal sector	Cash	15,000	Public	Workshop	Yes
2. Carpentry	Formal sector	Cash	45,000	Own	Workshop	Yes
3. Tailoring	Formal sector	Cash	25,000	Public	Workshop	Yes
4. Brick-moulding	Formal sector	Cash	48,000	Private hire	Home	Yes
5. Carpentry	Formal sector	Cash	10,000	Public	Workshop	Yes
6. Scrap-metal dealing	Formal sector	Cash	10,000	Own	Yard	Yes
7. Block builder	Formal sector	Cash	27,000	Private hire	Home/ Workshop	Yes
8. Spray-painter	Formal/Informal	Cash	20,000	Own	Home	Yes
9. Hairdresser	Formal/Informal	Cash	20,000	Public	Workshop	Yes
10. Hairdresser	Formal/Informal	Cash	15,000	Public	Home	Yes

Source: Survey, 1999–2000.

Table 4 gives details of the procurement of raw materials, transportation and storage. As the table shows, seven of the units get their raw materials entirely from the formal private sector. Four of these sources are well-established companies that are registered on the Zimbabwe Stock Exchange in Harare. Three units procure their raw materials from a mixture of informal and formal industries. Two of these three are hairdressing saloons. They obtain most of their chemicals from traders at the so-called flea markets, who are engaged in cross-border trading. Flea market is a local term for a trading place where (informal) sellers of goods rent stalls from the local authority or private individuals. The total average monthly expenditure on raw materials for the 10 units was Z$235,000, which translates to an average of Z$23,500 per unit.

All enterprises pay cash for their goods. Unlike their counterparts in the formal sector—and indeed some individual households—they do not have access to credit facilities. This may be both because they are perceived to have low credit-worthiness and because they lack collateral security. Half the units rely on public transport, principally privately owned and operated commuter omnibuses and conventional buses. Three use their own transport, and two prefer hiring private vehicles to transport their goods. Use of their own vehicles and private hire may indicate some degree of affluence among the operators.

Storage is done on business premises (5 cases), at home (3 cases), a mixture of home and premises (one case) and the home industry yard (one case). Some of these operators employ somebody to stay at the business premises overnight to guard the property because of the prevalence of burglary and theft. The availability of storage space seems to indicate that there is generous provision of space in home industries. In fact, the sizes of the units range from 70 to 400m².

All the units engage in operations that add value to their inputs. Even the scrap metal dealers do add value to their collections through cleaning and painting. This again emphasises the fact that home industry business operators are not mere middlemen and women who simply buy goods in bulk, add a mark-up and resell. This finding contradicts the views of many economists and industrialists who insist that there is no value adding in indigenous businesses

Table 5. Clients and Marketing Techniques in Home Industries

BUSINESS UNIT	PRINCIPAL CLIENTS IN PREVIOUS MONTH	CLIENT ACQUITIONS TECHNIQUES	CHARACTERISTICS OF ESTABLISHED CLIENTS	
			Formal	Informal
1. Welding	Local residents	None	None	Local Residents
2. Carpentry	Acquaintances Local residents	Advertising Workmanship	YWCA Spar[a]	Local Residents
3. Tailoring	Local residents Cairns[c]	Advertising Workmanship	Chitoko[b] Ashavangu	Local Residents
4. Brick-moulding	Construction company	Workmanship	Construction company	None
5. Carpentry	None	Former clients	None	None
6. Scrap-metal	4 companies	Advertising on truck and bill-boards	WS Craster[d]	None
7. Block builder	Local residents	Advertising	None	Local Residents
8. Spray-painter	Local residents	Advertising	None	None
9. Hairdresser	Local residents	Advertising Friends and relatives	None	Local Residents
10. Hairdresser	Tuck shop primary school	Advertising	None	Not yet established

[a] This is an international retail group and is the third largest retail organization in the country.
[b] Some formal sector medium-scale indigenous (black Zimbabwean-owned) companies.
[c] A large food processing company registered on the stock exchange.
[d] This is a large metal fabrication and manufacturing company.

Source: Survey, 1999–2000

(cf. MLGRUD, 1996). Thus these businesses have definitely responded to the advice handed out by government to local industries that they should add value to their goods before selling them.

Markets and Marketing Characteristics

With the exception of one unit (the welder) all units studied advertise themselves. The most common form of advertising, practiced in six of the units, are posters, notice boards and billboards (Table 5). The operators themselves write most of these, with a few being contracted to sign-writers, typists or word processing ventures within the home industries or in home-based enterprises. Another form of advertising is the use of friends, relatives and existing clients who put in a good word to acquaintances. Three of the operators emphasized the fact that the quality of their work is a very effective form of advertising themselves. According to them, good workmanship had attracted a number of customers.

In the month preceding the interviews four units—hairdresser, scrap metal dealer, tailor and the brick manufacturer—had had customers from a total of eight formal sector companies and/or institutions (Table 5). For the rest, their customers were local residents and individual friends, relatives and acquaintances. Four had an established relationship with formal private sector clients or public institutions. These four had a combined total of six large companies as their regular clients. Half the companies had an established customer base from residents of Warren Park or surrounding suburbs. Three units had no established clients. One of these, a hairdresser had just been set up at the time of the study.

RULES, ROLES AND RELATIONSHIPS

The study sought to examine the standing of the business units in home industries in terms of their legality and conformity to operating regulations, standards and requirements. The units were examined in seven areas, namely, land occupation, planning, building, finance, public health and safety, labour and trade.

Land occupation focuses on the legality of the occupation in terms of freehold, leasehold and other forms of legal tenure. Most of the operators legally occupied the land. Seven had been allocated the land by the local authority. One was renting from an individual who had obtained the land from the city council. Only two of the operators were squatters, legally speaking. Despite having legal tenure half the units openly violated planning regulations. They did not conform to existing statutory plans and subdivision and consolidation laws. The main violation was on subdivisions. Seven units were also in violation of building by-laws, having no approved plan and certificates of occupation, nor requisite infrastructure such as running water and sewer reticulation. The remaining three partially complied with the regulations in terms of having an approved structure. The main violation was on infrastructural services, which were almost non-existent. In all the cases there is absolutely no adherence to public health and safety regulations. The main problems relate to water, fire regulations, lighting, building materials and environmental sanitation.

By government regulation, businesses in home industries—and indeed the informal sector—are supposed to pay taxes (Kamete 1998). Only one unit, a scrap metal dealer paid taxes. None of the units complied with labour laws in terms of minimum wages, pension and other benefits as well as hiring and firing. None observed trade laws such as business hours, sales tax, standards and trading licences. It should be noted that not all violations could be traced to the business units themselves. Some are a result of the local authority not fulfilling its responsibilities. This is especially so in the case of building by-laws and public health regulations. Whereas the industrial units should conform to health, environmental sanitation and building regulations, it is the local authority that should have provided services and infrastructure such as access roads, storm-water drainage, water and sewer reticulation as well as waste collection. That the regulations are not observed here is thus partly of the local authority's own making.

Business relations between home industries and the formal sector as represented by the private sector and public institutions, were varied, but not extensive. During the week preceding the survey only four units had purchased goods from formal private sector enterprises and only two units had made sales to private sector enterprises and public institutions. The total value of goods purchased from the formal sector enterprise during this week Z$80,000 (about US$1,455), and the value of goods sold amounted to Z$60,000. In terms of finance, only one enterprise had managed to obtain a Z$5,000 loan from the Small Enterprises Development Corporation (SEDCO), a quasi-government fund that lends money to small and medium scale enterprises. Apart from this small loan there was virtually no relationship worth talking about between the financial sector and home industries in this particular week in 1999.

Contribution to Urban Development

The contribution of home industries to the urban system is summarized in Figure 1. Perhaps the most important contribution of home industries in the socio-economic sphere is the creation of employment and the provision of skills to the young. As noted above the ten units combined employ a total of 48 people excluding the owners. The wages in home industries compare favourably to those in the formal sector. At the time of writing, it needed considerably less money (Z\$3,000) to create a single job in the home industries than it would in the formal and public sector (Z\$200,000) (MLGRUD 1996). Associated with the creation of jobs and the imparting of skills is the question of reducing urban poverty which in Harare currently stands at over 50 per cent (cf. MPSLSW 1997:23). Thus in a way home industries do make a positive contribution to the beleaguered urban economy (see Kamete 1999).

Home industries have been blamed for making the city dirty. Indeed, their by-products in the form of solid and liquid waste are rarely taken care of in a way that is environmentally friendly. Litter spilling over from production sites into roads and open spaces is unsightly. Add to this the noise and the chaos and what comes up is a very negative picture. Nevertheless, the study also found out that the scrap metal dealers, carpenters and welders of the home industries, contribute positively to the cleaning up of the city. They pick up anything in metal and wood from industries, homes, dumpsites and open spaces and recycle this type of waste into usable products.

Home industries bring goods and services closer to the people. This means a saving in money and time for their customers, who otherwise would have to travel to the central business district or industrial sites. The goods are also available in the right quantities and at affordable prices. Goods in home industries are up to two thirds cheaper than they are elsewhere. Sometimes it is only at these outlets that scarce goods like vehicle spare parts can be obtained. This means that home industries satisfy the needs of the urban populace in three ways, namely, availability, affordability and accessibility.

Some established industrial concerns in the formal private sector have a buoyant market for their products in the home industries. The study unearthed more than a dozen companies that supply goods and services to home industries units. In 1999 alone these companies sold goods worth more than half a million dollars to businesses in home industries. In turn, some units in home industries have successfully managed to acquire established customers in the private sector. The carpenter and the scrap metal dealer are good examples. The former supplies wardrobes to Pelhams, a large furniture store, which is part of a retail chain owned by Delta, one of Zimbabwe's largest holding companies listed on the Stock Exchange. The scrap metal dealer has an established relationship with ZEMCO, a large steel company.

Figure 1. The Contribution of Home Industries to the Urban System

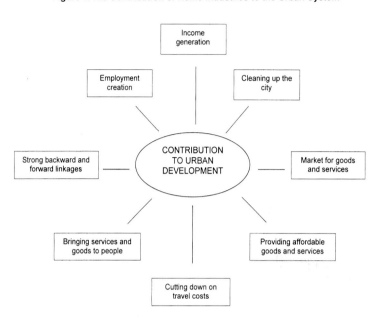

Businesses in home industries have strong backward and forward linkages that are truly local. They obtain their supplies from local suppliers and sell to local consumers. This is significant in that any benefits in terms of income and employment accruing from their operations are almost totally localized. In contrast some well-established industries in Zimbabwe have been accused of having little or no significance to the local economy because of the absence of these linkages (Kamete 1998). The above discussion demonstrates that home industries do make a significant contribution to the socio-economic fabric of the city.

INSTITUTIONAL REACTIONS TO HOME INDUSTRIES

The attitudes of established public and private institutions to home industries are of great importance to their operations. Institutional reactions also reflect and in a way affect the feelings, perceptions and convictions of other stakeholders such as politicians, ratepayers and consumers in general to home industries. The study examined responses from the private sector, the financial sector, the local authority and non-governmental and civic organizations.

The Private Sector

The attitude of the formal private sector is reflected in the business relationship between the two sectors. There is no technical, material or moral support by the formal sector to the units operating from home industries. However, as indicated above, quite a few large concerns are happy to sell their products to home industries. A few buy from home industries, as they are attracted by the price and availability of the products, or the good workmanship. In some cases the contracts given to enterprises in home industries are a result of 'connections' either through relatives or former work-mates. Not all of these dealings can be classified as shady or corrupt, although some do raise eyebrows in terms of the granting of the contract, amid accusations of kickbacks and associated benefits. Some established industries have gone on record as saying that home industries steal business from 'legal' industries that are properly registered and pay taxes. Notable in this category is the clothing and textile sector that has been facing numerous problems due to the opening up of the economy and the removal of state protection.

The usual scenario of financiers being averse to investing in the informal sector was confirmed in the study. Apart from the one loan from the semi-public institution SEDCO, the units in the study had largely failed to access funds in the financial sector in 1999. All the operators cited the lack of collateral, proper registration and risk as reasons why they had failed to qualify for loans. The situation of the operators of business units in home industries regarding collateral is unenviable. A good number of them do have assets in the form of houses, but the problem is that the houses do not have title deeds. If these are available, they are held by building societies as mortgage bonds. In either case the houses are useless as security pledges for loans.

The Local Authority

Harare City Council, the local authority, has a long history of dealing with the home industries. Figure 2 summarizes the various routes the urban planning and management system has been taking over the years, categorized into three types, namely, positive, negative and undefined. Positive and negative responses are easy to visualize because they are respectively for and against home industries. 'Undefined' denotes responses that are too vague to be classified as positive or negative. In this case the local authority's intentions cannot be easily figured out and comprehended.

Local authority responses were regarded as promotive if they actively encouraged activities and operations of home industries. They were classified as accommodative if they allowed these activities to proceed without hindrance (cf. Kamete et al. 1999). One typical instance of an accommodative response was the Statutory Instrument 216 of 1994.[1] This legislation partially deregulated commercial and industrial activities in residential areas (Kamete 1999). Another positive or accommodative measure was the national policy on indigenization (DSEI 1997). This policy calls for the economic empowerment of blacks. Local authorities have readily adopted this policy by recognising small scale informal business enterprises and giving them land from which to operate. The effect of the statutory instrument and the indigenization policy above is to compel the

---

1. Statutory Instruments (formerly called subsidiary legislation) are pieces of legislation added to existing acts of parliament (laws) to 'update' them.

local authority to at least tolerate home industries. The attitude of the urban planning and management system to home industries is to a large extent shaped by these accommodative policies. The local authority, in some cases, does actively promote home industries. This is done through layout planning and subdivisions where some parcels of land are set aside specifically for home industries. Harare City Council also levies preferential rents and service charges for home industries.

Repression takes place when the local authority curbs, puts down by force, stops or bars activities of business units in home industries. Restriction involves the placing of limits or controls on size, amount, operations, extent or effects of units in home industries (see Kamete et al. 1999). On many occasions the City of Harare has descended on some perceived excesses of home industries. These include boundary violations, illegal structures and squatting. Evictions, demolitions and forced relocations are strictly enforced. In addition, the local authority has an array of by-laws on building, health and environmental sanitation that it occasionally enthusiastically enforces.

'Hands-off' describes responses that are characterized by silence and inaction. Sometimes the local authority just decides to keep quiet and, as it were, 'let sleeping dogs lie'. These responses are notable especially when issues become political, volatile and sensitive. This seemed to have been the strategy adopted by the suspended council. Before its suspension in 1999,[1] council turned a 'blind eye' to the mushrooming of illegal structures and activities especially in the residential areas. The silence, inaction and resignation continued until the newly appointed commission decided to act to restore the city's reputation as a clean city. The suspended mayor openly acknowledged the economic problems facing the residents but fell short of applauding their efforts to make 'an honest living' (*The Herald* 1998).

For their part, the operators in the home industries did not have positive views on how the city was managed. They all agreed that the local authorities were inadequate, inefficient and ineffective. Six operators maintained that they had not been consulted in any decision that affected them. One said that they were consulted 'sometimes', and one pointed out that they are consulted but their views are not considered. They all agreed that they are decision-takers and not decision-makers, meaning that they have to accept what they are told. The consensus is that the local authority comes to them with ready-made decisions, which are not subject to negotiation. Classic cases of imposition were cited, such as the fixing of rents and service charges, imposed relocation, destruction of illegal structures and the drafting of by-laws. The operators of home industries were extremely dissatisfied with official decisions. According to them nothing in the council's way of reaching decisions is transparent, accountable, participatory and democratic.

1. The elected council was suspended in 1999 by the Minister of Local Government and National Housing following an unprecedented water crisis in some residential areas. Citing the water crisis and a list of other misdeeds (none of which referred to the informal sector) as evidence, the minister argued that the council had failed to manage the city. Using his legally enshrined powers, he appointed a commission to run the city (see Mubvami and Wekwete 2000; Kamete 2002).

Figure 2. The Responses of the Urban Planning and Management System to Home Industries

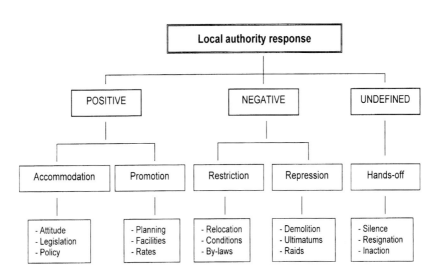

This may be related to the local authority's perception of home industries. During interviews both managers and policy makers made it clear that they did not view home industries as economic entities. There was unanimity that the plight or potential of home industries is a socio-political issue. The argument is based not on a study of the units but rather on the number of politically motivated decisions and 'favours' directed at home industries. The rationale behind this view seems to be that home industries are seen primarily as temporary cushions against poverty. The operators are not perceived to have managerial capacity, are not recognized by the financial sector and do not respond to economic policy in a 'sensible way' (Kamete 1998).

This view appears to have moulded the attitude of the local authority to home industries. Harare, like most other urban centres in the country has an economic development section that is specifically tasked with improving local economic development. One of the section's terms of reference is to invite and retain investment. It is this office that liases with and looks after industrial and commercial enterprises. Interestingly, home industries are looked after by the charity-like Department of Housing and Community Services (DHCS). What makes this even more intriguing is the fact that the DHCS is predominantly staffed by social workers and a few administrators, whereas the economic development office, which is in the city's treasury department, recruits its staff from applicants with an economics, industrial, commercial and financial background.

Consequently incentives that are offered to industry and commerce are not extended to home industries. These incentives include tax holidays, reduced rates and service charges as well as environmental regulations and employment conditions. On the other hand when politicians intervene in favour of home industries they do not include the formal sector enterprises in their demands. This is further complicated by the reaction of home industries to what they consider to be unfavourable decisions or an adverse operational environment. Whereas formal industry and commerce issue statements and engage in discussions where facts and figures are the point of discussion, home industry practitioners take to the streets in noisy demonstrations where the points of discussion are such emotive issues as livelihood, votes, poverty, politics, colonial rule, discrimination, black empowerment and threats (*The Herald* 1998; Kamete 1999).

Examples of formal sector lobbying include the issuing from the year 2000 of some proposals and position papers on price controls and the economic situation by such organizations as the Confederation of Zimbabwe Industries (CZI) and the millers and bakers associations. Cases where the informal sector has used their style of lobbying include the furore that accompanied the destruction of illegal tuck shops by the Harare City Council in 2001 (see Kamete 2002).

NGOs and Civic Associations

Non-governmental organizations in Harare are notable for advocating among other things, poverty eradication, free enterprise, promotion of the informal sector and small and medium scale industries. However, apart from holding conferences and supporting research there is no evidence of direct support such as funds and training programmes. The only dissenting voice comes from environmental groups who believe that uncontrolled informal activities damage the environment (Environment 2000, 2001, 2001a). The Hawkers and Vendors Association of Zimbabwe (HAVAZ) is an interest group that advances the cause of informal industries. HAVAZ has come out strongly in condemning some repressive actions of the local authority. It occasionally speaks emotionally (frequently appealing to history, politics and race) on the reluctance of financial institutions to lend to the informal sector, including home industries. Women's groups have on numerous cases stepped in with observations on the plight of women in the informal sector including those in home industries (Matshalaga 1997). Both enterprises in the formal sector and the local authority come under attack for their lethargy, discrimination and repression of female-owned or run businesses.

This study has revealed that the only NGO to provide material support to home industries is Zambuko Trust. Zambuko Trust offers credit and savings facilities. It is also used by organizations like the United States Agency for International Development (USAID) in specific projects (USAID 2003). Zambuko's mission is to work towards the promotion of informal sector enterprises. In home industries, the organization offers loans for both initial and working capital. Prospective borrowers must have at least Z$1,000 in their bank accounts. Thereafter they should maintain a debit balance of at least Z$1,500 in these accounts. The organization matches the borrowers' savings dollar for dollar. The maximum amount that can be lent without collateral is Z$2,500. At the time of the study the loan attracted an interest rate of 45 per cent (compared to around 52 per cent charged by commercial banks). Zambuko offers loans of up to Z$10,000, but demands collateral for these higher amounts. Obviously the loan sizes are too small for large ventures such as manufacturing. Zambuko justifies the small amounts in terms of its "small capital base" which constraint forces the NGO to "ration" loans. In addition, the repayment record of some of the borrowers is reported to be "atrocious" (Interview with Zambuko official, 2000). At the time of the study Zambuko had a client base of 15,500 and an outstanding portfolio of US$2.5 million (cf. Inafi 2002.)

CONCLUSION

This study has documented that business units in home industries are self-made both in terms of establishment and financing. They have had practically no assistance from the formal private sector, the local authority or non-governmental organizations. They have no access to regular credit schemes, make their purchases in cash and have to make do with very few facilities apart from land and temporary makeshift structures. Each unit manages transport and storage facilities separately. The popular perception of indigenous businesses being nothing more than a conduit between producers and consumers is, according to this study, a misconception, as all the units studied undertake some form of value adding in their processing.

Operators of home industries get most of their inputs from established industries in the private sector. This finding echoes what has been found by other studies, notably those sponsored by government (see MLGRUD 1996:6). Although home industries have markets in public institutions and the formal private sector, most of their clients are households.

From a legal and regulatory point of view, there are major irregularities and violations in terms of planning, public health and safety, as well as environmental, labour and trading laws and regulations. A lot of these can be traced to the operators of the business units, but as the study discovered, quite a few originate from the local authority's urban planning and management system. Home industries' relationships with the formal sector can be described as strictly businesslike; that with the financial sector as almost non-existent; that with NGOs as nondescript; while that with the local authority as multifaceted ranging from the very amicable to the confrontational. However, the contributions, in terms of products and employment opportunities, of these informal enterprises to society, industry and the urban system in general are significant. It is in the areas of decisions and decision-making that the major shortcomings were observed. The process of making decisions and the quality of the decisions made by the urban managers do not contribute to the smooth functioning of home industries. The decisions are invariably impositions. In addition, they are almost always insensitive if not irrelevant to the business operations in home industries.

A lot has to be done to redress and improve the situation. First it is necessary to make some adjustments. These major adjustments have to begin with re-defining the view of home industries by influential stakeholders, in particular the local authority and financiers. A look at the operational characteristics and workings of enterprises in home industries drives home the point that they are business entities in their own right. Granted, they do differ from their formal sector counterparts in some important aspects. This merely makes them different, but it certainly does not make them 'less business'.

It has been pointed out how formal sector players, like the local authority, view home industries as fundamentally political and social entities rather than economic ones. This has resulted in home industries being consigned to the sidelines when economic policies and strategies are proposed, initiated, discussed, adopted and implemented. This unflattering view has also made enterprises in home industries subject to shifts in the political and social climate rather than substantive partners in the business environment. Home industries may be different from other enterprises but they are still businesses. In view of the foregoing, when home industries do not respond as anticipated to the business environment they should not be condemned and marginalized offhand. Rather it may indicate that they need their own special set of decisions on incentives, rules, regulations, policies and laws. Failure to realize this can be said to be the root of all the problems facing the informal sector in general and home industries in particular.

From the above it is apparent that the interface between the formal and informal city is not sufficiently well conceptualized and well managed. This is fundamentally a result of the local authority treating enterprises in the informal sector as protégés while in contrast they treat the formal sector ones as partners. Consequently, home industries, which are an important part of the informal sector, find themselves being relegated to being 'looked after' by a lone district officer who is invariably a social worker under the Department of Housing and Community Services (DHCS). In contrast, the formal sector is taken on board and regarded as an equal by the high-powered Economic Development Office of the city council. This disdain should be discarded and the local authority should make an attempt to bring home industries aboard mainstream urban management as significant players rather than objects of sympathy, political convenience and arbitrary decisions.

The foregoing findings justify the need for a turnabout in the way the formal-informal city interface is managed and in the method by which decisions are made. This demands a complete redefinition of the terrain between the formal and the informal city. If it is the hope of the urban management system to nurture home industries so that they graduate into the large and viable formal sector industries that they aim for then this turnabout is a prerequisite.

References

Burgess, R., 1985, "The limits of state self-help housing programmes", *Development and Change* 16(2):271–312.

CCZ (The Consumer Council of Zimbabwe), 2001, *Poverty study report*. Harare: CCZ.

Daily News, 2001, "Harare council moves to regularise shacks". Harare, 5 May.

DSEI (Department of State Enterprises and Indigenization), 1997, *Policy Paper on Indigenization*. Harare: DSEI.

E2000, 2001, *Deforestation disturbing in Zimbabwe*. Harare: Environment 2000.

—, 2001a, *Now is the time to act on air pollution*. Harare: Environment 2000.

Gemini, 1991, *Micro and small-small enterprises in Zimbabwe: Results of a countrywide survey*. Gemini Technical Report 25. Maryland: Bethesda.

The Herald, 1998, "Relaxation of land uses brings mixed feelings". Harare, 3 July.

Inafi, 2002, "Detailed Profile". Available at http://www.inafi.org/html/zambuko.htm

Kamete, A.Y., 2002, *Governance for sustainability? Balancing social and environmental concerns in Harare*. CMI Report R 2002: 12. Bergen: Christian Michelsen Institute.

—, 1999, "Restrictive control of urban high-density housing in Zimbabwe: Deregulation and challenges and implications for urban design", *Housing, Theory and Society* 3(16):136–51.

—, 1998, "Revisiting urban local economic development in Zimbabwe". Paper presented at a staff seminar, the Department of City and Regional Planning, University of Wales, Cardiff, 30 October.

—, 1997, *Background to skills development in Zimbabwe*. Mimeo, Department of Rural and Urban planning, University of Zimbabwe, Harare.

Kamete, A.Y., M. Sidambe and M.N. Ndubiwa, 1999, *Managing the interface between urban councils and the surrounding rural district councils in Zimbabwe: The case of Bulawayo City Council and Umguza Rural District Council*. Municipal Development Programme, Harare.

Kumbawa, D., 2002, "Informal sector now Zimbabwe's biggest employer", *Financial Gazette*. Harare, 12 June.

Matshalaga, N.R., 1997, *The gender dimensions of urban poverty: The case of Dzivaresekwa*. Harare: Institute of Development Studies, University of Zimbabwe.

Mhone, G.C.Z., 1995, *The impact of structural adjustment on the urban informal sector in Zimbabwe*. Geneva: International Labour Organization.

MLGRUD (Ministry of Local Government Rural and Urban Development), 1996, *Prefeasibility study on informal small-scale/micro sector enterprises for development pilot industrial estates (sic) in selected urban centres of Zimbabwe*. Harare: MLGRUD.

MPSLSW (Ministry of the Public Service, Labour and Social Welfare), 1997, *Poverty assessment survey study* (Main report). Harare: Social Development Fund.

Mubvami, T. and K.H. Wekwete, 2000, *The challenge of managing towns and cities in Zimbabwe in the next millennium*. Mimeo.

UNCHS/ILO, 1995, *Shelter provision and employment generation*. Nairobi and Geneva: United Nations Centre for Human Settlements (Habitat) and the International Labour Organization.

USAID, 2003, "Office of Private and Voluntary Cooperation (PVC) Matching Grant". Available http://www.usaid.gov/hum_response/pvc/mg.html

SECTION III
LAND, HOUSING, AND PLANNING

In most African countries, the capacity of public agencies to guide and support urban development has decreased considerably over the last three to four decades. Shelter is primarily supplied through illegal occupation of land or subdivision of land in conflict with planning regulations, and construction of houses without permission and in contravention of building codes. Not only the poor find shelter outside the law. In recent years, middle and high standard housing areas have also been developed informally, mainly based on unauthorized subdivision of land, both public and private. There, as in low-income settlements, infrastructure is poor or non-existent. Informal settlements that appear to have emerged in defiance of the law may actually be based on a mixture of political patronage, tacit permission on behalf of the local administration and arbitrary application of some elements of existing regulatory frameworks but not of others. The law itself may be out of date and at variance with practice. Some activities may be formally extra-legal, but considered legitimate by the actors concerned.

The chapters in this section deal with planning, land acquisition for housing, land use and legalization of settlements. They exemplify various forms of co-operation and conflict between groups of residents, politicians and public authorities across a range of different urban contexts.

In a study of an informal settlement on the outskirts of Dar es Salaam, Tanzania, Marco Burra, describes how its residents had gradually occupied and subdivided state owned, agricultural land and developed a middle-income community with, and mechanisms for, management of services and resolution of conflicts. However, the official urban planning policy considers the unplanned peri-urban settlements as transitory, and thus still subject to the need for proper planning or upgrading. Consequently, the government prepared a plan for land development in the area, a plan that totally ignored land allocations and investments in housing and shared facilities that had already taken place. This state-led planning attempt was strongly resisted by local residents, and a committee composed of local land-owners and CBO leaders started negotiations with the planning authorities for permission to prepare an alternative plan. This was obtained, and with the help of outside consultants from the university and financial contributions from residents, a plan that respected existing properties and boundaries was drawn up. The approval process was lengthy, with standards for plot sizes and the need for preserving land for communal facilities being the main contentious issues. The case portrays the potential of local initiative and ingenuity when faced with the deficiencies in the formal systems for planning and service provision, but also how difficult it is for the formal system to change its approach from a top-down approach to an inclusive, participatory process. It also highlights the limited capacity of a local community to handle the complex planning issues on its own, and the crucial importance of having access to alternative expertise whose competence is recognized by the authorities.

Rose Gatabaki–Kamau and Sarah Karirah–Gitau analyse the actors and interests involved in the development of an informal settlement on the outskirts Nairobi, Kenya. They follow the development of the settlement from a small cluster of squatter shacks built on privately owned agricultural land in the early 1960s to the present day sprawling middle-income housing area. The central argument is that informal land supply and housing provision do not simply reflect inappropriate legal frameworks and institutional incapacity to enforce them, but a particular development context of falling incomes and commercialization of low cost housing. Large segments of the urban middle class are excluded from the formal urban development process, resulting in the emergence of informal settlements owned and rented by middle-income groups.

In the particular case under study, the process was realized through legal land ownership by a foreigner that was replaced with irregular land rights controlled by a group of politically influential Africans. After the realization that the initial developments would not be demolished, and that the development standards were high, middle-income investors were attracted to the settlement. As elsewhere in Nairobi, a feeling of security of tenure has developed, based on protection, patronage and unofficial assurances to settlements that can deliver votes for particular candidates in national and local elections.

Resetselemang Clement Leduka examines access to land for housing in Maseru, Lesotho, through the lens of the legislative instruments aimed at regulating and regularising the conversion of peri-urban agricultural land into urban plots. Not surprisingly, formal state rules at times impeded the delivery of land for urban housing. Formal rules were arbitrary and on occasion inconsistently enforced, which rendered the formal land delivery system less reliable than alternative systems. As a result of unmet demand and nonpayment for land that the state acquired for public projects, illegal subdivision of peri-urban land proliferated. Customary chiefs and landowners took advantage of the inconsistencies that were inherent in the formal rules, and subdivided plots informally. These processes are analysed within the theoretical framework of non-compliance, a subtle form of protest underwritten by its own rules of the game, contradicting some state rules and respecting others. Non-compliance is both a survival strategy and a strategy to gain access to resources that would otherwise be out of reach. In the case analysed here, it is a strategy resorted to by chiefs, plot-owners and plot-seekers alike. However, individuals in a disadvantaged position vis-à-vis the law were not the only ones responsible for the creation of Maseru's illegal city. State employees and legislators were all part of the process and used the ambiguity of both formal and informal rules. The illegal city is thus a manifestation of the interplay of both formal and informal rules and actors.

John Abbot's chapter reports on a pilot project which began as a desk study of informal settlement upgrading, but which subsequently led to the development of Cape Town's, South Africa, first pilot *in situ* upgrading programme. The original goal of the project was to explore the general applicability of a methodology for settlement upgrading which had been developed in the Brazilian city of Belo Horizonte. It was based on the following principles: minimum relocation of dwellings, partnership between the community and the local authority, promotion of social and economic development and internal relocation and layout of dwellings to be decided by the residents.

The project was a collaborative exercize between the engineering department of the local university, UN-HABITAT, a public water research institution and the City of Cape Town. Resistance to the concept of settlement upgrading was strong there, the predominant view being that informal settlements should be demolished and their occupants relocated to new sites. To obtain practical results, it was therefore necessary to change perceptions and attitudes not only among politicians and technical professionals but also in neighbouring communities. At the same time, partnership with residents and organizations within the settlement had to be forged, creating a basis for internal settlement transformation and its intergration into the city. The relative success of this project is attributed to the following elements: it was based on an elaborate and tested methodology and had an articulated, long term goal, it used highly competent technical personnel independent of, but respected by the city authorities and it demonstrated to those authorities the usefulness of pragmatism in setting technical standards.

In his study of access to land in Maputo, Mozambique, Paul Jenkins reviews how the various legal systems for allocation of urban land have functioned in urban Mozambique, from the colonial era through the socialist period to the present day market regime. The colonial legal system was incomplete and contradictory and formal access to land through state and market mechanisms for the African urban population was highly restricted. After independence in 1975, land was nationalized, and land could be rented. In peri-urban areas, largely non-monetary traditional forms of allocation persisted. The vast majority of these activities were classified as illegal, and the state attempted to abolish them. However, this was impossible due to their being so widespread and essential for people's livelihoods. The state then attempted to introduce a minimum of regulations. Later, structural adjustment measures led to the draining of the state's administrative and technical capacity and the state institutions for subdivision and allocation of land collapsed.

A survey undertaken in 1995 of how Maputo and Matola residents had obtained land for housing revealed that through the various changing regimes, a majority had obtained land informally. A market for land where the full monetary exchange value is paid, is still quite limited. Legal and administrative processes are ill-defined and complex, and hence are both exclusionary and open to abuse. The author argues for alternative systems for allocation, management and transfer of land that are not based primarily on the market or the state, but on the social mechanisms and structures whereby the majority of the population manage their survival.

CHAPTER 8

Land Use Planning and Governance in Dar es Salaam: A Case Study from Tanzania

Marco Burra

Tanzania is experiencing high rates of urbanization, the scale and pace of which have increased dramatically over the last three decades. In the same period, the capacity of the public sector to support and guide urban growth has decreased considerably. The greatest part of urban development is thus taking place in unplanned settlements beyond the control of the formal planning system. The outcome is the 'informal city' that is not regulated by public planning authorities and is hardly covered by urban services (Kironde 1995). The capital, Dar es Salaam, is a case in point. Unplanned settlements provide shelter to over 70 per cent the total city population (Hoek-Smit 1991; Wangwe 1996). The city covers some 1,350 square kilometres of land, encompassing coastal plains, tidal swamps, hills and small offshore islands of the Indian Ocean. Dar es Salaam represents about 10 per cent of the national total population and remains the commercial, industrial and transportation centre of the country. In the early 1990s, the population was approximately 3 million inhabitants and the annual growth rate was estimated to be 8 per cent. The city's land area was expanding by 7 per cent per year (DCC 1998; Kironde 1992; UNCHS 1987). According to the 2002 national population census preliminary analysis, the population of Dar es Salaam was then 3.4 million and was still growing at 7 per cent rate per annum.

INFORMAL PLANNING

As a reaction to the failure of the official planning system, people have developed local structures for informal planning, for acquiring land and providing services. Informal planning here connotes the popular practice of self-help based activities by which individuals, groups of people or local communities provide land rights, undertake spatial structuring or land subdivision, land transfers and service provision. They do this without deferring to the administrative or legal state structures, i.e. outside the conventional public sector planning and land development control mechanisms.

As in other countries, informal planning may take place with the tacit consent of the state even though formal recognition or acknowledgement is withheld (Vaa 1995; Abbott 1996). In Tanzania, "informal settlements" are not synonymous with "slums" or "squatter settlements", as many of these settlements accommodate middle and high-income groups and land is still officially owned by the state. Rather, this term connotes settlements that have developed outside the official land development process and planning procedures, the emphasis being not on the illegality of land ownership or occupation, but rather on the nature of the land development process that is employed. Therefore, the terms "informal" or "uncontrolled" settlement are preferred to connote the lack of influence over their development by the formal public sector planning.

The official planning tradition has been centralized and top-down, with the public sector as the main provider of infrastructure and overseer of land use, and with minimum participation by the private and popular sectors (Kombe 1995; Halla 1997; DCC 1998). In 1993, the City administration started to adopt a more strategic planning system for urban development, under the UNCHS' Sustainable Cities Programme (SCP). The Sustainable Dar es Salaam Project (SDP) was initiated with an overall objective of strengthening the City administration's capacity to plan and manage the growth and development of the city in partnership with other public, private and popular sectors on a 'sustainable basis' (UNDP 1993).

The Emergence of Community Based Organizations

By the end of the twentieth century, Dar es Salaam city had more than 42 unplanned settlements whose physical and living conditions needed to be improved (Lerise and Nnkya 1999; DCC 1998). In addition, there were several settlements located within the planned parts of the city but lacking key infrastructure and services. Most initiatives taken by the residents of Dar es Salaam's unplanned settlements over the last decade are directed at improving the environment or securing rights to land they already occupy. Another important dimension is to mobilize resources for the provision of facilities and services that have been lacking for many years (Mhamba and Titus 2001). Others deal with income generating or poverty alleviation activities. Some community-based organizations (CBOs) have taken initiatives to negotiate assistance from the local government, NGOs and external agencies. At the same time, communities may be seeking external expertise for the formal regularization of their settlements.

The city had by 1995 about 13 identified environmental CBOs. This number rose to over 70 in 1998. In addition, there were a number of other locality-based associations, both registered and unregistered, addressing development issues, such as gender and poverty. There are two main categories of community-based initiatives aimed at improving conditions in the settlements. The first involves projects started by voluntary groupings of individuals or associations residing in a particular neighbourhood, usually formed to gain access to specific services for their local area. Sometimes, they have external support from the beginning. The grouping then establishes a members' organization, open to everyone in the settlement and gets it registered as a CBO (Lerise and Nnkya 1999). The second category originates in projects initiated from outside. Here the residents of a settlement are mobilized by external agencies to implement projects supported by donors and NGOs. Donor requirements for local participation in project implementation are initial factors behind the establishment of these CBOs.

Map 1. Dar es Salaam: Urban Growth and Development

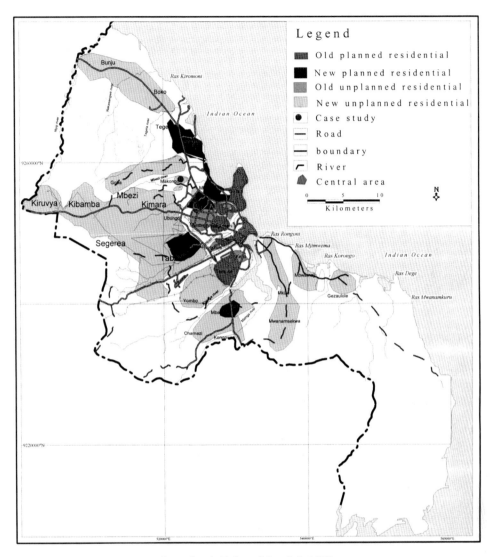

Source: Sustainable Dar es Salaam Project, 2000.

To have a CBO registered is a lengthy process, and according to existing records it takes between six months to two or more years. Applications are submitted to the Registrar of Societies in the Ministry of Home Affairs. Requirements for registration include 1) preparation of a constitution approved by the CBO members, 2) a list of not less than twelve founder members, 3) a supporting letter from the local government authority and 4) payment of registration fee of Tanzania Shillings 40,000 (ca. US$40). Submission of the paperwork and the registration fees complete the application process.

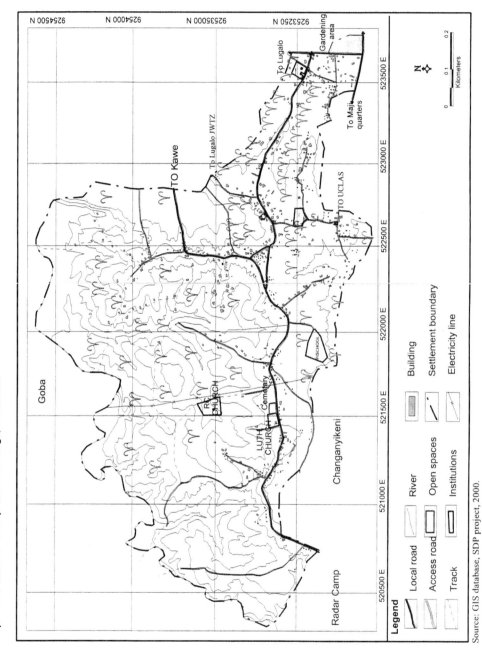

Map 2. Land Use and Development in Makongo, 1970s–2000

Legend

Local road	River	Building	
Access road	Open spaces	Settlement boundary	
Track	Institutions	Electricity line	

Source: GIS database, SDP project, 2000.

CBOs have emerged in both planned and unplanned settlements. Later in this chapter, the role of an organization called the Makongo Juu Development Association (MAJUDEA) in land use planning and overall development of an informal settlement will be presented. By contrast, the case of a CBO that has its basis in a planned settlement, will be briefly presented. This is the Tabata Development Fund (TDF), which operates in a suburb situated on the south western fringe of the city. Tabata is a newly planned residential area which over the past 15 years has attracted over 20,000 inhabitants. For a long time, however, it lacked key infrastructure and services. Another problem for the settlement and its residents was a city refuse dumpsite in its proximity. Its location was not compatible with residential use; between 1988 and 1993 it brought the residents onto a collision course with the City Council. A committee of elite and middle-class residents took the City Council to court and on 31 August 1991 the High Court in Dar es Salaam ordered the closure of the dumpsite. Based on this success, it was decided to form a society with a legal status—the TDF CBO, that was subsequently registered in March 1993 by the Registrar of Societies (Kessy 2000). The objective was to upgrade deficient infrastructure within Tabata through community initiatives and self-help. Among its achievements are the rehabilitation of 4 kilometres of the main road through the settlement and planting of trees in order to preserve the environment. There is also a committee dealing with night security in the area, other committees deal with education, social welfare, finance, health, trade and environment. The TDF is today a partner in development projects being implemented by the City Council, various donors and NGOs. TDF has also won international recognition by collaborating with the City Council to win the 1998 Dubai International Award on best practices during the World Habitat Day (Kessy 2000).

Many CBOs are still young and weak in capacity in terms of manpower, management structure and finance, with few mechanisms in place to enable them to operate effectively. Success of organizations seems to depend not so much on membership size but on the commitment of a few influential founding individuals (Lerise 1999). There is an emerging debate on issues of participation and democracy versus the prevalence of business interests or other motives (Andreasen 2001), and the problem of CBOs being sustained only by donor money (Kiondo 1994).

Addressing the Challenge of Governance in Urban Planning

At the international level as well as in Tanzania, the concept of planning is changing, from a centralized, bureaucratic exercise to a participatory and communicative process (Healey 1997). In Tanzania, the discussion on the role of community initiatives in land use planning and urban governance more generally has only begun. To some, it is self-evident that the only way to improve service provision and governance is to involve residents and their organizations in the planning and management of settlements. These new orientations are, however, posing significant normative challenges to land use planners and administrators, as the existing planning practice remains expert-oriented and top-down.

City authorities often impose planning decisions on settlements without due regard to local interests and aspirations. The plans then become a source of conflict between local communities and the public planning system.

Until now, planners have generally not been able to create a cooperative involvement with community-based initiatives. The questions of how such initiatives may become part of the planning practice and what such co-existence or intertwining of formal and informal planning structures means for urban management or governance remain largely unexplored. The case of Makongo is not only a story of a process of informal planning but also points to some issues entailed in the encounter with formal planning institutions.

Data and Methods

This chapter draws on data collected within the framework of a larger research programme at the University College of Lands and Architectural Studies (UCLAS) at the University of Dar es Salaam, on community and CBO initiatives in land use planning and management in Dar es Salaam city. They include documentation of planning and management projects, physical surveys and field observations, and interviews with community and CBO leaders, residents and officials. The author conducted reconnaissance visits and explorative surveys for several settlements and CBOs, and collected material on ongoing donor and locally funded projects focusing on community-based upgrading of settlements and studies covering characteristics of CBOs and NGOs in Dar es Salaam city. The Makongo settlement was first explored in a pilot study in 1996, and later in a survey in 1999, which revealed a rich record of local initiatives in land use planning, service provision and management of the environment for improving the urban space (Burra 1999).

THE MAKONGO SETTLEMENT

Makongo is located in the north-western, peri-urban zone of Dar es Salaam city, about 17 kilometres from the centre of the city. Its development spans years of spatial and socio-economic transition starting with informal acquisition, subdivision and development of land. Through this process, the local community has assumed land use planning activities and responsibilities, which normally are the duties of public authorities. These include organizing the use of land and acquiring land rights. Subsequently, procedures for land subdivision and mechanisms for locally sanctioned conflict resolution have been instituted by the residents themselves. Some provision of services and joint management of the built environment have also been achieved.

Makongo's land area was at one point in time covered with sisal, but over the years, members of indigenous communities and former sisal workers cleared the plantation and engaged in subsistence farming. Since the late 1960s and the 1970s, these original landholders have transformed the agricultural land into residential plots through land subdivision. In contrast to the original farming residents, the new landowners or land right holders in the settlement mainly comprise the elite class; well-educated public servants, retired civil servants and executives, most of them coming from other parts of the city. Low-income residents occupy the older, consolidated part of the settlement that evolved through customary land tenure and subsequent informal subdivisions. In 2000, the settlement was estimated to have over 1000 households with about 12,000 people, and covered approximately 400 hectares.

The settlement has a varied history. During the Villagization Programme (1974–76) it was designated a resettlement area, to accommodate people from other areas of the city. Later, it saw an accelerated influx of individual home seekers from adjacent institutions and from other parts of the city. One category of landowners evolved during the national campaign of "Human Resources Deployment" from the late 1970s and onwards, which aimed at resettling the urban unemployed, particularly youth, to engage in (agricultural) productive activities. Under this programme, land was distributed to the newcomers by the government. The 1979 City Master Plan incorporated Makongo within the city planning boundary and designated the settlement a green belt area, and later, in the 1985 version, it included both a green belt and institutional uses. However, development of the settlement has continued through informal acquisition and subdivision of the original customary and plantation land. Many of the original landholders have left or have been bought out by new plot buyers.

Prominent collective initiatives in the Makongo settlement include agreement on procedures for land use and provision of social and communal facilities. As in other informal settlements in Tanzania, landowners in Makongo are subdividing land and selling plots with at least a minimum of consideration for access, open spaces and other public uses, following locally accepted norms. There are observable mechanisms for solving conflicts that stem from disagreements over plot accesses, boundaries and land ownership.

Community Initiatives in Services and Infrastructure Provision

Makongo residents' initiatives for the settlement's improvement have concentrated on service provision particularly water supply, road access, land use planning and, more prominently, formation of a community-based organization in order to deal with these issues. With the increase in demands for development in the 1990s, Makongo residents realized that many projects in the settlement could not be implemented through normal government funds nor could they be maintained from individual contributions and the community's own resources locally. Besides, normal local administration channels were not successful in obtaining the required funds. In 1994, a group of Makongo residents formed an organization called Makongo Juu Development Association (MAJUDEA), which was registered in 1995.[1] Its primary purpose was to lobby through influential individuals or groups, both local and external agencies, for provision of finance to locally initiated projects. The association was formed by a core group

1. The name 'Makongo Juu' is used to differentiate this settlement which is located within the elevated ridges and valleys, from an adjacent area that encompasses the army area, a secondary school and other institutions. The other area is just referred to as Makongo.

of retired civil servants and officers, its objectives being "to improve the environment and secure basic services for the Makongo Juu community".[1] Through the active role of MAJUDEA leaders and elected members of the local administration there has been successful fund-raising for water supply and road improvement. There have also been further attempts to seek assistance from appropriate national agencies and service institutions and even foreign donors.

Water Supply Improvement

The water issue has dominated the efforts of the Makongo residents for many years due to chronic shortage and absence of any reliable source. The original settlers initiated a water supply system, which was incrementally extended to serve the growing settlement. Mains distribution lines followed the ridge road alignment while other spaces for laying pipes were made available by individual landholders who also secured connections to their buildings or properties. However with the increasing population and rapid development of the settlement, the system collapsed. The network was obsolete and its capacity insufficient, but there was also shortage of capital to revamp and extend the existing system.

The longstanding water problem was partly alleviated by a project funded through the Japanese Embassy. This comprised finance for connections to the trunk line, a pumping station and construction of reserve tanks and a supply network. Makongo residents contributed by providing manual labour. Water supply improvement initiatives covered plans and projects including sources augmentation, distribution network improvement and maintenance. A water supply committee was formed in order to mobilize resources, both local and external, for implementation of the various projects. MAJUDEA played an important role in lobbying for funds needed for water provision. This CBO has in many instances liased with government officials as well as making contacts that have been an influential factor in gaining access to services needed by the community. MAJUDEA leaders cite examples of water supply and roads improvement as cases in point, where senior officials in the water corporation, electricity company and the Ministry of Works were directly involved in assisting the community.[2]

Access Roads

The second initiative by Makongo residents was to improve roads within the settlement. The existing road network in Makongo was the result of a mixture of individual and collective initiatives since the early formation of the settlement. The main access road was developed in the 1950s–60s through the adjacent army area, linking the properties of the early settlers. Later, these early settlers bought land from the original owners to link the settlement with other parts of the city without having to pass through the army camp. This formed

1. Contained in the Memorandum of Understanding document concerning the registration of MAJUDEA, 1995.
2. Information based on the interview held with MAJUDEA secretary, March 1999.

part of the present trunk road, which later linked up with what was originally a cattle track, and is now linking the settlement to the outside areas and the city. With the passage of time, other settlers cleared smaller roads and parts of the ridge road to link their properties to an emerging network of roads.

The original traditional paths or tracks, which lead in and out of the area, are not planned in advance but are implemented when plots are sold, thereby creating an organic network. The road network in Makongo has therefore developed within existing ownership structures. Original paths and tracks, which are locally upgraded and maintained, are extended as needs arise. Roads or paths do not, however, cut across the structures except in the border between subdivisions or land holdings. When interviewed, the landholders in Makongo explained that the primary reason for maintaining access, apart from previous establishments, was pre-conditions set and mutually agreed upon between various parties i.e. original settlers, neighbours, owners and land sellers who are given conditions by buyers to provide accessibility when land transactions are made.[1]

The MAJUDEA cooperates with the local Sub-Ward leaders (see below) in mobilising the community to implement maintenance of roads, and to collect the annual contributions from residents towards this end. After rehabilitation of the main road, there was a successful campaign to introduce public bus transport service through the settlement.

Leadership and Community Mobilization

When the bulk of development initiatives started in the 1970s, there were no formal community based organizations in Makongo. Initiatives emerged from informal contacts and mutual trust among individual landholders, on the basis of which projects were planned and decisions taken. Projects such as water supply, ridge road and school construction were originally initiated by a group of settlers, who volunteered to contribute land and secure funding, through appeals to other volunteers and external agencies. Community 'action-planning' was thus limited to specific activities only, and effectuated through intermittent co-operation among individual landholders, based on their immediate common needs.

An active involvement of the *Chama Cha Mapinduzi* (CCM), the only political party that existed in the country until 1992, was instrumental in mobilizing residents in the ensuing period. The party supported mobilization for issues such as identifying locations and securing land for school buildings and other communal facilities. Earlier initiatives by core groups of the early settlers and individual landholders were later taken up by elected representatives to the Village/Sub-Ward administration. This is the lowest level of local government administration in Tanzania. It was introduced in 1993 and replaced the so-called "ten-cells" of the CCM. After the introduction of multi-party democracy in 1993, the

---

1. From a discussion held with Grace Mkandawire, one of the landowners who had just parcelled part of her land for selling to a prospective buyer, May 2000.

Sub-Ward or *Mtaa,* is the main unit of administration and for discussing communal matters. Through this unit, residents channel their daily issues regarding services, disputes, land and boundary authentication and other matters. The Sub-Ward administration in Makongo has an elected chairman, secretary and several other officers and committee members, who are all residents. They are assisted by development committees, which have the task of mobilizing residents for implementation of various government and donor-based projects in the area. These include construction and maintenance of roads, water supply improvement, construction of public facilities; and more recently, fund raising for the preparation of a local land use plan for the settlement.

In interviews with the residents of the settlement, it became clear that not everybody was aware of what MAJUDEA and other local leaders did to improve conditions in the settlement. About half of the interviewees claimed that they had no knowledge of the ongoing planning process, yet, it became clear through answers to other questions that they had contributed funds for the planning initiative and other projects. As is also observed elsewhere, not all community members automatically participate in meetings, planning or decision-making. As may be expected, there are differences in interests, perceptions and priorities, among the various categories of residents. The most active residents/groups seem to be those where the members were highly educated and had influential contacts. Yet, it is important to note that not only may different groups have divergent interests but also differing degrees of access to power to influence development decisions. Communities are not necessarily undifferentiated social units without conflicts and disparities in power (Friedmann 1992).

RESIDENTS' INITIATIVES MEET THE STATE PLANNING SYSTEM

The official urban planning policy and the law consider the unplanned peri-urban settlements as transitory, to be subjected to proper planning or upgrading in due course. Whenever that occurs, residents may risk eviction without warning, jeopardising the investments they have already made in housing, infrastructure and over-all development of their settlement. This is what happened in Makongo. On 10 October 1992, the residents/landholders in Makongo were informed through a local newspaper, that the government had declared their areas as urban settlements to be planned for residential use i.e. preparation of plot subdivision according to the Ministry of Lands standards. The declaration was made under the *Town and Country Ordinance* (TCO), Cap. 378, section 24–32. The Ministry's action came partly as the implementation of the change of use for Makongo and other areas that was announced in the *Government Gazette* No. 44, Vol. 66 published on 11 November 1985. By that declaration, it was implied that land developers and residents in Makongo (and other areas) now so-called planning areas, could not carry out construction or improvements without asking for permission from the City (planning) authority and that plans were going to be prepared for those areas. Indeed land subdivision plans to that effect were prepared by the beginning of 1991 and were officially adopted by the Ministry on 15 March 1991.

Thus, the government attempted to impose a scheme for land development in Makongo, including a plan for land subdivision. The plans prepared by planners initially totally ignored local developments on the ground. When their layout of building plots and location of roads were superimposed on the existing settlement, proposed plot boundaries and roads cut through buildings or across properties, indicating a need for demolitions. The Ministry's plan did not take into account existing land holdings and development. Other shortcomings included defective or inaccurate mapping. Either planners from the Ministry never visited the site or the base maps that were used for planning purposes were outdated or of poor quality.

The state-led planning attempt was, however, strongly resisted by the Makongo residents, forcing the Ministry of Lands to defer its implementation. Following an appeal made to the Minister for Lands, the Makongo community was allowed to prepare its own or alternative plan for the settlement. The community through a number of landholders, their Sub-Ward and CBO leaders, started negotiations with the formal planning authorities to regularize their settlement's land use so as to prepare the ground for formal subdivision, surveying and servicing of the settlement. It is the concern and insecurity about land, according to the then Sub-Ward secretary, Zuberi Mtemvu,[1] that gave Makongo residents the courage to reject the Ministry's 1991 plan:

> When we rejected that (Ministry's) plan (...) we appealed to the Government, which subsequently advised us to prepare an alternative plan as we saw it satisfactory to our needs. We told them that we need our land areas surveyed physically, our properties and boundaries should be respected, and then even when they do the subdivision in our areas, it should be done without causing boundary disputes later.

It should be noted that the law also provides for communities or residents to propose their own planning schemes to be approved by the Ministry of Lands and the City Council. Thus, in 1994, with help from private consultants affiliated to UCLAS, Makongo community started preparing an alternative plan. In the process of plan preparation between 1994 and 1996, the local leaders, landowners and influential groups were primarily observers. The plan was submitted to the City Commission and the Ministry for approval. In 1999, the plan was returned for amendments but is yet (spring 2002) to be approved by the authorities. It is to be noted that in the follow-up process, the local Sub-Ward leadership had been in the forefront in mobilizing residents to contribute to various stages of plan preparation, including making funds available for the required equipment and materials and paying an agreed token fee to the consultants. The consultants were paid only an agreed token fee for the preparation of the plan, in part, because Makongo community leaders were acquainted with people at UCLAS and made informal contacts with them, in the face of the impending government takeover of their settlement and land. Thus, UCLAS staff members were willing to help the neighbouring Makongo community without charging the actual costs of the plan preparation.

1. Interview held with Zuberi Mtemvu, the former Sub-Ward secretary, November 1999.

For the Makongo community and its residents, the starting point in elaborating an alternative plan was the preservation of their land rights and investments in housing and shared facilities, in contrast to the Ministry of Lands which disregarded the existing property boundaries and infrastructure and pretended there was a clean slate. The Ministry attempted to impose a plan upon the settlement, but the residents were able to reject that plan and successfully appealed for their democratic rights. Indeed the major aim of the Makongo residents has been to prepare a plan that will incorporate the residents' or landholders' rights as well as their existing investments and development. This was seen as the way to reduce risks of losing property rights, to avoid demolition of houses and displacement of people.

At the same time, during the approval process, the plan prepared by the community is required to meet some standards set by the Ministry and local authority. Notable in this process has been the required standards for plot sizes; according to the planning authorities, plots should be in the range of 400–800 square metres. However, plots with sizes up to ten times the required size standards could be found in the plan, which was submitted to the authorities, reflecting the fact that the settlement is built on former farming land.

The main contentious issues in the plan approval process are reported to be standards for plot sizes and the need to reserve land for communal facilities. This process has already taken five years and in the meantime, new developments and changes in land use are taking place due to the unabated process of land subdivision and sale to new developers.

The last two sections have demonstrated that although community initiatives within Makongo represent a new force in the management of the settlement, their potentials are yet to be recognized by the formal planning system. There is complacency of government action in dealing with those initiatives. Events from Makongo indicate that the community is aware and has realized the need for planning their settlement; they have successfully referred their case to the planning authorities to incorporate their needs and requirements. By way of the convergence of the formal and informal systems, this case shows how the community, CBO and the local leadership in serving the legitimate interests of their members, through their informal planning initiatives, may be able to link up for formal arrangements with the powers-that-be, making themselves part of the system rather than challenging its authority outright.

DISCUSSION AND REFLECTIONS

The emerging community initiatives in land use planning and management of urban settlements in Dar es Salaam are a response to the diminished capacity of the government to provide services and to manage urban development. The changing political and socio-economic environment in Tanzania since the mid-1980s has included the adoption of market-oriented policies, which have made the role of the State very different from the one it had during the previous socialist period, when it took the official responsibility for the provision of housing, services and infrastructure. In this changed role, the state is no longer the obvious provider of services and infrastructure in housing and in urban planning. These changes have enhanced the role of local actors: communities, CBOs, residents and other groups in the civil society in urban management and governance. Although there are numerous actors in housing and service provision and planning, there is still an uneasy interrelation between formal and informal planning systems.

Lessons emerging from local initiatives in Dar es Salaam indicate that the most common issue is the need to acquire missing services, particularly potable water, for the majority of settlements. Communities and CBOs are also galvanized into action by land rights issues, such as legitimising existing holdings and obtaining fair compensation for land or property affected by formal planning interventions in local areas. As the community based initiatives gain momentum, these efforts are increasingly based on the inhabitants' own initiatives and resources, albeit with some external help. The registration of CBOs makes it easier to establish networks that facilitate donors' channelling of assistance to the communities. CBOs also constitute a forum where authorities and donors hear the community's voice.

Makongo represents a case of an urban community taking land use planning and settlement management initiatives to address their problems, to promote their livelihood and to safeguard their rights to land and to a democratic space in planning. The case portrays the potentials and ingenuity of popular, community initiatives in their responses to the growing deficiencies in settlement management and provision of urban services by the public sector. This example illustrates some issues that surface as the popular initiatives interact with the formal planning system. It is a case of both insensitive planning which creates conflicts between the city government and groups of residents, and documents the inability of the local community to handle complex planning issues on its own. It demonstrates a lack of concrete initiatives from the formal planning structures to incorporate community initiatives in the decision-making processes for urban management.

One of the interesting aspects of the community-initiated land use plan for Makongo is that while some facets of both the planning process and the plan itself present a break with the conventional planning practice, it also demonstrates how difficult it is to change both ideas and forms of that practice. Providing a framework for democratic practices by the actors involved and creating an enabling environment for the communities and the civil society groups for urban governance, still poses significant challenges to the administrative institutions of both central and local government concerned and to planners in the field. The urban planning professionals sometimes respond to the changing context or 'environment' for planning practice by associating with stakeholders in the civil society.

The negotiations with the formal authorities represent interesting innovations on the part of communities. In the case of Makongo they do not actually amount to formal partnerships. Rather, these are informal undertakings by which the respective settlements can be informally planned, as when official planning regulations such as zoning and building standards, cannot be achieved.

These informal mechanisms may be far from partnerships of equals, but they in-dicate a changing relationship between public sector planning and local commu-nities. At the interface, we are beginning to see a tacit recognition that the com-munity initiatives should be incorporated into formal planning practice even if they do not conform to official norms and regulations. This is a far cry, how-ever, from the desired participation of local communities in local development, including planning. Much needs to be done to sensitize planners and adminis-trators and other actors in urban governance to community-led development issues and their role in urban development.

Looking at the whole process of land use planning initiatives in Makongo, it is evident that the state-led regularization attempt culminated in conflict with the community and prompted its rejection by the latter. So, how can the formal and informal planning co-exist in such circumstances of change? What initia-tives need to be taken by the public sector planning to offer advice and help to the local communities, developers or urban residents in general in their efforts to improve and regularize their settlements? The importance of acquiring knowledge and a better understanding of how local actors are shaping urban governance becomes paramount. There is therefore a need for undertaking fur-ther research through detailed case studies in order to gain better knowledge of alternative modes of urban planning and management. The increasing number of CBOs and NGOs in urban Tanzania provides a fertile ground for improved service provision and for collaborative planning. The challenge remains, how-ever, to integrate grass root initiatives into sustainable planning and manage-ment, and into the overall governance process in the country.

References

Abbott, John, 1996, *Sharing the City. Community Participation in Urban Management.* London: Earthscan.

Andreasen, Jorgen, 2001, "The Legacy of Mobilization from Above: Participation in a Zanzibar Neighbourhood" in Tostensen, Arne, Inge Tvedten and Mariken Vaa (eds), *Associational Life in African Cities. Popular Responses to the Urban Crisis.* Uppsala: Nordiska Afrikainstitutet.

Burra, Marco, 1999, "Autonomous Self-Initiated Planning and Local Spatial Management for the Informal Settlements. A Case Study of Makongo Settlement, Dar es Salaam" in Fred, Lerise, *Planning Issues in Dar es Salaam and Its Environs.* Research Report. Dar es Salaam: Department of Urban and Rural Planning, University College of Lands and Architectural Studies (UCLAS).

Dar es Salaam City Commission (DCC), 1998, *The Strategic Urban Development Plan for Dar es Salaam.* City Planning Documents.

Friedmann, John, 1992, *Empowerment: Politics of Alternative Development.* Cambridge, MA: Basil Blackwell.

Halla, Francos, 1997, *Institutional Arrangements for Urban Management: The Sustainable Dar es Salaam Project.* PhD thesis, Rutgers University, New Jersey.

Healey, Patsy, 1997, *Collaborative Planning: Shaping Places in Fragmented Societies.* London: Macmillan Press Ltd.

Hoek-Smit, Marja, 1991, "The Urban Housing Sector in Tanzania. Analysis of the 1990 Housing Survey". A World Bank commissioned study. Nairobi: World Bank.

Kessy, Joseph, 2000, "Promoting Good Urban Governance at Community Level: The Case of Tabata" in Suleiman Ngware and Lussuga Kironde, *Urbanizing Tanzania: Issues, Initiatives and Priorities*. Dar es Salaam: Dar es Salaam University Press.

Kiondo, Andrew, 1994, "The New Politics of Local Development in Tanzania" in Gibbon, P. (ed.), *The New Local Level Politics in East Africa: Studies on Uganda, Tanzania and Kenya*. Research Report No. 95. Uppsala: Scandinavian Institute of African Studies.

Kironde, Joseph, 1995, *Evolution of the Land Use Structure of Dar es Salaam 1890–1990: A Study on the Effects on Land Policy*. PhD thesis, University of Nairobi.

—, 1992, "Land Scarcity amid Land Abundance: The Paradoxes of Tanzania's Land Policy", *Open-House International* 17, 1.

Kombe, Wilbard, 1995, *Formal and Informal Land Management in Tanzania, the Case of Dar es Salaam City*. Spring Centre Research Series 15. Faculty of Spatial Planning, Dortmund University.

Lerise, Fred (ed.), 1999, *Planning Issues in Dar es Salaam and Its Environs*. Research Report. Dar es Salaam: Department of Urban and Rural Planning, University College of Lands and Architectural Studies (UCLAS).

Lerise, Fred and Nnkya, Tumsiph, 1999, "Characteristics of Dar es Salaam-Based CBOs and NGOs". A report for the Swedish Embassy. Dar es Salaam: University College of Lands and Architectural Studies (UCLAS).

Mhamba, Robert M. and Colman Titus, 2002, "Reactions to Deteriorating Public Services in Dar es Salaam" in Tostensen, Arne, Inge Tvedten and Mariken Vaa (eds), *Associational Life in African Cities. Popular Responses to the Urban Crisis*. Uppsala: Nordiska Afrikainstitutet.

UNCHS, 1987, "The Role of Community Participation in Human Settlements Work". UNCHS Report for the International Year of Shelter for the Homeless, Habitat, Nairobi.

UNDP and The United Republic of Tanzania, 1993, "Managing Sustainable Growth and Management in Dar es Salaam". Report/90/033. Dar es Salaam.

Vaa, Mariken, 1995, "Issues and Policies in the Development of Unauthorised Settlements", *The Norwegian Journal of Geography* 49:4, Oslo.

Wangwe, Sam, 1996, "Economic Reforms and Poverty Alleviation in Tanzania". Summary Report of the ILO Conference held in Geneva, 29–30 January 1996. Geneva: ILO.

CHAPTER 9

Actors and Interests: The Development of an Informal Settlement in Nairobi, Kenya

Rose Gatabaki-Kamau and Sarah Karirah-Gitau

This chapter examines the political and economic conditions underlying the proliferation of unauthorized land supply and provision through a case study of Zimmerman, a sprawling middle-income housing area on the north-eastern outskirts of Nairobi. The historical reconstruction of the emergence of this housing area between 1961 and 1993 provides the basis for the identification of actors, interests and the critical mechanisms underpinning informal land and housing supply and its consumption. More important for an understanding of urban change in postcolonial Nairobi, the case study provides insights into the formal and informal political processes involved. Thus the case study demonstrates how social groups that felt excluded from formal production and consumption of housing in Nairobi influenced both the local and the central state's decisions on urban land and housing development.

The central argument is that informal land supply and housing provision do not simply reflect inappropriate legal frameworks and institutional incapacity to enforce them as argued by the World Bank and UNCHS (Habitat) (Rodwin 1987; World Bank 1992, 1993). Rather as other research in Nairobi (Amis 1983, 1984 and 1996) and in other Third World cities shows (Angel 1983; Baross 1983; Gilbert, 1986), what takes place is first and foremost a process of commercialization of low-income housing. Secondly, as data from our study of Nairobi, and from other cities demonstrate (Gatabaki-Kamau 1995; El Kadi 1988; Oncü 1988; Chabbi, 1988), informalization of land supply and housing provision also involves a process of exclusion of large segments of the urban middle class from the formal urban development process. This exclusion has from the 1960s and onwards resulted in the emergence of informal settlements owned and rented by middle-income groups. This fact deviates from the norm where informal settlements are viewed to be developed by and for the low-income sector of the economy. The above notwithstanding, the informal systems of land and housing supply should be seen as a function of political intermediation of varied but mutually reinforcing interests in urban land and housing. They should also be seen as an historical form that has continued to dominate Nairobi's land and housing markets.

Future regularization of the proliferating informal developments may be difficult if not impossible if state capacity to intervene in housing remains constrained. Continued growth of unauthorized settlements also becomes unavoidable if workers' incomes remain low relative to the cost of housing and if both production and consumption interests converge and organize politically in collusion with officers of the development control agency. These were the key components of the mechanism that kept propelling the development of Zimmerman from a small squatter settlement in 1961 to a sprawling middle-income housing area by 1993 (Gatabaki-Kamau 1995).

Solutions to the problems involved should therefore not only be sought in the legal frameworks for land supply, housing development standards and the development control agency's capacity to enforce them. They must also be sought in the political-economic conjuncture. Physical development laws and standards are relative. To a large extent they are a product of value judgements and are informed by specific socio-structural relations. These relations are themselves constantly and spontaneously subject to question. The Zimmerman case study will demonstrate this.

Relevant literature from the last two decades highlights the need to examine further the processes of production and consumption in informal land and housing markets. It has been suggested that this should be done through identifying the actors and their motives as well as by scrutinizing the state and explicitly showing what role it plays (Payne 1989). Rakodi (1992) has further pointed out the need for future research in Third World housing markets to utilize both Marxist and neo-classical ideas in the analysis of these markets. Later, she urged that in the context of economic and political liberalization policies being adopted in Third World countries "understanding the relationship between formal and informal land markets and between these markets and the housing sector has become paramount" (Rakodi 1994, quoted in Jones 1994; Durand-Lasserve 1987). This chapter is informed by these approaches.

THE ORIGINS OF NAIROBI AND ITS GROWTH

The growth of present day Nairobi dates back to 1899 when the Mombasa/ Uganda railway line reached the site where the city is located. George White-house, the Chief Engineer in charge of the railway made the following observations regarding the site:

> It is about 5,500 feet above the level of the sea, which ensures a comparatively salubrious climate. There is ample space of level ground for all sorts of requirements and excellent sites for the quarters of officers and subordinates. (Quoted in Hake 1977:22)

The natural endowment with "excellent sites for the quarters of officers and subordinates" was given concrete expression through the plans for the city from 1905, 1927 and 1948. Thus Europeans came to typically occupy private houses on the spacious lots in the higher, cooler north-western sections of the city. Asians, who had come as workers for the railway construction, lived in large extended family houses near the city centre. Those Africans who were not domestic workers in European/Asian houses, were relegated to cramped rental quarters in the lower lying "Eastlands" (Temple and Temple 1980:225–26). This racial zoning, rationalized as "the need to achieve a disease free environment with minimum of public expenditure" (Amis 1990:86), was a major component of the 1948 Master Plan. Indeed, the 1948 Master Plan is to date the only comprehensive plan for the city. The 1973 Nairobi Metropolitan Growth Strategy was never implemented due to lack of political will (Syagga, Mitullah and Gitau 2001).

In as far as access to urban residential land was concerned, the racial zoning effectively set administrative limitations to what was otherwise perceived to be a free land market. After independence, segregation and distribution of residential land by race was merely replaced by segregation along socio-economic lines. Amazingly enough the 1973 "Metropolitan Growth Strategy for Nairobi" failed to recognize that effective development control along traditional lines would be a daunting if not impossible task. Furthermore "... the distribution of infrastructure in Nairobi has been dependent on income levels rather than density" (Obudho 1992:102). Thus even after independence, urban governance for the city continued to be characterized by serious democratic deficits. To a considerable extent the rise in the unauthorized land and housing supply from the 1970s onwards reflects popular struggles for fair distribution of available resources among the various socio-economic groups in the city. This was particularly inevitable after independence in 1963 given the changes in political conjuncture and the rapid increase in the urban population.

Nairobi has experienced sustained growth both in physical expansion and population from the time it became a settlement in 1901 to the present. Between 1899 and 1963 the city boundaries changed several times, in 1920, 1927 and 1963 (Gitau and Macoloo 2000). However, the major boundary extensions took place in 1963, which resulted in the inclusion of new areas such as Karen, Spring Valley, Nairobi National Park, Ruaraka, Njiru and Dagoretti (Salau 1988). Even before 1963 Karen, Spring Valley and Ruaraka, all of which were occupied by Europeans, were administered as part of the then Nairobi Urban District Council (NUDC), now replaced by Nairobi City Council (NCC). The population figures for the period 1899–1903 are 10,000 people on 18 square kilometres of land (Salau 1988). Before independence in 1962 the population was estimated at 350,000 people (Mbugua 2000). With independence in 1963, the population grew rapidly due to rural-urban migration and the population brought under the city's jurisdiction with the 1963 boundary extensions mentioned above. By 1969 the population was 509,286; in 1979 827,775 and 1989 1, 342,435 people. A steep increase in population occurred between 1990–92 attributed to the ethnic land clashes in various parts of the country. By 1999 the population of Nairobi had risen to 2,137,000 people (Gitau and Macoloo 2000).

THE EVOLUTION OF THE INFORMAL LAND AND HOUSING SUPPLY SYSTEM IN NAIROBI

Informal settlements commonly refer to agglomerations of residential structures that are constructed largely of temporary materials. The informality is construed to result from the fact that acquisition of land and/or housing development occur without formal approval from the relevant authorities either because the actual developments do not meet the required development requirements or are situated on land that does not belong to those who have built (squatters), or result from unapproved therefore illegal subdivisions, infiltration, accretion and engulfment (Gitau 1996).[1]

This definition fails to describe informal settlements developed by the middle-income groups comprising units of high standard (constructed of permanent materials with good workmanship) and serviced, as is the case in Zimmerman. Here, the process was realized through legal land ownership by a foreigner that was replaced with irregular land rights controlled by a group of politically influential Africans. Indeed, after the realization that the initial developments would not be demolished, and that the development standards were high, middle-income investors were attracted to the settlement so that, for example, by 1981 there emerged scattered three to five storied blocks of flats. The majority of the property owners who lived in Nairobi or in other parts of the country, were absentee landlords and sublet all their units.

The typology based on land acquisition processes and nature of development of Nairobi's informal settlements shows that there are more settlements that have resulted from commercial factors (unapproved subdivisions and developments) than the non-commercial (squatting, accretion, gradual infiltration and engulfment). Moreover, the large low-income settlements such as Kibera, Mathare and Korogocho are made of several villages of varying sizes, formed at different periods. However, it is difficult to distinguish the physical boundaries between the villages. The large settlements often comprise more than one formation process. For instance, in Mathare, the initial villages resulted from the non-commercial modes where pure squatting and gradual infiltration occurred on government land; later ones resulted from commercial modes through land buying companies and cooperatives, sale by squatters through illegal subdivisions and sub-subdivisions (Gitau 1996). It is worth noting that among the city's informal settlements only about 5 per cent provide housing for middle-income groups, e.g. Zimmerman, Kahawa and parts of Githurai. The middle-income settlements emerge through commercial transactions. Their illegality stems from failure to comply with stipulated land subdivision requirements or through unapproved developments, especially those in the areas that were engulfed after the boundary extensions that brought formerly customary owned land and freeholds under the city's jurisdiction. Kangemi, Waithaka and Dagorretti are cases in point (Gitau 1996).

Informal settlements in Nairobi are rooted in the contradictions of colonial and post-colonial labour policies, housing policies and economic relations. Since the colonial period, serviced land for residential development or/and houses, at the right location and affordable by both the middle-income and the low-income groups has been lacking in Nairobi. This has been the main contributing factor for the increasing number of informal settlements. Indeed, the earliest informal

---

1. Accretion is the process that responds to some historical circumstance e.g. tribal/civil clashes that result in squatting on vacant land anywhere within a city's morphology. Gradual infiltration/quiet encroachment results when a few people identify vacant public or private land and occupy it over time and are joined by others. Engulfment occurs when formerly existing villages are brought under the city's jurisdiction due to boundary extensions (Gitau 1996:52).

settlements are documented to have occurred through displacement of Africans in Nairobi in 1902 with the arrival of the European settlers who expropriated large tracts of land in Kiambu, Kikuyu, Limuru, Mbagathi, Ruiru and other areas close to Nairobi (Majale 2000:4). In this respect the informal settlements may be seen as a consequence of the growth of a capitalist system in Kenya.

In addition to the above, most of the problems of housing in Kenyan towns had been inherited from the colonial period. They were a direct result of colonial labour policies, which treated the African presence in towns as temporary. For instance, the implementation of the Vagrancy Act 1922 was meant to curtail the number of Africans who came to Nairobi illegally (Macharia 1992). The Africans' housing needs were only covered under labour laws such as the 1940 "Employment Ordinance". Such ordinances were vague and left the employer free to decide how to respond (Choka 1988). This is exemplified by the directive of the Municipal Native Affairs Officer and Senior Medical Officer who in 1941, had called for strict reinforcement of legal obligations of employers to house their employees (Kabagambe and Moughtin 1983).

The widespread non-provision of housing for Africans was expressed in the form of the extreme overcrowding that the 1965 UN Mission reported. The colonial government did not deem it necessary to provide housing for the Africans in Nairobi. Indeed, although the Legislative Council had voted for more funds to be spent on African housing in 1930, only 40,000 pounds was allocated to this as compared to 586,430 pounds allocated for additional European accommodation (Macharia 1992). The housing problem was real because in the Vagrancy Act of 1922, the colonial government had been authorized to demolish any illegal/informal housing in the city (Macharia 1992).

The housing shortage and institutional vacuum inherited from the colonial period were exacerbated by the removal of colonial restrictions on movement of people after independence in 1963 and accentuated by the creation of individual property rights in African reserves. The Swynnerton Plan of 1954 initiated this process, which resulted in the conversion of land into a form of private property held by individuals. Other African families migrated to the city after they were unable to participate in the market-based transfer of agricultural land that formed part of the independence bargain with Britain (Kenya Human Rights Commission 1998). Consequently, Africans dislocated from the rural areas through colonial land alienation flocked into the towns in the early 1960s. This resulted in an increase in the African population by 174 per cent between 1948 and 1962; when 350,000 were living in Nairobi. The heaviest rural urban migration has been shown to have occurred between 1963 and 1965 (Muganzi 1996; Syagga et al. 2001). The continued growth of the African population resulted in the emergence of temporary dwellings with no extension of water and sanitation in Kariokor around the old Carrier Corps camp in 1930–31. Consequently, the first informal housing that had occurred through gradual infiltration was in Kariokor. Indeed, the first recorded official demolition which occurred in Kariokor in 1931, became a spark plug for the formation of other new small informal settlements, for example, Pumwani and Mathare became the resettlement areas where those evicted moved to (Syagga et al. 2001).

On attainment of independence, the Government actions and omissions contributed to the increased numbers of informal settlements when it allowed the migrants who could not find accommodation in the formal low cost housing to put up shacks within the city as long as these were not close to the central business district. Indeed, the many squatter settlements situated along the Nairobi River emerged at this period (Shihembetsa 1989). Later, in the quest to maintain law and order, the government and NCC undertook slum demolitions near the city centre but allowed those affected to settle at the then city fringes mainly in Huruma and Korogocho both in Starehe division. However, double standards prevailed where the government and NCC demolished some informal settlements while at the same time extending protection to others (Gitau 1996). Indeed, the majority of the informal settlements survive through political patronage, tacit permission by the local administration and a few by defiance. For instance, from 1963, Mathare Valley enjoyed the protection of the first Kenyan president. Hence while other settlements were demolished Mathare was not affected. To obtain further government tolerance, the squatters in Mathare Valley formed land-buying companies that started buying the land from the 1960s (Gatabaki-Kamau 1995).

In Nairobi, a feeling of tenure security has since independence continued to be experienced in the settlements that receive unofficial assurances resulting from protection, patronage and social reciprocity. Such settlements are those considered to be important political bases during national and local elections. In some instances the structure owners have considered their settlements to be recognized by the authorities even when no ownership rights are extended. This occurs when the local authority and central government extend urban services and public utilities such as water, schools, markets and health centres to the settlements. Indeed, in Zimmerman discussed in this chapter, NCC had constructed a primary school yet it had not officially recognized the settlement as evidenced by the demolition and eviction orders. Moreover, the NCC grants licenses to small business operators in these settlements after some payment.

Given the above observations and many more cases in Nairobi, the informal systems of land and housing supply should be seen as a function of political intermediation of varied but mutually reinforcing interests in urban land and housing. Solutions to the problems involved should therefore not only be sought in the legal frameworks for land supply, housing development standards and the development control agency's capacity to enforce them. They must also be sought in the political-economic conjuncture. To a large extent, they are a product of a value judgment and are informed by specific socio-structural relations. These relations are themselves constantly and spontaneously subject to question.

Those unable to get entry to middle-income housing that is in short supply in Nairobi either as property owners or tenants tend to move into the informal settlements. In fact renting is not necessarily the culture of the poor (Amis,1996; Mugo 2000). Landlords make considerable profits from their rental units. Amis (1983) in his study of construction and profitability in Kibera estimated the returns at 86–130 per cent excluding the money paid to the chief to obtain the construction permit. In a later study, the same author established that a typical

10-room structure gave an annual return of 131 per cent (Syagga et al. 2002). Moreover, "even at modest rent levels, capital investment could be recouped within two years" (Menon 1982 in Amis 1990:87). The above figures illustrate the profits accruing from low-income informal settlements. Since no studies have been undertaken on the profitability of subletting middle-income informal houses, one would assume they are as profitable. The rapid growth of Zimmerman supports this.

The informal settlements have continued to increase in number, size and densification from 50 informal settlements in 1971 to 133 in 1995 (NACHU 1990; MATRIX 1993; Ngau 1995). This number has more or less been maintained due to the issuance in 2000 of a moratorium against demolitions and evictions by Nairobi Informal Settlement Coordinating Committee (NISCC) comprising representation of informal settlement residents, civil society, NCC and the government through the provincial administration (Syagga et al. 2001).

ACTORS AND INTERESTS IN THE DEVELOPMENT OF ZIMMERMAN HOUSING AREA, 1961–1993

Location and transfer of land

Zimmerman estate has been developed on what was until 1993 Land Reference Number (LR NO.) 8–345/6 Kamiti Road in Nairobi. This was a plot measuring 190 acres (76.7 hectares), located within a triangle formed between the Thika Road/Kamiti road junctions approximately 13 kilometres to the North East of Nairobi's Central Business District (CBD). The estate is within the general area of Ruaraka. Administratively the estate is located in Kahawa location in Kasarani Division of Nairobi. Politically it falls under the Mathare Parliamentary Constituency and the Kahawa civic ward.

Until 15 March 1966, it was a Mr. Donald Giovanni Destro who owned LR No. 8345/6. He was a European settler who for unknown reasons was nicknamed Mr. Zimmerman by the original squatters on his land. NCC's records of the early 1960s on LR No. 8345/6 indicate that the land was subjected to sporadic invasions during the period just before Kenya became independent in 1963. On 10 June 1961 Mr. Destro was served with a removal notice from the then Clerk to the then Nairobi Urban District Council. The notice referred to the removal of "20 partially or wholly constructed, unauthorized buildings in stone, timber or mud used for African occupation". Mr. Destro was given 14 days within which to remove the buildings or the council would enter the land and "remove the said structures and recover any cost as civil debt" (Removal notice served to Mr. Destro on 10 June 1961).

From subsequent communication it seems that Mr. Destro did not or could not comply with the removal notice. Thus after 14 days the council entered his land, demolished the structures and charged Mr. Destro Ksh. 947/10 (then approximately British £26). While Mr. Destro paid the charges he complained bitterly about his helplessness in controlling the sporadic invasions of his land:

Please find enclosed my cheque for Ksh. 947/10. I feel I must protest over this. In the first place I did not build the huts or give permission for them to be built. Furthermore, the huts have been rebuilt and as far as I can see every few months I will be paying for the demo-lition of huts built by trespassers on my land. I am unable to demolish them being sta-tioned in Nakuru … . (Letter from Mr. Destro to the then Nairobi Urban District Council, dated 15 July 1961.)

Thus on 15 March 1966 Mr. Destro was only too glad to transfer his land to a partnership of four Africans. Reliable sources informed us that the four Africans were politically well connected and that Mr. Destro sold his land at a give-away price to them. The partnership took over the land ownership under the name of "Tiabo Partnership". The four buyers signed the title deed as tenants-in-com-mon for a 99 year leasehold. Reliable informers revealed in 1993 that the land was at the time transferred for a consideration of Ksh. 100,000 (then about Brit-ish £2,976). By this time there was a sizeable squatter settlement on the land. No reliable information regarding the exact number of unauthorized structures was available.

Around 1970/71 the original squatters organized themselves into a Housing Company called the "New Roysambu Housing Company Limited". The objec-tive of the company was along similar lines to that of land buying companies, which had increased since independence. Land-buying companies/co-operatives are common in the Kenyan urban areas that are located in the former "White Highlands". The organizations have played crucial economic-cum-political roles in facilitating access to land by ordinary Kenyans. This was particularly important following independence in 1963 since many Africans found it impos-sible to participate individually in the market-based transfer of land from the white settlers in the highlands. State-funded schemes aimed at helping the poor could not adequately address the need and demand for land by people with modest and low incomes (Gitau 2001).

The objective of the founders of the Roysambu Housing Company was to acquire the land they were squatting on from Tiabo Partnership. Richer, better-educated people from other parts of Nairobi soon joined these original squat-ters. Mr. Ranju (real name not used), at the time an officer with NCC's Housing and Social Welfare Department, joined the Housing Company in the early 1970s. When interviewed in July 1993, he still owned one of the oldest perma-nent houses in Zimmerman estate. According to him, he had nevertheless put the house in the name of one of his daughters, as a measure of self-protection. Also according to him, he played a crucial role during the early 1970s in lobby-ing for support for the New Roysambu Housing Company within NCC. At the same time, Tiabo Partnership and the New Roysambu Housing Company entered into an informal process of land transfer.

The Informal Transfer and Subdivision in Zimmerman Estate

Transfer of land in Zimmerman estate started in 1972. Besides the squatters, anybody willing to take the risk of informally buying a plot in the area was wel-come to join the New Roysambu Housing Company Limited. The "directors" of the company were elected by the original squatters from among themselves but others were recruited from outside by the those who had been elected by the squatters. Recruits from outside included people such as Mr. Ranju. According to Mr. Ranju he was recruited into the Housing Company by a cousin of his who was among the original squatters and one of the elected "directors" of the Housing Company.

In the period 1972–1975, when most of the shares in the New Roysambu Housing Company were sold, the price of a full share was Ksh. 6,600. Out of this sum, Ksh. 4,000 was calculated to go into the purchase of the land while Ksh. 2,600 was supposed to go into the provision of services. A full share translated into a plot measuring approximately 350 square metres. The money could be paid in instalments for which the Housing Company issued receipts bearing its name. After a member had fully paid up for one share he or she was issued with a share certificate as a document of proof of ownership. While the share certificate served as the main instrument of exchange in this informal land market, trust and willingness to take risks also played a crucial role. Through mutual agreement, the New Roysambu Housing Company bought the land off Tiabo Partnership in phases. All of the land had been informally sold off to the New Roysambu Housing Company by 1976. By 1989 the housing company had a total of 1,300 shareholding/plot-owning members.

The need to seek a shortcut for legal recognition arose in 1989 when NCC lawyers, Kaplan and Stratton Advocates, issued Tiabo Partnership with a demand for rates arrears. The demand was for Ksh. 2,008,012 (US$105,263 at the 1989 exchange rate). On receiving this demand the partners of Tiabo Partnership teamed up with the directors of the New Roysambu Housing Company Limited and visited the NCC's lawyers. The objective of the visit was to explain that Tiabo Partnership was no longer the *de facto* owner of LR No. 8345/6 and thus should not be served with the demand for rates arrears. A letter written to NCC by Kaplan and Stratton, Advocates, on 30 April 1989 on the matter captures this simultaneous existence of formal and informal ownership of the same parcel of land very well. We will quote it here at length for illustration:

> Two of the partners of the rateable property namely, Mr. Henry Kiarie and Mr. Edward Kamau Nganga came to see us on the morning of 24 April 1989 in company of Mr. John Kangethe of New Roysambu Housing Company. Mr. Henry Njenga Kiarie and Mr. Edward Kamau Nganga informed us that they sold the property to New Roysambu Housing Company way back in 1976 but that the land has not been transferred in favour of the New Roysambu Housing Company Limited. The directors of the company also confirmed that they have purchased the said property and that they have subdivided the land into many small pieces and allocated them to its members who have already constructed houses thereon … . (Letter from Kaplan and Stratton advocates to NCC, dated 30 April 1989.)

On the basis of this revelation the two partners of Tiabo Partnership and the two directors of the New Roysambu made two interesting suggestions to the NCC lawyers. The first was that demands for rates arrears be served to members of the New Roysambu Housing Company Limited individually. The four officials of the two respective landholding organizations offered to provide a list of all the 1,300 members and their postal addresses. The second suggestion was that while they wished the NCC lawyers to accept this *de facto* position on the ownership of the land, they also wanted the rates to be adjusted to reflect the *de jure* status of the land, which was agricultural. NCC had in 1977 refused to grant the change of use for LR 8345/6 from agricultural to residential.

During a special technical meeting held on 22 April 1981, in the Chief Planning Officer's Office at NCC, the fact that informal surveying and parcelling out of the sub-plots in Zimmerman had been carried out by technically qualified employees of NCC was put on record. The meeting had been called to discuss illegal developments in Nairobi. In reference to the illegal construction of houses on LR 8345/6, (Zimmerman) the meeting noted that:

> A council employee surveyor did the layout plans as a private job but the plans were never submitted to the town Planning Section for Approval. (NCC Records, Minutes of a Special Technical Meeting held on 22 April 1981.)

Furthermore a report submitted to the same meeting on this particular illegal development also noted that:

> The sub-plots have been surveyed by the then Chief Land Surveyor in NCC and the plot beacons provided. The said subdivision plan has never been submitted to the Council for approval and hence is illegal. (As above)

The most probable interest of the NCC Land Surveyor in illegally developing his own city was a desire for private gain in the form of fees. However it is also possible that he may have worked in close consultation with the then Deputy Mayor of Nairobi. This Deputy Mayor's extension of patronage in unauthorized developments on LR 8345/6 is also found in NCC records. His interests were obviously political. This will become apparent from the discussion in the next section.

NCC lawyers could not agree to recognize the *de facto* position of the ownership of the land. Instead, they advised the officials of both Tiabo Partnership and the New Roysambu Housing Company that the "Nairobi City Commission would not involve themselves with such matters" (Letter from Kaplan and Stratton Advocates to NCC dated 30.4.1989). However, the lawyers advised NCC to adjust the rates arrears since the land was still officially recorded as agricultural. This adjustment resulted in the rates arrears on LR 8345/6 being reduced from Ksh. 2,008,012 to Ksh. 269,012.

One important point should be noted here. By 1989 the title deed for LR 8345/6 still showed that Tiabo Partnership owned the land. Furthermore neither the New Roysambu Housing Company Limited nor its individual shareholding members had placed any caveats (written expression of interest on a parcel of land) in the title deed. An examination of the title deed in July 1993 confirmed that it was not until 25.5.1990 that a caveat by the New Roysambu Housing Company was placed on the title deed for the first time. Trust therefore played a crucial role in instances of an informal land market operating.

First Attempt at Controlling the Growth of Zimmerman

According to the original members of the New Roysambu Housing Company whom we were able to contact, construction of unauthorized permanent housing in Zimmerman estate started in 1972. By 1973 there were an estimated 30 houses under various stages of construction. An NCC report on illegal housing development on LR 8345/6 observes that:

> Investigations on illegal housing development on the above plot (LR 8345/6) revealed that action by the Building Surveyor to stop the unauthorized development was initiated on 21st August 1973. The then Deputy Mayor, Mr. Ngumba stopped the demolition. (NCC Report from the Building Surveyor on illegal housing development LR 8345/6 Kamiti Road, dated 22 April 1981.)

Therefore, with the Deputy Mayor at the time extending protection, the shareholders of the New Roysambu Housing Company continued to build unauthorized housing on land whose subdivision had also not been legally approved or recognized.

The Town Planning Sub-Committee's refusal to change the use of the area from agricultural to residential was mainly based on the grounds that adequate services to support a residential estate did not exist in the area. However, unauthorized housing construction continued. In June 1978, most probably through the political influence of the Mayor (the former Deputy Mayor who had become Nairobi's Mayor in February 1977), the extension of water was granted by NCC's Water and Sewerage Department. In 1979 NCC also built a primary school in the settlement. The tender for construction of the school was formally awarded under Minute 33 of the chief officers meeting held on 27 November 1979. A Tender Committee also formally ratified it on 10 March 1980. However the plans for the school were never submitted to the Town Planning Section for approval.

The Mayor's motivations in extending patronage to the unauthorized builders in Zimmerman were obvious. For him, extending political protection and services to the illegal developers of Zimmerman carried considerable political value. In the first instance he was the Councillor of Kahawa civic ward, where Zimmerman estate was located. He was therefore delivering "state resources" to his immediate constituents. Furthermore he had higher political ambitions for which he was campaigning. In 1979 the patron Mayor of Zimmerman resigned from his mayoral and civic posts in order to contest the Mathare parliamentary seat in Nairobi. Most unauthorized settlements in Nairobi and particularly those developed by "land companies" were and still are located in this constituency. The constituency covers most of the newly developing areas in northeastern Nairobi including the original squatter settlement of Mathare Valley. Zimmerman was one of the newly growing settlements located in this particular parliamentary constituency.

From the late 1960s and throughout the 1970s the land companies in Mathare became important organizational bases for political campaigns for both local and national elections (Chege 1981:787–82). In his analysis of the 1979 elections in Mathare and Dagoretti Constituencies, Chege linked politics to the expansion of capitalism in unauthorized housing in Nairobi. In relation to the 1979 parliamentary election campaign in Mathare he notes:

> Probably at no time in Nairobi's history has the office of the Mayor been used for such nakedly calculated political ends. City projects were commandeered to Mathare constitu-

ency. Patronage was dished out to the Mayor's supporters, new and old, and denied those of Waiyaki. (Chege 1981:81)

In 1979, however, the ex-mayor failed to capture the Mathare parliamentary seat from the powerful and long-serving Dr. Munyua Waiyaki. After much more groundwork, this time involving the use of his private financial clout, the ex-mayor dislodged Waiyaki from Mathare constituency in the 1983 general elections.

Out of City Hall the ex-mayor used his personal financial power to gain advantage over the incumbent MP. To do so he made use of a financial institution in which he was the majority shareholder. In an innovative approach to Housing Finance in Kenya, this financial institution is recorded to have extended loans to builders of unauthorized housing in Mathare Constituency (Jorgensen et al. 1987:10, 65). The innovation was that the financial institution did not demand registered title deeds as security for loans. The share certificates were acceptable. Furthermore calculation of affordability was based on future rather than current incomes of the developers. This happened particularly in extension of loans to housing developers in Zimmerman and Githurai. Githurai is another unauthorized settlement in Kasarani constituency, which is close to the Zimmerman estate to the north (Jorgensen et al. 1987:10). Members of another landholding "company" have developed Githurai. Thus large scale finance capital was introduced into the unauthorized development of these areas.

Second Attempt at Controlling the Growth of Zimmerman

After the patron of Zimmerman (NCC mayor) left City Hall, fresh attempts to curb the estate's growth were initiated. On 22 April 1981 the Town Clerk of NCC issued a demolition notice to the developers of unauthorized housing on LR No. 8345/6. The demolition notice had been endorsed by a special technical meeting on illegal developments in the city. The meeting had been held on the same day. Among the senior technical officers present at the meeting were the Chief Planning Officer, Principal Planning Officer, Chief Assistant Engineer, Senior Building Inspector, Principal Assistant Engineer and Senior Public Health Officer. In issuing the notice the Town Clerk brought to the attention of the unauthorized developers of Zimmerman that they had contravened by-law 252 (1) of the Local Government (Building) By-Laws of 1968. They were therefore given 30 days to demolish the following:

1.   Unauthorized buildings approximately two hundred in number constructed of stonewalls, and roofed with G.C.I. sheets and concrete tiles and of a type design. The said buildings are used for living accommodation.

2.   Unauthorized buildings consisting of double storey structures with toilet block constructed of stone walls and roofed with concrete tiles and used as classrooms (Demolition notice issued by NCC to Tiabo Partnership on LR 8345/6 dated 22.4.1981.

The press took up the issue of this demolition order in May 1981. It generated heated public debate in Nairobi. On 19 May 1981 for instance the Daily Nation carried a very critical story on the matter. The story was sensationally headed "Pull down Houses, Orders Council". It went on to comment on the absurdity of the order given that production of formally produced housing lagged far behind need and that those houses which were being produced were unaffordable to most urban households. Furthermore, the press story argued, NCC had stopped producing the subsidized housing that could offer alternative accommodation.

Newspaper sensationalism aside, the 1970s had increasingly become characterized by growing non-affordability of formally produced housing. The waiting list for NCC housing had also grown longer (Stren 1979:182). At the close of the decade the situation had become even worse. The 1979–1983 Development Plan for instance indicated, "of the existing 440,000 urban households, only 30 per cent have sufficient incomes to afford minimum conventional housing" (Government of Kenya 1979:171).

As a consequence of the worsening housing problems, the residents in Zimmerman (who were mainly tenants) were willing to form an alliance with their landlords to protest against the demolition order. They too had an interest in unauthorized housing, since it provided affordable accommodation. The Daily Nation of 21 May 1981, for instance, carried this interesting story:

> Residents of the New Roysambu Housing Company near Kahawa army barracks yesterday protested against an order by Nairobi City Council to demolish the 200 houses in the estate. The residents who called on the Nation House expressed deep concern over the demolition order and termed it as crazy. They said they would combine their efforts with the landlords to block the proposed move …

While of course the residents felt threatened with possible homelessness, the people who stood to lose most from the imminent demolition were the landlords. One irate house-owner in the estate for instance wrote to the Town Clerk of NCC on 19 May 1981 protesting thus:

> I write to you because I have seen your letter ref. LR 8345/6–Kamiti Road telling us to demolish our houses. This cannot be so because I have borrowed Ksh. 300,000 to build my house and now it is complete. Now I would rather the City Council askari (law-enforcement officer) kill me or I kill them. Why do you agree to give us water if you do not want us to build these houses? What politics is this? (NCC, records, letter from a house owner in Zimmerman addressed to the Town Clerk, dated 19 May 1981.)

On 22 May 22 1981, the heated public debate on the issue culminated in a ministerial tour of Zimmerman estate. On this day, the then Minister for Urban Development and Housing, Mr. Charles Rubia, a former Nairobi mayor, imposed a demolition ban on the unauthorized development. He publicly overruled NCC's demolition order. However the Minister avoided giving any formal policy guideline on unauthorized developments such as Zimmerman. In a very carefully worded statement the Minister dwelt on the school rather than houses:

> We in the government cannot allow this school to be demolished. If it is demolished it will be a loss to Nairobi ratepayers since the Council also gave its share of the money used to build the school … . (*Daily Nation*, 22 May 1981).

The gist of the ministerial speech was that if the houses were demolished the school would also have to be demolished. This would be so because they had all been developed on land whose subdivision had not been officially endorsed. Thus with the ministerial tour the last demolition threat in Zimmerman was lifted while the policy vacuum on the informally produced housing still remained. The state had responded to the multiplicity of interests through non-decision making that was geared to avoid conflict. The government appeared to accept that there were large shortfalls in formal housing production, and that only a small proportion of the urban households could afford formally produced housing. This acceptance was interpreted as a signal that informal or unauthorized developments would be tolerated. The ministerial lifting of a highly orchestrated demolition order reinforced this signal. So, Zimmerman grew very rapidly after 1981. Furthermore the original single storey type design was increasingly replaced by a multi-storey design, which contravened both "future" plot coverage and plot ratio standards for the area. In addition professionals in the building industry, including architects and engineers became increasingly involved in the unauthorized development of the housing. Other land-buying companies in the area also took their cue and started constructing unauthorized houses for modest and lower income households.

Thus by 1993, the small scale investors had produced 2,628 middle-income dwelling units in the area. The majority (1,828) of these dwelling units were put up between 1981 and 1993. By May 2000, the number of dwelling units had more than doubled. This rate of middle-class housing output by small investors may be compared with the rate of housing produced by the formal private sector. The latest large scale project funded by the Housing Finance Company of Kenya (HFCK), called Komarock, produced 2,394 dwelling units between 1987 and 1995. However, unlike Zimmerman, Komarock is not affordable to the majority of middle-income families in Nairobi. Indeed, many of the households living in Zimmerman in 1993 had moved from formal housing areas to escape both overcrowding and non-affordability.

The impressive character of Zimmerman in terms of level of investment and the construction effort of the informal small scale investors should nevertheless not hide the fact that in many ways Zimmerman presents an environmental and safety nightmare. Most of the area is waterlogged. Yet all the households rely on septic tanks/soak pits for human waste disposal. During the rainy season pools of storm water mixed with raw sewage become a common sight on many "roads" and passageways. A few of the multi-storey houses have recently started sinking into the waterlogged ground while high voltage electric cables hang dangerously over some of the houses. The land left for infrastructural services and social amenities is insufficient.

CONCLUSION

The unauthorized development of Zimmerman reflects varied and mutually reinforcing interests in urban land and housing. These include the speculative interests of the legal landowners such as Mr. Destro and the Tiabo Partnership.

They also include the political and speculative interests of the organizers of land-buying/housing development "companies" such as the directors of the New Roysambu Housing Company, the interests of squatters who wished to access land at the lowest possible cost but who lost out to market pressure; the interests of the house builders/producers looking for opportunities for capital accumulation or chances for self provision of housing; the interests of housing consumers looking for affordable housing as their real incomes fell; local politicians in search of votes; professionals looking for opportunities to generate income and the state in its efforts to forge a consensus and to find someone to take over the responsibility for infrastructure investment and service provision.

From the case study of Zimmerman it does not therefore seem reasonable to argue that the housing area developed in its unauthorized form because of complicated land subdivision laws and high housing development standards only. Rather the unauthorized housing area is a product of a particular development context. This context is characterized by scarce and inequitably distributed resources for infrastructure investment and collective consumption. It is also characterized by low and declining workers' incomes. The development context thus encourages clientilistic transactions between the state, politicians and production interests in urban land and housing. Scarcity of resources leads to exclusive criteria being used for allocation.

It therefore seems that solutions to the proliferation of unregulated informal housing should be sought not only in lower and more effectively enforced land subdivision laws and housing development standards. They must also be sought in increased and more equitably distributed resources for infrastructural investment and collective consumption. Quite simply, the Kenyan economy will need to grow, create more and better paid jobs and provide alternative opportunities for investment while enabling the state to intervene much more in urban housing than it did over the last two decades of the twentieth century.

Note

This chapter is based on Rose Gatabaki-Kamau's PhD thesis *The Politics of an Expanding Informal Housing Sub-Market in Nairobi. The Informal Development of a Middle-Income Settlement, 1961–1993.* 1995: CURS, School of Public Policy, University of Birmingham. A paper about the Zimmerman case was presented by Rose at the Copenhagen conference in June 2000. After Rose's passing away in late December 2000, it has been prepared for publication by Sarah Karirah-Gitau.

References

Amis, P., 1996, "Long-Run Trends in Nairobi's Informal housing Market", *Third World Planning Review*, Vol. 18, No. 3:271–85.

—, 1990, "Administrative Control or Market Mechanisms: The Economics of Commercialised Rental Housing in Nairobi". Rental Housing: Proceedings of an Expert Group Meeting by UNCHS (Habitat), Nairobi.

—, 1984, "Squatters or Tenants: The Commercialization of Unauthorised Housing in Nairobi", *World Development,* Vol. 12, No. I:87–96.

—, 1983, *A Shanty Town of Tenants: The Commercialization of Unauthorized Housing in Nairobi, 1960–1980.* Unpublished PhD thesis, University of Kent at Canterbury, UK.

Angel, S. et al. (eds), 1983, *Land for Housing the Poor.* Singapore: Select Books.

Baross, P., 1983, "The Articulation of Land Supply for Popular Settlements in Third World Cities," in Angel et al., 1983.

Bloomberg, L. and C. Abram, 1965, *United Nations Mission to Kenya on Housing.* Nairobi: Government Printers.

Bujra, J., 1992, "Ethnicity and Class: The Case of East African Asians" in Allen, T. and A. Thomas (eds), *Poverty and Development in the 1990s.* Oxford: Oxford University Press in association with Open University.

Chabbi, M., 1988, "The Pirate Sub-Developer: A New Form of Land Development in Tunis", *International Journal for Urban and Regional Research*, Vol. 12, No. I:8–12.

Chege, M., 1987, "The State and Labour in Kenya", in Nyong'o, A. (ed.), *Popular Struggles for Democracy in Africa*, pp. 248–64. London: Zed Books.

—, 1981, "A Tale of Two Slums: Electoral Politics in Mathare and Dagoretti," *Review of African Political Economy*, No. 20:74–88.

Choka, J.M., 1988, *Employer Housing in Kenya: Case Study of Selected Organizations Nairobi.* Unpublished MA thesis, University of Nairobi.

Durand-Lasserve, A., 1987, "Land and Housing in Third World Cities. Are Public and Private Strategies Contradictory?" *Cities*, Vol. 4, No. 4:325–38.

El Kadi, G., 1988) "Market Mechanisms and Spontaneous Urbanization in Egypt: The Cairo Case,", *International Journal of Urban and Regional Research*, Vol. 12, No. I:22–37.

Gatabaki-Kamau, R., 1995, *The Politics of an Expanding Informal Housing Sub-Market in Nairobi: The Informal Development of a Middle-Income Settlement, 1961–1993.* Unpublished PhD thesis, CURS, School of Public Policy, University of Birmingham, UK.

Gilbert, A.G., 1986, "Self-Help Housing and State Intervention: Illustrated Reflection on Petty Commodity Production Debate" in Drakakis-Smith, D. (ed.), *Urbanization in Developing World*, pp. 175–94. London: Croom Helm.

Gitau, S.K., 2001, "Land-Buying Companies for Urban Housing Development in Eldoret, Kenya" in Tostensen, A. et al., *Associational Life in African Cities. Popular Responses to the Urban Crisis*, pp. 144–61. Uppsala: Nordiska Afrikainstitutet.

—, 1996, *Community Participation in Informal Settlements Development in Kenya.* Unpublished PhD thesis, UCE, Birmingham, UK.

Gitau S.K. and C.G. Macoloo, 2000, *Human Settlements in Nairobi in the Last 100 years.* Nairobi.

Government of Kenya, 1996, *National Census Data for 1989.*

—, 1989, *National Development Plan 1989–93.*

—, 1979, *National Development Plan 1979–83.*

—, 1970, *National Development Plan 1974–78.*

Hake, A., 1977, *African Metropolis: Nairobi's Self-Help City.* London: Sussex University Press.

Jorgensen, N.O. et al., 1987, *Informal Sector Housing Finance: A Survey of Two Informal Settlements Combined with Literature.* Nairobi: USAID/RHUDO.

Jones G., 1994, "Urban Land Management: Panacea or Myth?" Paper presented at the 2nd Symposium on Housing for the Urban Poor, Birmingham, UK, 11–14 April 1994.

Kabagambe, D. and C. Moughtin, 1983, "Housing the Poor: Case Study of Nairobi", *Third World Planning Review*, Vol. 5. No. 3:227–48.

Kenya Government/UNICEF, 1990, *Social-Economic Profiles*. Ministry of Planning and National Development, Kenya Government.

Kenya Human Rights Commission, 1998, *Behind the Curtain, A Study of Squatters, Slums and Slum Dwellers*. Nairobi: Land Rights Program.

Kiamba C.M., 1986, *The Role of the State in Control of Urbanization: Urban Land Policy for Nairobi*. Unpublished PhD dissertation, University of Cambridge, UK.

Macharia, K., 1992, "Slum Clearance and the Informal Economy in Nairobi", *Journal of Modern African Studies*, No. 30(3):221–36.

Macoloo, G.C., 1991, "The Transformation of Production and Retail of Building Materials for Low-Income Housing in Mombasa, Kenya", *Development and Change*, Vol. 22, No. 3, July 1991, pp. 445–73.

Majale M.M., 2000, "Origins of Nairobi's Informal Settlements", *Vijijini Newsletter*, Nairobi.

MATRIX Development Consultants, 1993, An Overview of Informal Settlements in Nairobi. An Inventory. USAID: Office of Housing and Development Programmes.

Mbugua, J.P., 2000, "Problems of Shelter and the Planning Constraints in the City of Nairobi". Paper presented at the Annual Convention of the Architectural Association of Kenya.

Muganzi, Z.S., 1996, "Migration, Urbanization and Development", *Population Studies Research Series*, Vol. V., University of Nairobi

Mugo, P.N., 2000, "An analysis of the real estate market in the slums: A case study of Kibera slums, Nairobi", A Research Project, Department of Land Development, University of Nairobi.

Nairobi City Council/NCC, 1974, *Nairobi Metropolitan Growth Strategy*, Vol. II and I.

National Housing Cooperative Union (NACHU), 1990, *A Survey of Informal Settlements in Nairobi*.

Obudho, R.A, 1992, "The nature of the urbanization process and urbanism in the city of Nairobi, Kenya", *African Urban Quarterly* 7 (1/2):50–62.

Ngau, P., 1995, *Informal Settlements in Nairobi: A Baseline Survey of Slums and Squatter Settlements. An Inventory of NGO's and CBO's Activities*. Nairobi: IDRC.

Oncü, A., 1988, "The Politics of the Urban Land Market in Turkey: 1950–1980", *International Journal of Urban and Regional Research*, Vol. 12, No. I:38–64.

Payne, G., 1989, *Informal Housing and Land Subdivisions in Third World Cities: A Review of Literature*, Centre for Development and Environmental Planning (CENDEP), Oxford Polytechnic, Headington, Oxford.

Rakodi, C., 1992, "Housing Markets in Third World Cities: Research and Policy in the 1990s", *World Development*, Vol. 20, No. I:39–55.

Rodwin, L. (ed.), 1987, *Shelter, Settlement and Development*. Boston: Allen and Unwin.

Salau, A.T., 1988, "Nairobi and Lagos: A Comparative Analysis of Growth of Two African Capital Cities". First International Conference on Urban Growth and Spatial Planning of Nairobi, Kenya.

Shihembetsa, L.U., 1989, "Urban Developments and Dwelling Environments. Brief notes on Dandora, Kariobangi and Eastleigh". International Workshop on Housing, KU–Leuven, UNCHS–PGCHS–HRDU.

Stren, R., 1979, "Urban Policy" in Barkan, J.P. and J. Akumu (eds), *Politics and Public Policy in Kenya and Tanzania*, pp. 180–208. New York: Praeger Publishers.

Syagga, P.M., W.V. Mitullah and S.K. Gitau, 2002, *Nairobi Rental Study Report For U-Habitat, Nairobi*. Consultative Report. Nairobi: UN-HABITAT.

—, 2001, *Nairobi Situation Analysis: Consultative Report*. Nairobi: GOK/UNCHS

(Habitat), Collaborative Nairobi Slum Upgrading Initiative.

Temple, N. and F. Temple, 1980, "The politics of Public Housing in Nairobi" in Grindle, M.S. (ed.), 1980, *Politics and Policy Implementation in the Third World*, pp. 235–50. Princeton NJ: Princeton University Press.

Werlin, H.H., 1974, *Governing an African City: A Study of Nairobi*. New York: Holmes and Meyer Publishers.

World Bank, 1993, *Housing: Enabling Markets to Work*. Washington DC: World Bank.

—, 1992, *Urban Policy and Economic Development: An Agenda for the 1990s*. Washington DC: World Bank.

Media References and Office File Records

Daily Nation, as given in the text.

Various files from the records of the Nairobi City Council (NCC) as given in the text.

CHAPTER 10

The Law and Access to Land for Housing in Maseru, Lesotho

Resetselemang Clement Leduka

A majority of urban residents in the cities of the developing countries find it difficult to obtain land and housing through established legal or formal processes. They therefore step outside the law in order to gain access to land and housing. As a result, some major African cities accommodate more than 70 per cent of their population in illegal settlements (Durand-Lasserve and Clerc 1996; Kombe and Kreibich 2000). Although much is known about the morphology of these settlements, and the type of people living in them, a lot is still unknown about many of the processes that structure and sustain the development of these settlements, especially the legal process. However, the magnitude of illegality in Sub-Saharan African (SSA) cities, which extends to both housing and employment, makes the 'law' an appropriate focus for urban research (McAuslan 1998; Leduka 1998). Drawing on experiences of how the rules of the game as defined by state law and those that are defined by other norms underwrite access to urban housing land in Maseru, I show that both state law and state agents, as well as informal norms and actors in society, are implicated in the development of the so-called illegal city.

The chapter commences with a conceptual framework that explains strategies that are often adopted by disadvantaged members of society to cope with formal state rules and enforcement methods. This is followed by a brief account of policy context and the methods used to collect data. A short description of Maseru is then provided, followed by a detailed analysis and discussion of the rules of the game in action and their outcomes. The last section summarizes the argument.

The study draws on recent research on the enforcement of formal state rules in Lesotho, aiming at analysing and explaining social actors' experiences, opinions and response strategies to the enforcement of the Land Act of 1979 (LA 1979) with respect to access to urban housing land. The fieldwork for the research was carried out between December 1998 and April 1999 in Maseru. The data collection strategy involved the use of multiple methods: extensive secondary data search from published and unpublished archival and current documents, primary data from focus groups, semi-structured interviews and a questionnaire survey. Here, data from documentary sources and semi-structured interviews with selected state office bearers, including those who are retired, of legal private practitioners, traditional authorities and members of development committees in the study areas are analysed. Examples are drawn from the neighbourhoods of Maqalika/Mapeleng and Ha Mabote (Figure 1) because they are some of the earliest and best-documented areas of enforcement of the LA 1979.

CONCEPTUAL FRAMEWORK

This section outlines the conceptual framework for explaining coping strategies by subjects or victims of formal state rules and how such strategies might in turn give rise to the so-called illegal city. The framework is based on the idea of societal non-compliance and draws on Scott's (1985, 1987) notion of the 'weapons of the weak'. In the context of this framework, non-compliance is considered as a form of protest, albeit a subtle protest that is underwritten by its own rules of the game, which might be used to contradict or complement those of the state. Non-compliance is defined in similar terms by Razzaz (1994), who suggests that it is a stance that entails more than mere protest against or deviance from state law, because a non-compliant group might devise rules that contradict or preempt certain state rules, while at the same time observing and respecting other state rules. Whilst contradicting or pre-empting state rules, non-compliant groups are adept at exploiting "whatever areas [in state rules] there are of inconsistency, contradiction, conflict, ambiguity, or open areas that are normatively indeterminate to achieve immediate situational ends" (Razzaz 1994:11).

Scott (1985, 1987) and Tripp (1997) argue that a good deal of social science work on social conflict focuses on confrontational protest by organized social movements and thereby misses important aspects of non-compliant strategies that assume covert or quiet strategies with no discernible form of organization. To Scott (1985, 1987) and Tripp (1997), overt protest by organized groups represents only a small proportion of what often counts as resistance to state imposed rules and regulations.

Scott (1987:419) defines resistance as "... any act ... that is intended either to mitigate or deny claims ... made on [a subordinate] class by superordinate classes ... or to advance [subordinate] ... claims vis-à-vis these superordinate classes". Viewed this way then, resistance can assume a variety of forms, ranging from "small, individual acts of resistance in response to immediate problems to highly organized movements with clear ideological goals, sustained over a long period of time" (Tripp 1997:5). Resistance by marginalized individuals, therefore, defies conventional understanding of social movements or overt collective action, because it often takes the form of the 'weapons of the weak', which might be symbolized by "foot-dragging, dissimulation, false compliance, pilfering, feigned ignorance, slander, arson, sabotage, and so forth" (Scott, 1987:419; also Tripp 1997). These forms of protest

> require little or no planning, they often represent forms of individual self-help, and they typically avoid any direct symbolic confrontation with authority or elite norms. Their execution depends on little more than a bit of room to manoeuvre, a healthy self-interest and a favourable climate of opinion amongst one's neighbors. (Scott 1987:420)

Scott (1987) and Tripp (1997) are concerned to show that non-compliance by disadvantaged groups is a strategy of first and, in many respects, last resort. They argue that non-compliant behaviour is often not aimed at changing macro-rules because disadvantaged individuals have neither the resources nor the organizational skills to do so. Instead, such non-compliance is a survival strategy, as well as a strategy to gain access to resources that would otherwise remain outside their reach. Moreover, given their lack of input or voice in the formulation of policy, action by disadvantaged groups is most effective if directed at policy implementation, where non-compliance becomes their only instrument for defeating or mitigating the negative effects of state policies. Therefore, it is by undermining the bargaining power of state authorities that non-compliance gives agency to marginalized groups and thereby compensates for deficiencies in the resources and organizational skills required to sustain open confrontation with the state.

However, it is important to note, first, that silent protest occurs within a framework of macro-rules, which are often not entirely ignored, but might be used alongside informal rules in ways that advance the interests of disadvantaged groups. Second, that disadvantaged individuals have no monopoly of the 'weapons of the weak', as these are available for use by any group of individuals to resist state policies that might appear to threaten their interests (Scott, 1985).

The idea of non-compliance has important implications, given the history of urban development in the less developed countries, which has often involved open acts of confrontation by way of land invasions and illegal or clandestine land markets, all underwritten by non-compliant strategies. The illegal city, therefore, could be considered as an outcome of societal non-compliance and illustrates how the 'weapons of the weak' might have enabled popular access to urban housing land by a majority of urban residents, irrespective of socio-economic status. Indeed, as Razzaz observes, "... non-compliance with some aspect of the law (*de facto* possession in particular) has been one of the few avenues through which disadvantaged groups have been able to gain access to land and housing" (1994:345).

Therefore, the notion of non-compliance brings into sharp relief the various ways in which quiet, often taken-for-granted everyday survival strategies by people who are marginalized by formal state rules and enforcement methods, might work to challenge such rules, which might in turn lead to various responses from the state. For instance, the rules might be changed to reflect more realistic expectations (Scott 1985:36) or "supplemented by positive incentives [aimed at] inducing voluntary compliance [or] ... the state may simply choose to employ more coercion" (Scott 1985:36). However, irrespective of how the state might respond, non-compliance significantly constrains state policy options and room for manoeuvre (Scott 1985).

POLICY CONTEXT

Despite increasing rates of urbanization in the past twenty years, the population of Lesotho is still essentially rural. For instance, in 1976, 11 per cent of a population of 1.2 million was urban. In 1986, this proportion had increased to 15 per cent of a national population of 1.6 million and to 17 per cent of a population of 1.8 million in 1996 (Bureau of Statistics 1996). However, these figures relate only to the population within legally declared urban area boundaries and, therefore, conceal the gravity of the problem posed by the growth of peri-urban settlements. Although it is difficult to provide reasonable estimates of the population living in urban peripheries, because it is officially classified as rural, an example might suffice to illustrate the extent of such growth. The 1991 Planning Study for the town of Maputsoe indicates that, in 1986, the town had 11,200 people within urban administrative boundaries and a peri-urban population of about 18,000, thereby showing that in reality the town had over 29,000 people (Government of Lesotho 1991). Similar situations where the peri-urban population was found to be more than double the official urban population have also been reported for other towns as well (Leduka 1995).

Therefore, a significant proportion of recent population increase is accommodated within peri-urban settlements, where agricultural land is privately subdivided into plots for sale under the authority of traditional chiefs. Given the general scarcity of cultivable land (9 per cent of total area) and the location of the most attractive urban centres on prime agricultural land, the need to preserve this resource has been widely acknowledged by state policy-makers. Other concerns relate to the perceived lack of a market in land, which has militated against land going to its most productive use; the unattractive structure and form of the built environment resulting from the subdivisions sanctioned by the chiefs; and uncontrolled low-density urban sprawl, which is inarticulate, haphazard and messy.

In order to address these problems, the Lesotho government has, on various occasions attempted to introduce legislative instruments aimed at regulating and regularising the conversion of peri-urban agricultural land into urban plots. The most drastic legislative measure was put in place in 1980 with the enactment of the Land Act of 1979 (LA 1979). In very general terms, the LA 1979 introduced three forms of tenure: *state leaseholds*, which are granted by the Minister for Lands, following allocation by urban land committees; *licences*,[1] which are for agricultural land within legally gazetted urban area boundaries; and *allocations* for rural agricultural land, which, similar to tenure under customary law, guaranteed only use rights in perpetuity. The LA 1979 effectively nationalized all land, with rights and privileges in land to be leased from the state.

The Act also provided for the designation of 'Selected Development Areas' (SDAs)[2] for the purpose of facilitating land acquisition for new residential, commercial, and industrial development, as well as to facilitate upgrading of un-

---

1. The licence as title to urban agricultural land was purposely meant to be an insecure title that could be terminated on three months notice without the need for the state to pay compensation. The rationale was that agricultural land in towns was a transient land use. Since fields had been allocated freely under customary law allottees were expected to freely surrender them to the public sector in the public interest. The licence was repealed in 1986 (see Land (Amendment) Order, 1986, Order No. 27 of 1986).
2. The rural opposite of SDAs are called Selected Agricultural Areas (SAAs), defined as areas of land set aside for the development of agriculture by modern farming methods.

planned urban settlements. The effect of the SDA declaration was to cancel existing rights and interests in land, pending direct grant of substitute leasehold rights by the Minister for Lands.

The Act further provided for the extension of urban area boundaries to cover the problem of peri-urban growth, as well as the declaration of 'new towns' for a similar purpose. It was hoped that the Act would effectively streamline the land delivery system, reduce the loss of agricultural land to illegal urban development and thereby promote orderly urban growth. However, the anticipated regulation did not occur, as a result of various forms of subversion by the state itself, customary authorities and the owners of use rights to peri-urban cropland (field-owners).

MASERU: A BRIEF PROFILE

Maseru was founded in March 1869 as a police camp and the colonial capital during the period of Cape Colony rule and British protection until independence in 1966, when it became the capital of the Kingdom of Lesotho and until 1996, one of the fastest growing towns. Colonial town reserve boundaries were drawn in 1905, and remained unchanged until 1980, when they were extended using powers derived from the Land Act of 1979, to incorporate peri-urban villages that were apparently urbanising fast. Maseru currently occupies an area of approximately 138km², which is almost five times the area originally set apart as a colonial reserve (Figure 1).

Prior to independence, Maseru's growth was well contained within the colonial reserve boundaries. However, it grew relatively rapidly following independence, maintaining an annual growth rate of 7 per cent over the census years of 1966, 1976 and 1986, while smaller towns grew by an annual average of less than 2 per cent. Between 1976 and 1986, national urban population increased by about 67,000 people and Maseru accommodated over 80 per cent of this increase. Between 1986 and 1996, Maseru's annual growth rate dropped to 3.5 per cent.[1] By 1996, it had a population of 140,000 people, which was approximately 44 per cent of the total urban population (Bureau of Statistics 1996).

Similar to other towns, recent urban population growth is accommodated in areas outside the former colonial urban reserve. It is these former peri-urban villages and their recent extensions, which constitute the core of the illegal city, where arable land is illegally subdivided by field-owners under the authority of traditional chiefs. Popular opinion is that individual field-owners are encouraged by their local customary chiefs to sell their agricultural land (fields) or face state appropriation without compensation. In turn chiefs issue certificates of allocation—the Form Cs[2]—to plot buyers (for which chiefs regularly charge a

---

1. Although the Bureau of Statistics does not explain the factors leading to the decline in the growth of Maseru's population, one plausible explanation could be that the Lesotho Highlands Water Project (LHWP) has diverted many rural-urban migrants away from Maseru to the towns within the project's activity corridors, namely Maputsoe and Hlotse, which grew by about 13 and 11 per cent per year respectively between 1986 and 1996 (BOS, 1996).
2. Form Cs are certificates of land allocation that were issued by customary authorities (chiefs) for land that was allocated in rural areas under provisions of the Land Act of 1973, which was repealed by the Land Act of 1979 in June 1980.

fee), backdated to periods prior to June 1980, when the LA 1979 came into force (personal communication, March 1999).[1]

FORMAL RULES IN THE FORMER COLONIAL RESERVE

Generally, the implementation of the LA 1979 can be divided into two phases. Phase I covers from June 1980 to January 1986, when Lesotho was under civilian government. Phase II stretches from 1986 to 1992, when Lesotho was under military rule. The distinguishing feature between these two phases is the method that was predominantly used to make new urban land grants (plots) under the committee system and by the Minister for Lands. Similarly, experiences from the implementation of the LA 1979 differ between those relating to Maseru's former colonial urban reserve and the peri-urban areas that were incorporated into the city's new administrative boundaries in 1980. These phases and implementation experiences are discussed in some detail in the ensuing sections of this chapter.

Phase I: The Committee System (June 1980–December 1985)[2]

In order to monitor the progress of implementation of the new LA 1979, Cabinet instructed the Minister for Lands to submit periodic progress reports. The first report (25 August 1980) alluded only to partial implementation of the Act and a series of activities that had been put together into a programme of action. In the main, the programme covered activities relating to new land grants, title conversions for applicants who intended to transact in land, and specifically those who had prior arrangements for loans or mortgage finance, as well as the designation of areas for selected development (SDAs). Another major policy decision was that, for new land grants by committees, land would first be serviced and thereafter advertized. The aim was to give every individual an equal opportunity to apply for a grant, as well as to make prospective applicants aware of their expected contribution towards the costs of land servicing.

Available records show that in the first two years of implementation, an average of 400 plots per year was potentially available for new grants.[3] During the same period, the number of people that were annually added to the urban population was estimated to be of the order of 6 500 people or 1,350 households (Leduka 1995), given a household size of 4.8 persons (Bureau of Statistics 1996). This means that an average annual supply of 400 plots would have met about 30 per cent of this potential demand for urban housing land. However,

---

1. In order to ensure confidentiality, names to all 'personal communication' references have been withheld, but the full identities of the respondents are available with the author
2. Although declared official policy was to create democratic structures of allocation, this appears not to have been the case with respect to urban land committees, as indicated by their membership:
   a) the Principal Chief within whose jurisdiction an urban area falls, who is to act as chairman (sic);
   b) the District Administrator or Town Clerk as secretary to the Committee;
   c) three persons appointed by the Minister (LA 1979, Section 24[2]).
3. These plots are considered to have been potentially available for committee allocation because some of them were ultimately allocated by the Minister for Lands and not the committees.

Figure 1. Marseru Urban Area

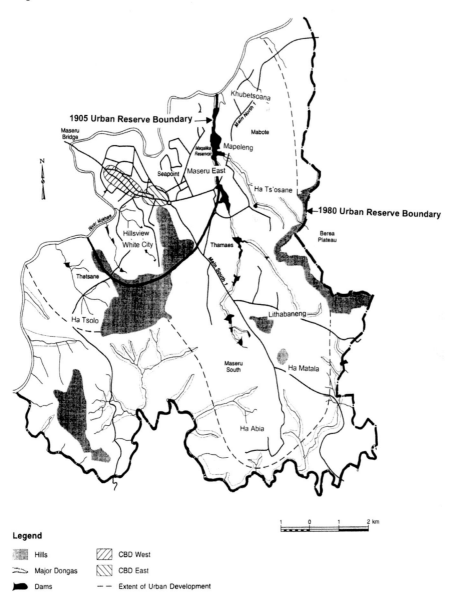

Legend

- Hills
- Major Dongas
- Dams
- CBD West
- CBD East
- − − Extent of Urban Development

Source of original figure: Romaa and Brown 1999.

even this estimate is unrealistic, since it implicitly assumes that, when the LA 1979 came into force, there was no backlog of demand for urban residential plots. It came as no surprise, therefore, when early in 1983, Cabinet concluded that the policy of advertising plots only after services had been provided had stalled the land delivery process and had to be discontinued, and with it the requirement for periodic reports.

The latest available general reports (1993) show that from June 1980 to September 1991, 10,237 new land grants, or 780 plots per year,[1] were made (although the authority that made the grants is not specified) and that 2,884 of these or 28 per cent, had registered titles. In 1991, annual demand by the urban population for registered titles was estimated at 75,000,[2] and, the LSPP had aimed to process at least 10 per cent (7,500) of this annual demand. However, the LSPP was only able to register less than 10 per cent (750) of this target per year, which represented less than 1 per cent of estimated demand for registered titles. With respect to title conversions by those who were surrendering their old titles in favour of the LA 1979 leaseholds, it is shown that since June 1980, 11,000 applications had been received and 4,900 (45 per cent) leasehold documents had been issued by the middle of 1991 (LSPP Archives, File Ref. INT/LS/9/17), which represents an average of 445 title conversions per year. By the LSPP's own admission, measured against targets, their performance "presented a sorry picture" (LSPP Archives, File Ref: INT/LS/9/17, 1993:no page).

Phase II: Direct Ministerial Grants (1986–1992)

Direct grants were possible through the use of SDA powers that the Minister derived from Part V, Sections 44 and 49 of the LA 1979.[3] According to Mosaase (1984) and Bruce (1984), these clauses were conceived in order to achieve specific policy objectives, such as the development or reconstruction of existing built-up areas (upgrading); construction or development of new residential, commercial or industrial areas; readjustment of town boundaries for purposes of town planning and belatedly, the correction of defective titles. However, someone fortuitously discovered that SDA powers could be used to make new grants to virtually anyone as long as a 'public interest' declaration was made, which was left to the sole discretion of the Minister for Lands to define.

---

1. If averaged over this entire period, the production of plots appears higher than it actually was, due to grants made under projects such as Mabote, where grants were made outside established formal channels (committees and Minister). It, therefore, represents a distorted picture of the land delivery under formal rule systems.
2. The CLO's estimated demand seems rather odd because between the 1966 and 1986 census years, urban population grew by an addition at about 7,000 people per year, and by about 13,000 per year between 1986 and 1996. An estimated demand for 75,000 registered titles per year, therefore, seems to have no rational basis. For example, there were 10,237 new land grants between June 1980 and mid-1991 that automatically had to be registered, and 11,000 applications for title conversion over the same period. Based on these figures, actual urban demand for registered titles over this period (11 years) works out to approximately 1,900 ($\cong$2,000) titles per annum.
3. Section 44 of the LA 1979 provides that:
   Where it appears to the Minister in the public interest so to do for purposes of selected development, the Minister may, by notice in the Gazette declare any area of land to be a selected development area and, thereupon all titles to land within the area shall be extinguished but substitute rights may be granted as provided under this Part.
   Section 49 provides further that:
   Titles to land within a selected development area shall be granted by the Minister and shall be evidenced by a lease, which shall be prepared by the Commissioner and executed in the manner prescribed.

A question, therefore, arises as to how the SDA clause came to serve a purpose that was obviously not anticipated when it was originally conceived. A narrative by one respondent, a former senior employee of the LSPP, shows that when the LA 1979 came into force on the eve of 16 June 1980, committees and procedural rules for allocation were not in place. As a result, land allocation was suspended for some time while preparations were in progress. However, there were people who could not wait or be made to wait, as well as those who felt that the Minister could, in the meantime, allocate land on a one-to-one basis, as he used to do in the past, a ministerial privilege that the LA 1979 had apparently overlooked. However, having carefully scrutinized the Act, the ODA's (British Overseas Development Administration, which is now the Department for International Development–DFID) Advisor to the Commissioner of Lands came across the SDA clause and realized that if land was declared a selected area in the public interest, existing interests in that land would be nullified and that only the Minister would thereafter have power to make direct grants. According to the respondent, although the initial idea was to use the clause only as a temporary measure, over time, it became a permanent feature of the implementation process, because

> Ministers began to enjoy it and the demand for land was there. And when the Ministers started enjoying it, people assumed the law was designed for that purpose, and it took time to get Ministers to drop it and only following terrible abuses, especially by all those Ministers who were also chiefs. They were the worst culprits … . (Personal communication, Maseru, March 1999.)

How then can we explain the apparent misuse of what was a well-intended legal instrument? This phase marks a period when the military took control of the state apparatus and initially honoured the monarchy with legislative and executive power as a legitimization strategy. Although the monarchy-military coalition was short-lived (Mothibe 1998), the King swiftly seized this opportunity to appoint members of his family and close friends to Cabinet positions, including his uncle as Minister for Lands. Therefore, customary chiefs, especially senior ones, were overnight thrown into the political and economic limelight, and in terms of land administration, the SDA clause became a perfect instrument that customary chiefs could use to reassert their control over the distribution of urban land. In describing the use of the SDA clause, one Maseru legal practitioner had this to say:

> Direct grants deprived lawful allocation structures of their power to do so [allocate land] … .This is because the Minister who took control then [1986] was not only a senior chief and senior member of the royal household, but was equally a staunch traditionalist who believed that the right to allocate land in Lesotho had never and would never be a commoner's role. The functions of committees were, therefore, taken over by the person who should have been the custodian of the law. (Personal communication, Maseru, April 1999.)

Many respondents suggested that the absence of criteria by which to choose between applicants in making grants by allocation committees and the Minister left too much room for discretionary decisions. For instance, according to one senior civil servant, in a typical committee interview, it was not unusual for an applicant to be asked questions that had nothing to do with the subject of the interview. This particular respondent indicated that in one of the committee meetings that he attended as an observer,

> ... applicants would be asked questions such as: Whose child are you? Do you know me? I used to work with your father! and so forth, and not a single question would relate to land development or matters of the interview. But then committee members believe that questions such as these actually assist them in choosing who qualifies for a grant ... . (Personal communication, March, 1999.)

However, despite claims that there were no criteria by which to choose between applicants, a close scrutiny of the above extract shows that criteria exist, although they neither derive from the LA 1979 nor the rules of procedure of allocation committees, because none of these rules specify such criteria. A complex permutation of rules of allocation is, therefore, possible. For example, the question 'Whose child are you?' could mean a lot of things: Is your parent someone whom I (committee member) might not wish offend by denying you land? Or is he/she someone from whom I might expect something in return?

Criteria for Minister's grants would seem to have been essentially similar. One respondent observed that "if I was a poor man ... who never greeted the Minister or did not know how to get access to him, then I would never be allocated any land" (personal communication, March 1999). To yet another respondent, "the Minister's office was not like a post-office, where anyone could just go" (personal communication, March 1999). Therefore, the first criterion, seemed to be access to the Minister or his office, which could only be secured through means that the Minister knew or were known to those who kept constant watch over his office. The second was that apparently one had to be a Minister's crony, or be a crony of the Minister's other cronies, since it was only through such connections that access to the Minister was possible. It is in view of these many possibilities that one respondent concluded that "invariably those who already have land, who are known to have land, who are slightly higher in rank in society, these are the people who are always favoured" (personal communication, March, 1999). It appears equally legitimate to conclude that, as the process of land allocation under formal rules draws closer to the actual act of making a land grant, it degenerates into personalized relations of reciprocity that are supported by informal *ad hoc* acts of exchange.

Therefore, while formal rules established by the LA 1979 stalled the land delivery system, so-called illegal subdivision and allocation of land under informal rules in the former peri-urban areas was gaining momentum, and to a majority of would-be plot-owners, informal systems became the only source of plots on which to build a house or invest in rental units. Non-compliant strategies by customary chiefs and landowners, therefore, became significant in the process, as discussed in detail below.

FORMAL RULES IN THE FORMER PERI-URBAN AREAS

As indicated earlier, Maseru's colonial reserve boundaries were extended in 1980 using powers derived from the LA 1979 to enclose hitherto peri-urban village areas that were experiencing the greatest pressures of urban expansion. Whereas residential plots that were allocated by committees and the Minister were confined almost exclusively to areas within the former colonial urban reserve boundaries, for residential plots within the former peri-urban areas, a slightly different approach was adopted, the SDA approach, which is discussed in detail below.

In his first progress report tabled before Cabinet in August 1980, the Minister for Lands had indicated that over and above preparations for new land grants and title conversions, work was in progress to designate certain areas in Maseru for purposes of selected development under the SDA provisions of the LA 1979. One of these areas was Mapeleng/Maqalika Reservoir (Figure 1).

The Mapeleng selected development area (SDA) was meant to provide substitute plots to people who had been displaced from the immediate perimeter of the Maqalika Reservoir, which had recently been commissioned as a main water supply source for the city. In order to prevent possible pollution, residential development in the immediate perimeter of the reservoir was to be prohibited, and approximately 300 plots were provided for the purpose of resettling plot-owners who had already been allocated land by chiefs and field-owners. The Minister initially granted about 200 resettlement plots, but soon a chain of claims for substitute plots came forth, even from people who never had land in the vicinity of the water reservoir. Each of these claims was evidenced by a Form C, duly bearing the chief's official stamp, although backdated to periods prior to June 1980. However, not every claimant was able to relate his/her certificate to a specific piece of land around the reservoir. The resettlement process was temporarily suspended in order to restore order, but when it appeared impossible to do so, the resettlement was quietly dropped. In his last report to Cabinet (1982), the Commissioner of Lands had openly admitted that the Mapeleng area was being invaded illegally, thwarting plans for orderly development and that without tough measures to restore order, such plans would soon become meaningless. The report had also added that some of the individuals who had been given substitute plots at Mapeleng were re-occupying or selling their former plots around the Maqalika reservoir (Mosaase 1984).

Non-compliant strategies that were adopted by actors involved in clandestine subdivisions at Mapeleng are nowhere captured as neatly as in a 1982 report to the Permanent Secretary of the Ministry of the Interior (then responsible for Lands) by the then Deputy Commissioner of Lands. The report relates to Lithabaneng (another erstwhile peri-urban neighbourhood) and the Mapeleng/Maqalika SDA. It states that:

> Some of the land which has recently been allocated [by the chief] was being prepared for certain projects which both the Planning Division (LSPP) and the Ministry of Agriculture (Woodlot) have agreed (sic). Corner posts [fence poles] have been placed to mark the boundaries of this newly allocated land and the marks on the concrete show "May, 1979". We, however, have prove (sic) that this land in question was not allocated in May 1979 nor were the corner posts placed then. (LSPP Archives, File Ref. INT/LS/9/21, 1982: no page)

Interestingly, the inscription of dates and reference codes on concrete bench-marks that mark property boundaries is a practice of government cadastral surveyors, which was, by the look of things, adopted by the local people to good effect. For Mapeleng, the report pointedly shows that "land allocations are within the selected development area...[and]...are done at night, over the weekends and during holidays, as was the case on the 1st, 2nd and 3rd May, 1982" (LSPP Archives, File Ref: INT/LS/9/21, 1982: no page).

The report then proceeds to identify actors or, according to the reporting officer, the 'culprits':

> Most people who were shown or allocated sites on those dates seemed to come from the Republic of South Africa [although] (they may be Basotho working in R.S.A). ... On the 3rd May, the Khubetsoana chief was showing new allottees sites and one of the allottees was driving a green Mercedes Benz with O.G. registration numbers[1]. ... It is further rumoured that some of the new allottees are members of the Interim National Assembly [although] of course this still has to be investigated and a more detailed report to be (sic) submitted. (LSPP Archives, File Ref. INT/LS/9/21, 1982: no page)

This report is significant in many respects, least of which being the apparent distress that the reporting officer obviously felt about what his/her espionage into erstwhile peri-urban territory revealed. First, it shows strategies that people adopted in order to assert rights to what they considered to be their legitimate property (agricultural fields), including rights to dispose of such property according to the dictates of the market that they understand best, even if it was a clandestine market (Mosaase 1984; Theko 1998). Second, it illustrates the strategies that people adopted in order to gain access to housing land when formal rules appeared to impede such access. Third, it demonstrates that such strategies might often mimic official land parcelling practice, in this case, survey practice. Fourth, it shows that 'clandestine' subdivision strategies aim to avoid direct confrontation with the state law enforcement machinery, as well as to ensure that some degree of anonymity and safety is guaranteed. This explains why subdivisions are usually at their peak during the odd hours of the day (night) or during weekends and public holidays, when the enforcement machinery of the state is less likely to intervene. Fifth, although the report shrewdly attempts to absolve members of parliament from direct involvement in clandestine land markets, it provides an interesting account of the actors involved: chiefs, field-owners, migrant workers,[2] people of above average wealth, as well as members of the National Assembly—the law-makers themselves. "If the law-maker violates the law, then people will follow the lead!" quipped a respondent (personal communication, Maseru, March 1999).

Two former LSPP senior officers who were directly involved in the implementation of the Act, were particularly outspoken with respect to the role of state employees in relentlessly working against effective implementation of the LA 1979, especially junior officers who were constantly in contact with the pub-

---

1. These are the old vehicle registration letters for the town of Ficksburg in South Africa.
2. Since prior allegiance to a chief is no longer a prerequisite for land allocation, it is possible that South African citizens were also able to buy land in Lesotho, as some of them might have held dual citizenship.

lic. The reason, as seen by these two respondents, was (and probably still is) that these officers derived benefits by way of unofficial income:[1]

> People in government, and those specifically charged with the responsibility of implementing and enforcing the Act, the street-level bureaucrats, were themselves buying and selling land outside there [former peri-urban areas] and even replenishing the chiefs' supply of Form Cs when their stationery had run out. (Personal communication, Maseru, March 1999)

However, it transpired from the interviews that the Form C racket was much more complex than was ever thought in that it involved not only the duplication of Form Cs in the LSPP office, but also the Government Printers, where new Form C booklets were printed for distribution to the customary chiefs. "When the beneficiaries of the Form Cs are the very civil servants who should be upholding the law, then you realize that you are in deep trouble!" quipped yet another respondent (personal communication, Maseru, March, 1999).

Another area that was declared an SDA in 1984, is a 640-hectare site at Ha Mabote,[2] which is adjacent to the Khubetsoana World Bank low-income housing project area, where land was taken without compensation for the project (Figure 1). Devas argues that the development of Ha Mabote was thus set in motion by the experiences at Khubetsoana:[3]

> When the field-owners in Mabote area (which at that stage was virtually undeveloped) saw that their neighbours in Khubetsoana had lost their land without compensation, they feared the same fate and rushed to sub-divide their fields and sell plots for private development. (Devas 1989:210)

Indeed, as Devas (1989) suggests, government had to act, and in 1984 Ha Mabote was declared a selected area. Project activities commenced in September of the same year under the co-sponsorship of the British Overseas Development Administration (ODA) and the Lesotho government. Although the project was initially conceived as a site-and-service scheme, it ended up as a form of 'guided development' that aimed "to work with—rather than ignore the existing processes of private subdivision" (Devas 1989:211).

However, Theko (1998) sees illegal subdivision at Ha Mabote as having been "triggered by the anger of the traditional leaders following the usurpation of their authority" (1998:10) and not, as Devas (1989 above) and this author would argue, by the appropriation of land without compensation at Khubetsoana across the road. Nevertheless, whatever factors lie behind the illegal devel-

---

1. This unofficial income regularly takes the form of cash for 'lunch', and it is not uncommon to see junior officers discretely accompanying clients (members of the public) through the LSPP main gate to their cars where cash would quickly exchange hands as a 'thank you', either for successfully negotiating a client's request for service quickly through the bureaucratic red-tape or in lieu of a 'promise' to do so.
2. The author was a member of the counterpart team that was seconded by the LSPP to the project when it was launched in 1984–1985, and participated in the feasibility studies commissioned by the ODA, as well as the compilation of an inventory of land allocations by chiefs. The author is, therefore, reasonably conversant with many of the issues involved.
3. The area known as Mabote Project includes arable land belonging to three villages, Khubetsoana, Ha Mabote and Sekamaneng and some of the people of Khubetsoana village who lost their land to the low-income project, also had land in the area falling under the Mabote Project and had, therefore, lost land once and were apparently not willing to lose it for the second time.

opment at Ha Mabote, experiences from the implementation process are interesting in their own right because they illustrate how chiefs and their subjects were able to cope with onerous state rules: first, by threatening to mobilize the state's own oppressive apparatus, the army,[1] when forced removal was imminent; second, by manipulating the project to their advantage through 'false compliance' (Scott 1985), which was made possible by the indeterminacies of formal rules, as well as inconsistencies in state enforcement methods.

According to Theko (1998), following the declaration of Ha Mabote as a selected area in 1984, the Minister for Lands was advised to remove illegal occupations from the project area. However, while preparations for eviction were in progress, one of the chiefs of the area had secretly informed the army that the price of plots in her area had been reduced to a quarter of the then going price (US$400 to US$100 for a 900m^2 plot). "Her aim, she discloses, was to ensure that government would find the place too hot to touch... .[And] on the morning that trucks and convict labour [prisoners] were being assembled for action on the site, the Minister [for Lands] called off the process" (Theko 1998:14) in response to a directive from the office of the Prime Minister. It was thereafter decided that illegal allocations would be accepted and regularized. According to Theko (1998) chiefs and their subjects accepted the project only after a pledge that existing subdivisions would be recognized, with the price to land owners being reduced plot sizes that would result from the re-planning process.

However, from the author's personal experience, Theko (1998) stops short of indicating further that in order to sell the project to the Ha Mabote field-owners and their chiefs, the executing officers did not only deliberately ignore on-going illegal subdivisions, but as an additional sweetener, actually encouraged field-owners who had not sub-divided, to do so quickly whilst allowing for road reserves to be demarcated.

Theko (1998) argues, therefore, that chiefs embraced the project not because of benefits that were likely to accrue from it, but only as a ploy to focus demand for housing land on their area and were thereby able to extract the greatest pecuniary benefits. To the chiefs, these benefits were fees for backdated allocation certificates (about US$20 in 1984/85 prices for each certificate) and a plot from every field sub-divided for the chief to sell for him/herself (Theko 1998).

Although Theko's (1998) observation is legitimate, it does not tell the whole story. To this author, it would seem that chiefs and land-owners merely took advantage of the inconsistencies that are inherent in formal rules, which, in some cases, recognized certificates provided under repealed law as evidence of valid allocation and withheld similar recognition in other cases.[2] Therefore, with so much room for manoeuvre, chiefs, field-owners and their clients did not only

---

1. The army has been described by many as unruly and easily corruptible (see, for example, Matlosa, 1999).

2. For example, to legally register an illegally acquired plot of land under the LA 1979 (Section 22(1)(c)) requires a Form C, with or without a supporting letter from a chief, or a sworn affidavit from a local chief or three people who have resided in the area in question for at least 30 years. The irony here is that most people who purchase plots from illegal subdivisions are recent in-migrants and, therefore, people with 30 years of continuous residence are none other than the field-owners themselves [see Section 21(1) (c) of the Land Act of 1979].

rush the subdivision process, but it soon became possible for people to buy certificates of allocation that did not relate to any plot of land, as well as numerous certificates relating to a single plot, leaving it to the project to accommodate such excesses. Unfortunately for the project, the emerging chaos (Theko 1998:16), which the project management could not resolve, forced the ODA to withdraw its support and consequently the infrastructure component of the project collapsed.

Devas (1989) observes, however, that despite the technical problems that confronted the implementation of the project, it was by working with, rather than against existing property interests that the Mabote Project achieved some success in ensuring a rational layout of plots. Indeed, when the project was changed to a department of Urban Development Services (UDS) in 1990, it had provided 3,600 planned sites for a beneficiary population of 18,360 people (4,400 households). This represents an average of 900 plots per year over four years (1986–1990), quite a feat compared to the committee system and the direct grants by the Minister for Lands. Theko concludes, and correctly so, that, "[i]n the end, it was not the designation of the area as a Selected Development Area that allowed the project to work, but it was the patience with negotiations and the readiness to adapt to prevailing circumstances" (1998:16). However, Theko (1998) appears reluctant to equally acknowledge that the initial implementation of the project was a hazardous undertaking, in which the executing officers had to endure incessant verbal and physical abuses from field owners. Therefore, over and above painstaking negotiations and readiness to adapt to existing circumstances, it is fitting to indicate that there was equally a risk premium that had to be paid as a price for people's compliance.

CONCLUSIONS

The aim of this chapter was to show how formal and informal rules of the game are implicated in the development of the so-called illegal city. This aim was achieved by examining how the rules govern access to urban housing land. In the main, the chapter has shown that formal state rules have impeded the delivery of urban housing land and that, as a result of unmet demand, coupled with the non-payment of compensation for land that the state acquired for public projects, the growth of the illegal city through illegal private subdivision of hitherto peri-urban land has proliferated. In addition, formal rules have been shown to be arbitrary and inconsistently enforced, which has rendered the formal land delivery system less reliable than alternative systems. However, disadvantaged individuals have not been the only active actors in the creation of the illegal city, nor have informal rules been the overriding rules. As the chapter shows, state employees and legislators have all been part of the process and have taken advantage of the ambiguity of both formal and informal rules. It, therefore, seems plausible to conclude that the illegal city is a manifestation of the interplay of formal and informal rules and actors.

Using non-compliance as a conceptual foundation to explain the coping strategies of actors faced with enforcement of formal rules, the chapter has dem onstrated the deployment of silent protest by field-owners whose land was appropriated without compensation, as well as by prospective plot owners who found it difficult to negotiate the land delivery system established by formal state rules. The study has, for instance, demonstrated the potency of false compliance, such as the backdated Form Cs and sabotage, such as allocating land under cover of darkness or over the weekends and public holidays. As a result of these non-compliant strategies, disadvantaged groups of plot-seekers and field-owners, assisted by their chiefs, have been able to extract substantial concessions from the state and to engender significant changes in formal state rules.

References

Bruce, John, W., 1984, "A Layman's Guide to the Land Act 1979", in *Proceedings: The Land Act 1979 Policy Review Seminar*, pp. 52–54. Maseru: Ministry of Local Government.

Bureau of Statistics (BOS), 1996, *Population Census Analytical Report, Vol. IIIA: Population Dynamics*. Maseru.

Devas, Nick, 1989, "The Evolution of Urban Housing Projects in Lesotho: The Tale of 5 Schemes", *Land Use Policy* 6:203–216.

Directorate of Lands, Surveys and Physical Planning (LSPP), *Various Files (Archives), 1999 Search*. Maseru.

Durand-Lasserve, Alain and Valerie Clerc, 1996, *Regulation and Integration of Irregular Settlements: Lessons from Experience*. Working Paper 6. Washington: UMP UNDP/ UNCHS (Habitat)/ World Bank.

Government of Lesotho, 1991, *Maputsoe Planning Study*. Maseru.

—, 1979, *The Land Act 1979*, Act No. 17 of 1979. Maseru: Government Printers.

Kombe, Wilbard and Kreibich, Volker, 2000, *Informal Land Management in Tanzania*. Spring Research Series 29. University of Dortmund, Faculty of Spatial Planning, Dortmund.

Leduka, Clement R., 1998, "Law and the Social Production of Urban Space: A Case for Critical Legal Geography in Sub-Saharan Africa (SSA)", *Lesotho Law Journal* 1:1–24.

—, 1995, "Land policy in post-independence Lesotho with special reference to the urban sector", *National University of Lesotho Journal of Research 5*, pp. 1–43.

Matlosa, Khabele, 1999, "Conflict and Conflict Management: Lesotho's Political Crisis after the 1998 Elections". Paper presented to a Regional Conference on "The Lesotho Crisis", SAPES, Maseru, 5–6 February.

McAuslan, Patrick, 1998, "Urbanization, Law and Development: A Record of Research" in Fernandes, Edesio and Ann Varley (eds,) *Illegal Cities*, pp. 18–52. London and New York: Zed Books.

Mosaase, Abner, 1984, "Experiences from Implementation of the Land Act 1979 in Urban Areas", *Proceedings: The Land Act 1979 Policy Review Seminar*, pp. 55–67. Maseru: Ministry of Local Government.

Mothibe, Tefetso, H., 1998, "The Military and the 1994 Constitutional Crisis: A Question of Trust?", *Review of Southern African Studies* 2:1–23.

Razzaz, Omar, 1998, "Land Disputes in the Absence of Ownership Rights: Insights from Jordan", in Fernandes, Edesio and Ann Varley (eds), *Illegal Cities*, pp. 69–88. London and New York: Zed Books.

—, 1994, "Contestation and Mutual Adjustment: The Process of Controlling Land in Yajouz, Jordan", *Law and Society Review* 28:7–39.

Romaya, Sam and Alison Brown, 1990, "City Profile: Maseru", *Cities* 16:123–33.

Scott, James C., 1987, "Resistance without Protest and without Organization: Peasant Opposition to Islamic Zakat and the Christian Tithe", *Journal for Comparative Study of Society and History* 29:417–52.

—, 1985, *The Weapons of the Weak: Everyday Forms of Peasant Resistance.* New Haven and London: Yale University Press.

Theko, Makalo, 1998, *Example of Best Practice: Mabote Project.* Maseru: Urban Development Services.

Tripp, Aili Mari, 1997, *Changing the Rules: The Political Economy of Liberalization and the Urban Informal Economy in Tanzania.* London and Los Angeles: University of California Press.

CHAPTER 11

Upgrading an Informal Settlement in Cape Town, South Africa

John Abbott

This chapter reports on a pilot project which began as a desk study of informal settlement upgrading, but which subsequently led to the development of Cape Town's first pilot *in situ* upgrading programme.[1] Obtaining support for the upgrading programme from both the local authority and the community was remarkably easy. However, it quickly became clear that the reason for this was due in both cases to a rather simplistic, and certainly idealized view of what constituted upgrading. Furthermore, the two sets of perceptions were quite different. This highlighted the importance of creating a partnership between the community and the local authority. At the same time, it also highlighted the need for flexibility and change on the part of the local authority. The way to achieve this was seen to be through the creation of a shared vision. What this means in practice is building a shared understanding of upgrading as a settlement transformation process, rather than a series of short-term *ad hoc* interventions. To date the discussion has focused on the community and the local authority. In reality there are also other actors whose views are important, and the process of changing perceptions had to be extended to them also.

The settlement to be upgraded is an area called New Rest, which is a well-located settlement occupying 18ha of land, and situated approximately 12km from the centre of Cape Town.

There are many different ways of approaching informal settlement upgrading (see Abbott 2002a, b, for a discussion of this). This project is probably the first outside of Latin America to draw heavily upon the Brazilian experience of upgrading, and in particular the experience of Belo Horizonte. Here, the improvement of infrastructure and shelter was supplemented by social and economic development interventions (see Abbott et al. 2001). The nature of informal settlements in Latin America is quite different to that of, say, African cities. The majority are located in pockets of urban land surrounded by or adjacent to formal areas. Furthermore, although informal settlements may be extensive, the formal areas still comprise the major part of the city. This compares to the situation (in Dar Es Salaam for example) where informal settlements may occupy the major part of the city, and the formal serviced area is reduced virtu-

---

1. The term programme is used here to describe a comprehensive set of actions that comprise both specific projects and development processes.

ally to a core. South African cities, in the main, follow the Latin American model, although Durban has elements of both types. In addition South African cities have an economic profile and technical support base similar to Latin American cities.

An important element of Brazilian informal settlements which is replicated, albeit to a lesser extent in South African cities, is their insulation from the surrounding formal areas. This exclusion from the rest of the city covers physical exclusion, through the absence of any infrastructure and services, spatial exclusion, through the creation of hard boundaries, and social exclusion. Within that context, a crucial element of informal settlement upgrading was seen to be what was termed 'the integration of the informal city' (Recife International Meeting on Urban Poverty, 1996, section 6). The New Rest programme has attempted to place that concept at the centre of the upgrading process. In doing so, it has sought to explore the full range of relationships between the formal and the informal, arguing that settlement upgrading was primarily about social and economic development rather than physical development, although the latter was perceived initially to be the dominant issue. This then highlighted the importance of exploring spatial development from within the context of institutional change. In turn, this meant that the project had to overcome a widespread scepticism concerning the need for informal settlement upgrading. It was present at all levels of government and in neighbouring settlements.

Based upon the New Rest experience it is argued that the creation of an effective interface between the formal and the informal city is determined by two distinct issues, which may appear to be different roots, but which are actually interlinked. The first issue could be described as institutional, in that it relates to the perception of different actors in the formal city, and the need to change these perceptions. The second issue is that of social-spatial relationships, which in turn is related to the upgrading process itself.

During the pilot project, we identified three different levels which may constitute barriers to integration in the formal city. These were found at the level of local politicians, with the officials of the local authority and in the surrounding settlements. It was first necessary to convince the political authorities of the need to recognize the permanence of informal settlements, and thence create a climate for the political acceptance of upgrading. It was working with the officials of the local authority that turned out to be the most difficult and complex. This was due mainly to the fact that there were different professionals involved, each of whom had a different perspective and a different set of priorities. Success was achieved at this level by gaining acceptance that the choice of an area for upgrading should be based upon residents' support for upgrading rather than the physical condition of the area. It was problematic because it was in conflict with the local authority's statutory obligation to reduce physical risk and provide services. We also obtained acceptance in principle for a method-based approach based upon long-term goals of social and economic development, even if such an approach cut across more traditional sector-based interventions which underpin current practice and many of the accepted norms by which professionals operate.

At the third level, that of residents, the key turned out to be the creation, with the community, of a spatially integrative physical development plan, that allows people both inside and outside the settlement to begin to see the informal settlement as part of the formal city. A major problem with informal settlement upgrading is that the focus is turned inwards, towards what needs to be done. Often this is incremental, and while it may have a major impact on the quality of life of residents, it will not necessarily impact on those outside the settlement, nor on their perceptions. Thus they will continue to see the area as an informal settlement and therefore problematic. The way to address this issue is for those living in the settlement to have a long-term vision of settlement transformation, which they can impart to their neighbours.

The sections that follow expand on this concept of changing perceptions. This in turn lays the foundation for the creation of a structured (method-based) integrated approach to informal settlement upgrading.

THE POLITICAL CONTEXT

The South African Constitution of 1996 identifies three distinct levels of government, National, Provincial and Local, and defines the role of each of them in the governing of local areas. It does not, however, define the organizational structure of government, which is the prerogative of National Government. Until 1990, South African cities and towns were divided along racial lines, both spatially and institutionally. With the unbanning of the ANC in 1990 the integration of urban areas became a high priority. However, this could not be achieved in a single step, if there was to be democratic government at a local level by 1994, the time of the first national democratic election. Hence the transformation of local government in South Africa was planned as a three-phase process. The first phase would provide for joint councils, from the previous White and Black Local Authorities. The second phase was the creation of interim local government structures in 1996–2000, which sought to provide spatially functional and integrated urban areas with representative local government. The third phase, complete with elections in December 2000, concentrated on geographical rationalization and consolidation, which reduced the number of local authorities as well as the number of councillors.

The result has been a series of major changes in the political and institutional landscape. The large metropolitan centres, including Cape Town, have moved from joint councils, through a two-tier structure, to the current single tier metropolitan authority model. In the two-tier system, the powers and duties of local government had been divided between a metropolitan authority and area-based metropolitan local authorities. In all cities except Cape Town the two tier structure was hierarchical, in that the metropolitan authority was clearly responsible for planning and development functions across the entire area, and local authorities had to operate within this wider framework. In Cape Town however, the situation was different. Nominally, the broad division of responsibilities applied. The problem was that the relationship was not hierarchical. Rather, the (Cape) Metropolitan Council (CMC), the metropolitan authority, was seen as 'first among equals', a situation that gave the six Metropolitan Local Councils (MLCs) a great deal of autonomy. The net result was that the division of responsibility became a more practical one, whereby the metropolitan authority took responsibility for bulk services while the MLCs were responsible for local planning and service delivery. The result was extensive duplication in areas such as housing and social services.

The change to a single tier should therefore have provided an opportunity for rationalization. In the other cities this was the case. For a mixture of political and administrative reasons, in Cape Town, the process has been extremely slow, with the result that almost two years after the elections for a single tier authority (December 2000) the city had still not achieved a comprehensive restructuring of staff and functions.

All of this has had a major impact on the debate about how to deal with informal settlements. On the one hand, there have been changing political groupings with different views on the issue. In addition, decisions relating to these settlements involve both the Provincial Government, which has overall responsibility for housing, and the two tiers of interim local government. Furthermore, all three tiers used a system of government that separates the political and administrative functions. The political structure at the provincial level is controlled by a Cabinet, at the local government level by an Executive Committee. The administrative structure is managed by a Director General at the provincial level, and by a Chief Executive Officer at the metropolitan level (CMC) or City Manager at the municipal level (MLC). This is extremely relevant to the current discussion, since much of the experience described here took place under that interim structure. This meant that there were six sets of external parties that played a role in the development of informal settlements in Cape Town, and acceptance had to be obtained, to differing degrees, from all of them. It then had to be re-negotiated with the new political and administrative structures. So the outcome is the result of a complex and fluid governance framework.

BACKGROUND TO THE PROJECT

The original goal of the project was to explore the general applicability of a methodology for settlement upgrading to the South African situation. This methodology had been developed in the Brazilian city of Belo Horizonte, and was based on the following principles:

– There would be the absolute minimum of relocation of dwellings, based upon the need to reduce physical risk (primarily flooding) and create a sustainable, long-term movement/access network.

– The upgrading programme would be a partnership between the community and the local authority.

– Development would be demand driven and recognize the centrality of social and economic development.

– The upgrading programme would seek to retain the social integrity of the settlement.

- There would be opportunities for relocation for those families not wishing to stay in the area.
- Internal relocation, and the final layout of dwellings, would be decided by the residents.

The initial project began in 1996 as a collaborative exercize between the Department of Civil Engineering at the University of Cape Town (UCT), the United Nations Centre for Human Settlements (UNCHS–Habitat), and the Water Research Commission of South Africa (WRC). The City of Cape Town, which is the metropolitan local council containing the majority of informal settlements in Cape Town, supported the study in principle and agreed to provide all necessary background and supporting information on their area.

The preparatory discussions emphasized the necessity to address the needs of informal settlements through a structured approach to *in situ* upgrading. Initially the emphasis was placed upon the spatial element, and specifically the need to develop the use of Geospatial Information Management Systems (GIMS) for settlement upgrading. The objective was to use the development of the GIMS as the basis for a broader methodology for *in situ* upgrading. This is seen as important for a number of reasons. A multi-pronged upgrading approach is dependent upon a large amount of information being available. By capturing this information in a geographic information system, it becomes easier to manage, being spatially referenced, it is easily updated, and moves the settlement planning process close to real time, in the sense that decisions are made based upon the situation at that point in time as opposed to being based on historical information. This approach is empowering for communities, because it gives them access to information about their settlement and it assists them in decision-making, because it makes use of a visual medium of communication.

The need for an accelerated programme of this type, which runs implementation of the programme together with the development of a methodology, was given impetus by the severity of the housing crisis in Cape Town. There was a need to explore alternative methods of housing delivery in order to speed up the overall delivery process. The term methodology is used here to describe a structured approach to a multifaceted intervention, which identifies the key elements, both products and processes, and structures them in such a way that they lead to a definable outcome, and defines them in such a way as to make the approach replicable.

The objective of the original desk study was quite specific. This was to explore whether the approach to informal settlement upgrading then being developed in Belo Horizonte, Brazil, and known as Visual Settlement Planning (ViSP) could be applied to South African cities. This required an in-depth study of the ViSP approach as well as an international review of informal settlement upgrading. As this research progressed during 1996, and work on the development of the wider methodology began, it became clear that there was some commonality, and that sufficient information and expertise existed to begin the implementation of an upgrading programme, in parallel with the ongoing development of the methodology.

In July 1996 a series of meetings was held with AVSI (Associazione Volontari per il Servizio Internatiozionale/ Voluntary Association for International Service) the major NGO working on the Belo Horizonte *in situ* upgrading project, and the University of Bologna, as well as the UNCHS. These confirmed the viability of moving towards an implementation phase, drawing upon the experiences of Belo Horizonte. A presentation of the Belo Horizonte experience and the UCT work was made to the City of Cape Town Municipality on 31 July 1996. This presentation was favourably received, and the Council requested UCT to develop the ideas in greater detail. The first step was to open discussions with SANCO (the South African National Civics Association) in Gugulethu, a major locus for informal settlements in Cape Town. Arising from these discussions, a number of informal settlements were identified as suitable for the programme and approaches were made to the communities to explain the concept of *in situ* upgrading and see if there was a sufficient level of interest to take the process forward.

This was an interesting exercise in its own right. There is an accepted wisdom, certainly among development NGOs and academics, that 'communities should decide their development priorities'. But how do residents of settlements learn about alternatives? It was found in these discussions that the residents did not even know that there was an option of *in situ* upgrading. All of them were waiting for the government to provide houses.

The level of interest in *in situ* upgrading varied quite widely. Finally, the adjacent settlements of Kanana and New Rest were chosen as programme pilot areas as they had expressed the greatest interest in the concept and created development committees (of their own accord) to take the process forward. This led to an extensive community consultation process, to initiate the programme, which began in August 1997.

At the same time, a proposal was prepared and presented to the Municipality's Housing Committee (a committee of the Council) which in March 1997 passed a resolution giving conditional support to the New Rest component of the programme as an officially recognized pilot project. Following the discussions within the New Rest settlement, a feasibility study proposal was prepared, submitted to the Council, and formally adopted in December 1997. New Rest had then 1,250 dwellings with an average of 4 persons per dwelling. For more information about the settlement, see Abott 1996.

This background already brings out some key issues. The first is the slow pace of change. Here was a Council that recognized the need to deal with the informal settlements in a positive manner. Yet it took 18 months of constant meetings, presentations and lobbying to have the principle of *in situ* upgrading accepted. And even then this acceptance was conditional upon the technical professionals giving their approval. This in turn required a new and different strategy to be adopted, to gain the acceptance and approval of the engineers and planners.

At the same time that this process was taking place, the researchers also initiated a major campaign to win support for the upgrading concept from the other tiers of government in Cape Town. Here it quickly became apparent that there was still immense resistance to the concept of settlement upgrading, and a predominant view that informal settlements should be demolished and their occupants relocated to new sites. It is also important to note that this view was held by a substantial minority within the City of Cape Town Municipality, even though official support had been given to the project.

Changing the Attitude and Perceptions of Politicians

Once the extent of the opposition to informal settlements was fully recognized the research project opened up a new area of activity. The project had received support from Intergraph®,[1] a major supplier of GIS software,[2] and was thus equipped with extensive GIS capabilities. This provided the capacity to widen the scope of the study to look at the wider metropolitan context and thus explore the extent of informal settlement growth at a metropolitan level. This began initially by using the data provided by the City of Cape Town Municipality, but this was later extended through a grant from the Cape Metropolitan Council. This then permitted a detailed study of growth and trends of informal settlements across the city as whole.

The results (Abbott and Douglas 1999) showed that informal settlements were growing faster than formal housing was being supplied, and that this situation was unlikely to be reversed in the foreseeable future. These findings were presented to the Provincial Cabinet and to the various local authorities. Finally, in late 1999, there was broad consensus among politicians at all levels of government that they should support the principle of upgrading informal settlements in the Metropolitan Area *in situ*. To obtain support such as this was neither simple nor straightforward and took four years to achieve.

Providing a contextual framework for informal settlement growth, and being able to demonstrate clearly the existing trends, proved to be an important element of the upgrading strategy. For it was only by illustrating clearly the nature and extent of the 'problem', demonstrating that alternatives to upgrading were inadequate, and then showing that a feasible upgrading methodology existed, that the official view began to change. In the case of Cape Town, the strategy led to a situation where the politicians went from thinking of informal settlements only as areas to be cleared and the residents relocated, to a situation where *in situ* upgrading became the City's highest priority in terms of addressing housing needs. This was in spite of a number of major political shifts at both the provincial and the local level.

---

1. Intergraph® is a developer and supplier of geo-spatial information technology. It is US based and has a South African subsidiary. Like many US and American corporations it has a social responsibility policy, whereby donations in cash or kind are allocated to social projects. Our project fitted this program well as it worked with the urban poor yet used the company's technology, which allowed it some free marketing.
2. The term GIS stands for a geographic information system. At its simplest this is a software system that allows the digital representation of physical data. These data can then be used in conjunction with other data to create information about the nature of a physical environment. Using GIS, extensive social data sets can be analysed within the context of a spatial environment.

Ironically though this change brought its own problems, for once the politicians had accepted the principle of upgrading, they wanted speedy results, placing products such as infrastructure before critical processes of social and economic development. This made the role and the perceptions of the local authority officials even more crucial.

Changing the Attitude and Perceptions of Technical Professionals

The project was fortunate to the extent that the attitude of the technical professionals was sceptical rather than hostile. It also helped that the University was involved, as there was already a working relationship and a degree of trust established between the relevant professionals, particularly in the civil engineering sector. There is very little information on and experience of informal settlement upgrading available to officials in local government in South Africa. There are also no design standards, as there are for conventional developments. All of this makes informal settlements very threatening at a professional level. The result is that engineers still have a tendency to impose technical solutions. This has led to a backlash from NGOs in particular. Thus the literature on projects such as Orangi in Karachi emphasizes the concept of community-driven processes, taking this to the point where local authorities are excluded from the process (Hasan 1992).

The experience in Cape Town has been that neither of these positions is appropriate in the long term. From the beginning the New Rest upgrading programme has aimed at building a partnership between the community and the local authority. The concerns of engineers and planners were taken into account, but did not drive the process. For this was contrasted with the development needs of the community and the constraints imposed by a minimum relocation policy, which all parties accepted as the basis for development. The result was a compromise position and a change in technical standards rather than a complete abandonment of standard.

Two examples serve to illustrate this dynamic. The first is the issue of roads. Before this project, the conventional approach to roads was to provide vehicular access to every dwelling, irrespective of need, car ownership or income level. The approach taken in New Rest was one that emphasized pedestrian movement and access, and which sought to strengthen and formalize existing movement networks. The major roads, with the exception of one road created over a service pipe to a water main, which is the only straight road in the settlement, are all situated over existing movement routes. Apart from these roads, all other access routes are 2m wide paths, which was the minimum width acceptable to the local authority.

The process of relocation of shacks to accommodate the improved road network was managed by the Residents Committee, starting when the upgrading programme began in 1997. Over the next three years the existing network of roads was widened and improved locally, with the local authority occasionally providing assistance with a mechanical scraper. The network was then formalized by engineers to provide the final layout.

The second example relates to the planning process. There had been a high level of agreement with the city planners around the need to integrate the settlement spatially with the surrounding areas. However, when they became involved in looking at spatial relationships within the settlement their whole approach suddenly changed. They abandoned the methodology, which they had previously agreed in principle to follow, and reverted to conventional practice. This meant demanding a full development plan before approval of any implementation activity would be given. Such a position was totally unacceptable. The only way that any form of 'development plan' could be created was through an organic process linked to the participatory planning that was being initiated within the community at that point. And the time scale for this process could not be pre-defined.

This created an impasse. The research group, supported by the community, objected to the planning approach and refused to endorse it. In the meantime the city's planner had actually given the brief to consultants to carry out a development planning process. They had done this without any wider consultation. At this stage, a high level meeting was held with the Deputy City Planner and the full city team (i.e. representatives from the three core departments of Planning, Housing and Engineering Services) and the previous position of requiring a development plan was overturned.

The interesting question that arises here is just how a community and their support team, whether this is a CBO, NGO or an academic grouping, *can* win in the face of such an intransigent position (on the part of city officials). The experience here is that it cannot be done solely by falling back on principles, or even by emphasizing the over-arching importance of process, even though this may be an important element. Ultimately what enabled the community/university team to force the withdrawal of the rigid development planning approach was the fact that there was an agreed upgrading approach and the proposed development planning process deviated from this agreed methodology.

The relative success achieved by this upgrading programme in being able to confront and modify entrenched positions and attitudes of city officials was built upon three key elements. The first has been mentioned. The upgrading had a methodology, and inherent within this was a long-term goal (i.e. the upgrading programme is seeking to create a sustainable settlement; it is not simply a series of *ad hoc* interventions). However, central as they may be, a methodology and a long term goal are not of themselves sufficient. The second element was the use of highly competent technical professionals on the side of the settlement upgrading programme who are independent of the City. These were people who supported the principles behind the upgrading, yet also shared a technical base with the City's professionals. This fact, when coupled with the methodology and goal, meant that the process was carried out in a structured and professional way. It was not an *ad hoc* process, although it was still extremely flexible.

And then there was the third element. It was crucial to demonstrate a benefit to the City, which was that the outcome would be a new set of standards that could be applied to informal settlements across the city. The creation of a new set of standards might appear counter-productive (given the historical association of standards with rigidity), but it is important to be pragmatic. Local authorities have a legislative role to perform and certain mandatory requirements that have to be adhered to. These need regulations and standards. The important point is that such standards have to be appropriate and, if at all possible, flexible. This project was defining those standards and that would be what the city would gain from supporting this process.

These three underpinning elements provided a degree of reassurance to the technical team in the City. This meant that, time after time, the community group was able to move the project from a confrontational stance to a collaborative one, whilst at the same time still being able to lead the process. This was only made possible because the project had a 'champion' within the city administration who was able to keep the channels of communication open. He was a civil engineer whose task it was to facilitate development of low-income settlements. Once he saw that the project was technically feasible, he became a strong proponent of it. In spite of these successes however, there are also concerns. The greatest of these relates to the City's attitude to partnerships, the City here comprising both politicians, technical and administrative officers. The project is constantly opposing a tendency within the city administration to revert to the 'default' position, which for many is control of the process by the city with community participation through consultation. In this regard the planning and housing departments were more prone to reversion than the engineering department. One possible reason for this is that the engineering department output remains quantitative. Once standards have been revised and agreement reached then this is a clearly defined position. With the planning and housing departments there remains an ongoing commitment to process as a mechanism for reaching solutions. Hence there is a much more qualitative element. And the housing and planning officials wanted their components quantified.

There are three lessons to be learnt from this experience. The first is that it is essential to build a strategic alliance with at least one key player in the local authority. The second lesson is that, if there is going to be a successful project, then it is crucial that everyone has the opportunity to share in that success. Finally the third, and in many ways the most important lesson, is that dealing with a local authority is an ongoing process. There is a constant pressure from within the organization to revert back to a product/delivery driven approach, and the only way to deal with this is to have a clearly articulated, method-based approach of one's own which is accepted by all parties, and which provides the anchor for a process-driven development.

Changing the Attitude and Perceptions of Neighbouring Communities

The New Rest informal settlement is situated on the edge of a township called Gugulethu, which was part of the Black Local Authority of Ikapa under the apartheid regime. The area itself was a buffer zone at the edge of the 'black' township, and is bounded on its other three sides by an urban freeway, a railway line and a suburban road. It was planned with part of it as a school site and part for business development. Hence its occupation in a land invasion was a contentious issue with many residents in Gugulethu, who are extremely wary of the informal settlement that has arisen. On the other hand the area is now well established, having been settled first around 1990–91, and the average length of stay of the current occupants is 7 years (in 2002). The people living there constitute a settled and relatively stable community.

From the time the pilot area was first identified, the project targeted key people in the surrounding areas, such as representatives of the local civic movement, development forums and business people. The first step was to explain the nature of *in situ* upgrading. An important element was the concept of the long-term goal or vision described earlier. It was the concept of an informal settlement that people had difficulty with. It is clear from the discussions that were held during this project that it is not just that such settlements are seen to be the base for criminal activity. There is a much deeper underlying fear, which stems from the randomness of the settlement. It is proposed here that it is the lack of physical order that many people find threatening. Thus the most influential factor in changing local perceptions was the fact that there was a plan to formalize the settlement. That people inside the settlement were driving this was equally important. It appeared to change the attitudes of those outside from opposition to one in which they took collective pride in what was happening. New Rest is no longer an excluded and distinctive area, but is considered a part of Gugulethu.

INTEGRATING ACROSS THE INTERFACE: THE NEED FOR A STRUCTURED APPROACH

At the end of the desk study in 1998, the project found itself caught between two quite divergent positions (Abbott 2002a). The one was the Belo Horizonte approach referred to earlier, which was constructed around what is termed in Portuguese a 'plano global', a form of masterplan. This was having major success in Brazil, but it also had shortcomings, not least of which was the lack of funding to implement all facets of the masterplan, since the success of the approach is dependent on addressing all facets of physical upgrading simultaneously. This in turn created quite serious problems in allocating priorities and programming actions.

The other position saw upgrading as a people-driven process, and responsibility and control lying with the community. This was the preferred approach of most NGOs in South Africa, as well as of the influential South Africa grassroots organization the Homeless People's Federation. But this too had problems. It was not that effective on the ground, while those projects that were successful did not necessarily lead to replicable models. If anything the total focus on process virtually precluded a replicable project model (Abbott 2002a, b). This is because it is driven by short-term goals identified by the community, and it can by no means be assumed that there is an automatic linkage between a series of independent interventions and long-term sustainability of a settlement, even when those interventions are determined by a community.

This project attempted to identify and integrate the strengths of both of the above approaches. Thus it saw the need to have some form of long-term goal, defining what was required for a settlement to become formalized, whilst recognising the centrality of the community in the decision-making process. The result was the creation of a new method-based approach to informal settlement upgrading that attempted to integrate identifiable physical outcomes with a process of ongoing social and economic development.

The difficulty with attempting to create a structured, method-based approach to informal settlement upgrading derives from the multiplicity of needs and the competition for resources. The Brazilian master planning approach works as well as it does for four reasons. Firstly, the majority of structures are constructed of permanent materials, which makes any physical intervention involving demolition and removal expensive. This in turn forces the local authority to adopt a more pragmatic approach to planning and services, based upon what is termed a minimum relocation policy. Secondly, the Brazilian authorities (at all tiers of government and including parastatals and/or private utilities suppliers) are now investing large sums of money in settlement, which gives them the means to address a wide range of issues simultaneously. Thirdly, advances in GIS and geospatial information management systems have provided the tools to manage complex upgrading processes. And finally, the local authorities are allocating significant resources to supporting social and economic development programmes.

South Africa is still in the early stages of informal settlement formation. This means that dwellings are, in the main, constructed of temporary materials of poor quality, and there is still a high level of movement both into and within settlements. In addition South Africa has not yet made the same level of commitment to informal settlement upgrading, while experience in Cape Town indicates that the local authority has not yet recognized the need to invest in social capital and economic development.

The approach taken in the Indian sub-continent, on the other hand, sees communities acting independently of government, as well as operating with minimal state expenditure on services. In addition the communities accept basic levels of services and housing, which keeps the capital requirement low. In Cape Town the physical condition of most settlements is such that some external interrvention is necessary to reduce risk (e.g. from flooding), while the demands and expectations in respect of services and housing are significantly higher. On the other hand, Cape Town does have a relatively high technical support capacity, the ability to use GIS-based technologies, and a high level of community mobilization. The methodology that has emerged seeks to optimize these strengths. Underpinning the methodology is a recognition of the importance of scale in development, and the ability of GIS to utilize this. Thus it is a multi-scalar approach.

Finally, given the marginal quality of the land on which the majority of informal settlements are situated, and the high level of associated physical risk, particularly from flooding, some degree of external intervention is necessary. The challenge is to keep this to a minimum, and ensure that it does interfere with the underpinning focus on social and economic development discussed earlier. This can only be achieved if there is a clear understanding of roles and relationships of those involved in the upgrading programme.

This development paradigm also defines the roles of different actors and the relationship between them. For upgrading under these conditions can only be achieved through a partnership of residents and the local authority. It also means that development professionals have an important role to play in upgrading. It is all very well for academics and others outside of communities to argue for community control and the self-sufficiency of communities. The reality, however, is that poor communities, like their more affluent neighbours, have a right to, and can benefit from, a professional support system. At the same time development professionals can only play this role if they change their attitude towards informal settlements, and see them in the context of a new planning paradigm.

THE KEY ELEMENTS OF A METHOD-BASED PLANNING APPROACH

The rationale for a method-based approach to informal settlement upgrading has been described in detail by Abbott (2002a, b). Essentially the argument runs that the only way in which progress can be made in addressing upgrading needs is through a programme that can be replicated, and that replication requires a structured approach. There are already different approaches that can be classified in this way (Abbott 2002a:309–11), each of which has strengths and weaknesses. This work in New Rest attempted to draw different elements of these approaches together to create a more generic approach, which was then tested in the settlement upgrading programme.

The methodology sought to create a balance between the need for a long-term development strategy on the one hand, and the optimization of community-based decision-making through short-term interventions on the other. The power of geo-spatial analysis was used to identify, in the first instance, which families would be affected and possibly have to be relocated. Through this process of visualization, residents were able to gain an understanding of, and approve, major structural changes. This made it possible to generate a long-term "vision" for the settlement, and to create a spatial development framework that will enable this to take place over a period of time, at a pace determined by the community's resources and commitment.

In practical terms, this means three things. Firstly the problems of physical risk associated with living in an informal settlement have to be addressed. In New Rest this meant dealing with the issue of flooding caused by a high water table in the winter rainfall period. Secondly, there needs to be a clearly definable primary access network within the settlement. Ease of movement through the settlement is a pre-requisite for long-term social and economic sustainability. However, this does require some relocation to take place. And thirdly, there needs to be an economic core activity to provide the community with a focus. This is a significant departure from current thinking. The current view, expressed, for example, through the national People's Housing Process (PHP) guidelines, emphasizes the importance of a social centre. The intention is to provide a venue that will allow for better community interaction. In New Rest there was already a small community hall that the residents had built themselves, so a different approach was taken. What was considered most important was the need to identify and understand local livelihood strategies. Interventions could then be designed to facilitate the process of improving livelihoods (Bauman 2001). Spatial interventions then emerge from this. The access network provides opportunities through its structuring elements, but the form that this takes will flow out of a participatory planning process that incorporates the livelihood study. This type of approach may encourage the softening of the formal-informal interface, because it necessitates an exploration of what is happening in the areas around the settlement.

The elements described above apply to the settlement as a whole. Once these have been defined, then the blocks formed by the intersection of roads and external boundaries could be developed by the people themselves at their own pace. The livelihoods study was linked to a broader socio-economic study of every household. This revealed that there were families that did not have a source of income. This group as well as other vulnerable groups were at risk. A poverty alleviation programme was required, addressing those who were the most marginalized. Informal settlements are not necessarily homogeneous entities, but socially and economically stratified like most other areas. Thus identifying ways of integrating vulnerable groups is an important facet of making settlements sustainable.

Strengthening the Interface —Experiences of the Cape Town Project

It was mentioned in the introduction that South Africa does have some advantages that support the process outlined here. Although many people opposed the idea of upgrading, the broader political climate provides a more sympathetic framework. South Africa is a middle-income country, and therefore there is funding available, as there was in Brazil, in a way that might not be possible in poorer countries. Nonetheless it is felt that these factors do not prevent the approach from being adopted in areas where resources are more constrained.

From its inception the Cape Town project sought to identify what might constitute the basic elements or building blocks of a replicable methodology for *in situ* upgrading. Thus it sought to avoid being locked into any particular ideology. The methodology recognized the centrality of people to the process, but was also mindful of the need to find a balance between an imposed project and a totally community driven project. Central to the successful achievement of this balance was the ability to reach consensus among different actors, and an acceptance of the process by all those actors. What emerged provided an interesting lesson about what happens at the interface between the formal and the informal city.

The first important factor that emerges from this study would seem to indicate that the point of contact between the formal and the informal cities is characterized by tension and mistrust, particularly on the part of those residents in the formal areas surrounding the settlement. The primary issue then becomes one of moving beyond that condition and finding common ground. This means that it should move beyond simply the needs of the informal settlement to take into account the needs of those outside. There needs to be a recognition that others outside of the settlement have an interest in what happens inside. Hence the approach needs to move beyond one that simply provides unconditional support for community driven initiatives to upgrade.

Informal settlements are threatening environments to the majority of people who dwell outside of them, because they appear to lack both form and structure, which provide the basis for security. *Ad hoc* improvements do not necessarily change this negative perception. Hence *ad hoc* improvements are not going to improve relations at the interface. On the contrary, there is a serious risk that they may deepen the divide further. Hence it is argued here that the primary task should be to seek common ground from the beginning, and that this can be achieved through the creation of a plan that defines the settlement within the context of the formal city. This is not simply a pandering to the formal city residents outside. Experience from this project indicates that the residents themselves do not wish to live in an informal settlement for ever.

Until recently the creation of such a plan was not possible, because the planning tools did not exist to make it happen. The power of GIS-based development makes this possible. GIS integrates images of the settlement with potential development activity. It is the vehicle that provides the link between those inside and outside the settlement, and allows both to explore what upgrading means to them in a way that is visible and transparent to the other party.

By creating a shared vision, based upon a view of how the settlement will develop in the future, it becomes possible to obtain acceptance of the informal settlement and its upgrading from all stakeholders. It also means that the focus of upgrading is turned from fulfilling basic needs to a longer term goal of creating a sustainable living environment. The implementation may begin at the level of basic needs provision, the long-term goal is sustainability.

Within the settlement, the upgrading programme found that there was a willingness on the part of residents to move, provided the reason was clear and the process leading up to the decision was inclusive and transparent. There were three sets of outcomes that residents were willing to relocate their shacks to achieve. These were:

– To relocate within the cadastral boundary that defined the perimeter of the site. This was linked to increased security of tenure.

– To move from areas that were prone to flooding in winter. This provided enhanced physical security and an improved quality of life.

– To improve the access (road and path) network. Here the importance, and benefits, of a good access network were perceived by all. In a broader context, an adequate, well-defined access (road and path) network, both within the settlement and across the formal-informal divide, was seen to be a core element of the upgrading process. It begins to define the form of the future settlement, as well as opening the settlement up to economic opportunities.

The key to success in the relocation policy lay in finding a balance between individual and collective needs. Opening up and consolidating the settlement should not lead to the destruction of social networks. Hence there needs to be seamless integration between physical planning, economic planning and social development. Physical development of an informal settlement should probably *not* take place unless there are also plans for economic and social development in place.

To sum up, the experience gained from this project, in relation to the wider theme of the book, is that building linkages across the formal/informal divide, depend not only on what is done, but how it is done. Those in power need encouragement to create a policy framework for upgrading. Those supporting the upgrading should approach the debate from a strategic, rather than from an ideological perspective. Creating bridges across a divide that is both social, economic and physical is a two way process. Those supporting the process have to go out to meet those who do not understand the process, and show them the way, rather than merely demanding their support. This is not always easy, but this project indicates that it can be done, and that the result is to the benefit of all residents in informal settlements. Many people in the formal city are unlikely ever to support informal settlements as they stand. Yet those same people can be won over to a strategic vision that is seen as a win-win situation. The barriers between the formal and the informal city can only be broken down if there is a shared vision of the future and a common understanding of the way forward.

Acknowledgements

The early desk-study work was funded by the Water Research Commission of South Africa, while financial support for the testing and implementation of the methodology was funded by Cordaid of the Netherlands as part of a community capacity building and economic development project. I would also like to thank my research students, Iuma Martinez and David Douglas, for their input into aspects of this project, the project social worker, Vuyiswa Mokwena, the community's project coordinator, Morrison Mvumvu, and the residents of New Rest. This project has been supported from its inception by Intergraph Corporation and by Intergraph Systems Southern Africa, and its success owes much to the continued support provided by these companies. Acknowledgement is also given to UNCHS (Habitat) and AVSI (Associazione Volontari per il Servizio Internatiozionale/ Voluntary Association for International Service), who provided links with the Belo Horizonte project and openly shared information and experiences in GIS with my research group.

References

Abbott, John, 2002a, "The Development of a Generic Integrated Approach to Informal Settlement Upgrading", *Habitat International* 26(3):303–15.

—, 2002b, "An Analysis of Informal Settlement Upgrading and Critique of Existing Methodological Approaches", *Habitat International* 26(3):317–33.

Abbott, John and David J. Douglas, 2002, "The use of GIS for spatial trends analysis of informal settlement growth", *Development SA* 19(5).

—, 2001, *A methodological approach to the upgrading, in-situ, of informal settlements in South Africa*. Pretoria: Water Research Commission. WRC Report Number 786/2/01.

—, 1999, "A trends analysis of informal settlement growth in the Cape Metropolitan Area, 1993–1998". A report prepared for the Cape Metropolitan Council, Spatial Planning, Housing, and Environment Directorate, unpublished.

Abbott, John, Iuma Martinez and Marie Huchzermeyer, 2001, *An analysis of informal settlements and applicability of Visual Settlement Planning (ViSP) in South Africa*. Pretoria: Water Research Commission. WRC Report Number 786/1/01.

Baumann, Ted, 2001, "Supporting local economic development in New Rest, Cape Town", unpublished.

Hasan, Arif, 1992, "Manual for Rehabilitation Programmes for Informal Settlements based on Orangi Pilot Project", *Environment and Urbanization*, 5(1).

Recife International Meeting on Urban Poverty, 1996, *The Recife Declaration*. Nairobi: UNCHS (Habitat).

Republic of South Africa, 1996, *Constitution of the Republic of South Africa*. Pretoria: Government Printer.

CHAPTER 12

Beyond the Formal/Informal Dichotomy:
Access to Land in Maputo, Mozambique

Paul Jenkins

The concepts of formal and informal need clarification before they can be applied in any analysis of actual cities. In this chapter it is argued that the concept of formality is particularly problematic, because of its basis in legal and regulatory systems whose legitimacy for the majority of the urban population may be doubtful. The formal/informal dichotomy is too simplistic to capture the social, economic and political complexities of urban situations. Its application in urban development may lead to marginalization and social exclusion. Research in Maputo, Mozambique, with specific reference to access to land for housing, leads to a questioning of the forms of socio-economic exchange which underlie the concepts of "formal/informal". An alternative approach to these concepts is suggested which is felt to be more widely applicable. This is based on the concept of different forms of socio-economic exchange: reciprocity, redistribution and the market. An approach which is based on strengthening forms of socio-economic exchange which are socially, culturally and politically more appropriate than the formal/informal dichotomy, needs to be developed.

WHAT DOES "FORMAL" MEAN?

The legality and legitimacy of what is labelled "formal" is discussed in a number of recent approaches to urban development. Fernandes and Varley (1998), for example, query the "legality" of laws and regulations that effectively marginalize the majority. In fact these laws have been inherited in many cases from colonial regimes, with little change to their fundamental nature, which privileges an elite. In addition the fact that the colonial legal system was often incomplete and contradictory has led to ever more complexity in the definition of legality. However, in many countries the post-independence political and economic elite favours the retention of existing complex legal systems which, while cumbersome, can be worked to their advantage due to their greater access to resources and power. The nature of state capacity also underpins this: the state is politically weak and its legal system has low administrative and technical capacity. This leads to bureaucratic groups also manipulating regulatory regimes to their comparative advantage. In addition to querying the legitimacy of legal structures which effectively marginalize the majority, there is also a growing literature on governance, state legitimacy and the relationship between the state and civil society, which queries the legitimacy of the regimes and social groups which draw benefits from the state (e.g. Harbeson et al. 1994; Hyden and Bratton 1992).

As noted above, in many situations the level of legality is itself complex. Different legal rights can coincide due to historical and socio-cultural circumstances. Equally, different components of any specific urban manifestation can have differing degrees of legality, and in any geographic area different legal and regulatory codes can exist for different spatial areas. In reality, levels of legality range from full illegality through complex matrices of levels of legality. The proportion of urban situations that could be seen as fully legal in the latter sense is a small minority in many African cities. The fact that the inapplicability of such legal definitions has not been challenged to any really significant degree is rooted in the strength of the state vis-à-vis civil society; powerful vested interests in maintaining the system; and weak socio-political structures for challenging illegitimacy. Drawing on the concepts introduced by Hirschmann (1970), the result is urban residents' varying degrees of "exit" from the system, as opposed to application of "voice" to change it.

An important lead to a new approach comes from Coquery-Vidrovitch's predominantly historical perspective, which has led her to query the validity of the concept of the informal sector. Her analysis derives from articulation theory and she states that through time and space prevalent modes of production and exchange can be distinguished, supported by distinct structures of power and ideology, and that each of these is reflected in differing processes of urbanization, with specific city models. Coquery-Vidrovitch argues that the phenomenon now termed the informal sector is rooted in history, pointing out the universality of co-existence of wage and non-wage labour, with a complex evolution of mechanisms of survival from ancient times to modern capitalism.

> As long as we lack a theoretical and historical account of the forces that underpin global differentiations, we remain unable to account for processes that lie at the heart of African urban underdevelopment: the integration of the household into new networks of capitalist production; the invention of a new web of concepts and practice on land and land laws, on housing and rental; new patterns of foodstuff consumption; new regulations governing social and political life; all of these processes involving new relationships to the broader political economy which is definitely neither Western nor native behaviour. (Coquery-Vidrovitch 1991:73)

A top-down approach still strongly underpins orthodox development practice, including the development of urban planning, urban management and housing delivery. The most recent manifestation of this is in the growing literature on how cities need to change, especially in the context of weaker nation-states and stronger trans-national economic and cultural flows (Friedmann 1986; Knox and Taylor 1995; Sassen 1991, 1994). However, it can also be argued that the focus in future should be on how African urban dwellers have continuously adapted the city to something more suitable to their needs, means and aspirations and not how cities can adapt to globalization. This is the core of the approach suggested here, with a focus on access to land by the majority.

Modes of Access to Urban Land

Rapid urbanization without correspondent economic growth and distribution of wealth has made access to land for housing increasingly difficult for a growing proportion of the population in cities in the developing world. In this context many writers cite informal urban land access as a dominant feature of many developing countries (Payne 1989, 1997). However, the degree of illegality varies enormously, from illegal occupation ("squatting") through to situations where some relatively minor aspect of legal regulations is not complied with (UNCHS 1996). As noted above, the widespread nature on "illegality" in some situations has led to queries on whether this should be termed "illegal", particularly where there are potentially different entities bestowing legality.

In Sub-Saharan Africa relatively high proportions of residents obtain land through informal processes. These are generally considered informal for the simple reason that they are not recognized in the modern legal system, although they may be recognized in traditional legal systems, and be widely practiced and accepted. Land supplied in these ways generally has limitations of ownership and is not registered in a modern, technical way. It is therefore not included in the market based, formal economic system. This is probably true more for West Africa than Eastern and Southern Africa, as traditional land tenure still applies in large tracts of urban land, overlapping with imported models of land legislation. However, across Sub-Saharan Africa, there are large areas in which no modern legal system of land tenure operates *de facto*, including significant portions of urban areas. In these situations different land rights operate, often not full freehold rights, but the right to occupy either temporarily or permanently.

The fact that customary land cannot be transacted in formal land markets does not mean it cannot be commercialized. In these situations often a mix of monetary and non-monetary forms of land acquisition co-exist with non-monetary forms tending to become commercialized, although not always in monetary form, but as "gifts", once symbolic, now of more commercial or "realisable" value. In fact, within the broad definition of informal land access, commercialization of customary land has often given rise to a set of brokers who act as intermediaries with those holding traditional rights. Other informal and/or illegal sources of land can be politicians, who also often act through brokers, and also staff within government agencies responsible for land control. In these latter situations some form of documentation of transfer may well be allocated, which may in itself be illegal. Examples are double allocations of the same plot or allocations of land not formally registered. Private developers also work on the fringes of the legal system in these situations, and provide land at lower prices than the formal, usually cumbersome, systems do. In many urban situations this is the growing tendency, rather than direct occupation based on political or customary allocations. However, these systems of land access are also still usually looked on as informal.

In general traditional and customary rights begin to enter the commodification system, without, however, necessarily the facility for easy onward transfer, particularly sale. While the majority of those needing land are primarily interested in the "use value" this poses no particular problem, but when there is significant need for transfer of land, the process to do this may become more complicated—certainly any legal resolution will do so. Thus informal markets work well when the land use value predominates, but are not as effective when exchange values grow more important.

At the *Global Conference on Access to Land and Security of Tenure* held in New Delhi in January 1996 it was recognized that informal land development is a solution for access to land by the urban poor, where formal supply is inadequate and inflexible. The resulting New Delhi Declaration recommended that "... a base be created for more efficient relationships between the formal and informal sectors" (Sinha 1997:7). Based on the dominant neo-liberal development paradigms of the 1980s and 1990s, however, international agencies have still tended to push exclusively for land tenure regularization with full transferable land rights as the basis for land and housing markets to operate more efficiently (e.g. World Bank 1993). There are, however, a series of crucial questions not often investigated within the development discourse: To what extent is it possible, politically, legally and administratively, to implement this regularization? Is it desirable in the light of other well-established forms of rights and traditions of land tenure? Would it lead to social exclusion for a majority?

The concept of "less alienating" paths to property reform has been advocated by Howard Stein (1995). He points out how a central aim of neo-liberalist policies, as implemented in structural adjustment programmes, is to remove "impediments" caused by state interference in market operations. This, however, increasingly includes recognition of the role of state institutions as guarantors of the rights of private property and contract. Stein criticizes the resulting emphasis on the legalization of property rights without the equally important social institutionalization of these; property rights must not only become established, but legitimate. He suggests that to expand market-based exchange of property and encourage investment and accumulation on this basis needs stability in the accepted "mental models" which these are based on. This is particularly so with respect to land rights, which are based on a complex web of social interaction. Coincidental and competing claims thus do not disappear with a shift to private property, there are rights to ownership, the right to claim ownership, the right to use and dispose of land, and the right to use and enjoy the fruits of the land. These rights are often more legitimate than the market transferable rights such as freehold. Land tenure can be seen as a "collection of rights", such as: rights of use, rights of development, rights of transfer, rights of lease or rental and rights to mortgage (Angel et al. 1983:543).

There is thus a growing realization of the importance of informal land markets, especially for the urban poor, leading to the recent calls to regularize these without "unifying" them as one formal market system. However, the increasing involvement of governments in legitimising informal housing arrangements will only be effective as long as informal arrangements themselves continue to be effective (Angel et al. 1983). It is thus argued that new forms of association and new forms of partnership across the formal boundary are required. Recent international research in urban land markets in the developing world has thus begun to investigate using informal land markets as a basis for widening access to land as a key element of urban development (Durand-Lasserve 1997; Fourie 1997). Recent research undertaken into access to land in Maputo, forms the basis of a discussion of how this might be approached in Mozambique.

THE MOZAMBICAN CONTEXT

The concept of informality in Mozambique can be applied in a broad way, in that a majority of the activities of the majority of the population have limited interaction with the state and modern market systems, even in urban areas. Space does not permit a wider exposition of this argument here, but the sub-ordination of traditional forms of socio-political organization and economic production and exchange in the colonial period was essentially followed by a not dissimilar subordination of these activities in the post-independence period, whether under "proto-socialist"[1] (1975–84), "market socialist" (1984–90), or "open market" regimes. A recent expression of this in urban life is the proportion of the population voting in the first local government elections (1998). Less than 15 per cent of the electorate turned out nation-wide. It has been argued that this reflects the extent to which civil society has lost trust in the electoral system and political representation, and in the state in general terms (Braathen and Jörgensen 1998). Similarly, a rather low proportion of the urban, active population is employed in the formal economy, the estimate for Maputo is 32 per cent. The definition of formal here is employment registered by the state (Euroconsult 1999).

In a study of urban survival strategies in Mozambique during the war of destabilization, Lundin observed that kinship is the basis of a wide variety of social organizations in Mozambique and that in fact this has been the basis for survival of the majority for centuries. Her research showed that kinship forms continued to contribute to social cohesion and remained the focal point for many individuals and groups both in rural and urban areas. Her work illustrated how social networks based on kinship, both real and classificatory, were the underlying basis for support in all spheres of life of the majority of the population of Maputo (Lundin 1991, 2001).

This study indicated that not only did kinship relations persist in Maputo, they had become more important. Lundin argued that the concept of kin was extended horizontally and vertically in the urban situation in relation to the needs of individuals, households and other groupings sharing the same social space. This meant that principles developed in rural domestic society were being applied in the urban space. She observed that this world of socio-cultural and socio-economic values and actions, regulated by essentially rurally developed norms, rules and laws, was evolving into a new way of living or new form of urbanization which she termed "rururban". However, she queries whether this is rather a form of "ruralization" of the city as opposed to urbanization. In this

1. Proto-socialism" is a term used by White (1985) with reference to various developing countries which aspired to socialism, including Mozambique. The term indicates that only certain steps towards socialism have been taken. For application to Mozambique, see Jenkins (1990:176).

she echoes the position put forward by Coquery-Vidrovitch concerning new socio-cultural forms that are appearing. Thus, instead of investigating the African adaptation to urban life this approach looks at how the population has adapted both urban realities and rural socio-cultural values in innovative and more appropriate ways.

A Brief Background to Urban Land Access in Mozambique

The evolution of urban areas and an overview of historical access to land in urban areas in Mozambique has been detailed elsewhere (Jenkins 1999a, 2001b). Urban settlements were an exogenous development, initially founded by traders along the coast, and later by Portuguese colonists. State-based urban land registers and control mechanisms were only set up in the late 19th century with the "Scramble for Africa" and the development of urban-based mining economies in neighbouring states. This led to military consolidation of Portuguese colonial interests, development of transport and labour markets based in urban areas, immigration from the metropolis to the colony and the beginnings of urban planning and regulation of development. In all of this the state favoured the settler population, and the elite within this.

Formal access to land through state and market mechanisms for the rapidly growing African urban population was highly restricted in the urban centres during most of the colonial period. Limited urban land rights for Africans were made possible in the mid-1950s and generally only used for special cases. This situation continued to independence in 1975. Access to land was achieved through renting of land and/or temporary housing in peri-urban areas, which were largely ignored by the state. The only other form of urban land access was on the urban periphery where traditional forms of authority, subordinated to the colonial state, continued land allocation on a predominantly non-monetary basis. Towards the end of the colonial period, with the exacerbated costs of the liberation war and international pressures, Portugal changed its investment regulations, leading to a surge in inward foreign investment and rapid urban expansion. This took place both horizontally and vertically in the main urban centres of Maputo and Beira, which were the only two cities to develop any significant industrial base. In this period, the colonial state began some programmes of urban expansion with land allocation for lower-income groups, although these were soon interrupted by independence.

After independence there was a period of considerable economic and social turbulence with many settlers abandoning the country. A series of nationalizations included land, and abandoned and rented housing. The state continued some of the local level programmes in land subdivision, however the raising of colonial restrictions on internal migration led to a rapid rise in the urban population. Due to the weak nature of the state and the land supply mechanism, the traditional form of allocation persisted in peri-urban areas, where many households settled. In the early 1980s the state, having taken over all land supply functions due to the now illegal nature of the previous formal land market, attempted to develop previous low-cost land supply mechanisms as well as cater to the widespread other land needs. However as most urban areas had virtually no capacity within local government, and central government was also very weak, the impact of this was very limited, except in the capital Maputo. The legal rights of land allocation were henceforth with the local state. But it had virtually no administrative and technical capacity, and urban land regulation had low political priority. This resulted in a general acceptance of modified traditional forms of land allocation in all but the inner "cement cities".

The modification to the traditional system was the *de facto*, but not *de jure* transference of traditional land allocation rights to new institutions, the Grupos Dinamizadores ("Dynamising Groups" or GDs). After independence the governing party FRELIMO established a series of these groups in neighbourhoods, workplaces and institutions, initially as a form of social mobilization. The GDs continued to develop their role in community organization during the latter part of the 1970s and the early 1980s, but increasingly became responsible for a myriad of basic local administrative controls, ranging from registry of residency and permission to travel, to ration card distribution. Their role generally during this period became less that of popular mobilization and more of administrative control (Jenkins 1990 and 1998). The GDs varied widely in competence and capacity, however they normally operated within an environment of consensus, in that land rights were underpinned by social acceptance, whether between neighbours or between the household and the GD. Again in general this system was non-monetary, although some cases of corruption may have existed.

This land allocation system, however, began to suffer extreme strains during the period of transition between socialism and the current market regime (1984–1990). One important reason for this was the effect of the civil war on internal migration and subsequent urban growth. The larger urban agglomerations grew rapidly as rural and small town residents migrated in to these, and indeed the residents in peripheral locations of these cities also migrated inward as they came under increased attacks. In addition the economic decline of the country and the acceptance of structural adjustment measures had severe repercussions for urban living in terms of access to the basics of social reproduction—food, water, education and health facilities, and later, employment. Overall the smaller urban areas were less affected as there were still opportunities for the residents to practise agriculture, but in the larger ones urban agriculture was not possible as there was no suitable land available. The result was a rapidly growing monetarization of socio-economic interchange and a veritable explosion of small scale commercial and service activities.

The vast majority of these activities were classified as illegal, and at first the state attempted to abolish them. However, this was impossible due to their being so widespread and essential for people's livelihoods. The state attempted to introduce a minimum of regulations in the informal sector, albeit with little success. Structural adjustment measures led to the draining of the limited administrative and technical capacity the state had managed to build up since independence, and hence the state institutions for subdivision and allocation of land collapsed. In the general climate of commercialization, the pressures on relatively scarce urban land began to lead to its commodification. In this case the state did nothing to adapt the strict formal access mechanisms or regulate the informal sector.

By the mid-1990s there was an awareness within some state institutions that informal access to land was being commercialized, but little actual understanding of the situation. Some initial research into access to urban agricultural land indicated an increase in conflicts over land—especially in the bigger cities, such as Maputo, where land suitable for agriculture was limited (Boucher et al. 1995; Myers 1994). Thus, when the World Bank promoted the development of several new "Structure Plans" for key urban areas, the question of formal and informal land markets was identified as needing research. The research reported below was done in 1998/99, primarily in Maputo, the capital, and its satellite city, Matola.

Recent Research into Land Access Mechanisms in Maputo

The investigation was part of a wider socio-economic survey of Maputo. In total, 995 households with some 6,500 members were surveyed, using random sampling. The survey included questions concerning how urban households had accessed the plot they occupied, or in some cases in the central city, their flat. The response rate was very high. The households were then grouped by the area where they lived at the time of the survey, although some questions investigated where they had lived previously. The surveyed areas then were classified by the period they became settled and the nature of their infrastructure development. The first was the pre-independence period, up to 1975, when market forces dominated the supply of land and housing in infrastructure and service provision, albeit with strong state control in favour of a settler minority. The second was the early post-independence period 1975–1987, under centrally planned development, with state dominance of land, housing, infrastructure and service supply. The third was the later post-independence period, from 1987 to the time of the survey, representing the period of structural adjustment, opening up to market activity in housing services and infrastructure supply. Only a few settlements dating from before independence had fully developed infrastructure. Some colonial settlements and settlements created later might be located on formally allocated land or on spontaneously occupied land, and had only partially developed infrastructure.

The survey revealed a wide range of possible access mechanisms, with a majority in all periods obtaining land informally. Table 1 shows the main forms of access by period, and Table 2 shows the breakdown of the various forms of informal access by period. The formal access pathway through the municipality, which legally is the only entity with the right to allocate land, only represented at best 33 per cent of cases. The largest other proportion achieved access via other local administrative institutions which were considered as informal mechanisms of access as no register is kept of such allocations and these were not permitted to allocate land in the modern legal system. This means of access ranged from 20 per cent to 39 per cent. Monetary payment to another individual represented only between 5 per cent and 12 per cent of cases. Other informal forms of access, such as inheritance or ceding within the family, direct occupation and exchange, were used by between 18–25 per cent of respondents.

Table 1. Access to Residential Land in Maputo, by period of establishment (per cent)

FORM OF ACCESS	PERIOD		
	pre-1975	1975–1982	post-1987
Obtained from city administration	32	33	14
Purchased	9	5	12
Obtained informally[a]	59	62	74
Total	101	100	100
(N)	(295)	(283)	(417)

[a.] This includes houses allocated or bought for which there was no related land registry—see Table 2.

Source: Survey of Maputo residents 1998/99 (Jenkins 1999b)

Formal access dropped significantly in the post-1987 period, while direct purchase decreased after independence. It increased again in the latter period, but still remains relatively low. Informal access has stayed predominant, and increased sharply in later years. The incidence of direct purchase of land from private individuals is low, but between one third and one half responded positively to a separate question on whether they paid something for access to land. In areas developed recently, the proportion was even higher. This suggests that a significant number paid for access to land within both the formal and informal mechanisms, whereas land is meant to be formally free of any taxation. Cross-tabulating the responses to this question with those concerning forms of access shows that approximately one third of those who got land through the formal mechanisms indicated they also paid for access, as did slightly less than half of those who got land from local level authorities.

Table 2. Informal Access to Residential Land in Maputo, by period of establishment (per cent)

FORM OF ACCESS	PERIOD		
	pre-1975	1975–1982	post-1987
Obtained from local level administration	40	47	54
Directly occupied, swopped, ceded, inherited	35	40	40
Other	3	2	1
Occupied with house	22	11	5
Total	100	100	100
(N)	(176)	(175)	(309)

Source: Survey of Maputo residents 1998/99 (Jenkins 1999b)

Access to land for housing based on allocation by local authorities and through family ties has thus remained predominant throughout, although these allocations may also involve monetary transfers. In most of these cases, however, it would appear that the payment has been for the right to be allocated the land, rather than a payment for the land itself. This form of land access has roots within traditional means to access land in rural areas.

Concerning formalization of land tenure and sense of security, the survey asked about ownership and proof of ownership of the property. Between some 40 and 50 per cent of the respondents indicated they had some form of land allocation documents. This was significantly higher in older established areas compared with the more recent areas, where some 60 per cent of respondents did not have, or did not know if they had, documentation. In general therefore, the findings support those above concerning the decrease in formal access. However, the proportion claiming documentary rights to land is higher than those claiming formal allocation through the municipality, which suggests that informal rights also have some form of documentation. The most likely is a declaration from the local Dynamising Group acknowledging right of residence.

Despite the lack of clarity on land rights and the high proportion of occupants who claimed no documentary proof of land occupancy rights, the incidence of conflict was very low, only 1–2 per cent. The few conflicts that were reported were primarily resolved locally, with few reaching the city council. Hence, while there have been reported conflicts concerning access to agricultural land in the metropolitan area, no significant evidence has been found concerning residential land conflicts, despite the lack of secure proof concerning land rights.

Follow-up research, however, has revealed a rapidly growing incidence of conflict over housing land, closely allied to increased commodification. However, in relatively few cases were these conflicts dealt with through any formal legal system. The local District Administrators were generally the final recourse. They represent the lowest level of the formal urban government, but rely heavily on the remains of the Dynamising Groups, which have often survived at the local level (Jenkins 2001a). The experience in Maputo thus illustrates the difficulty of simple definitions of formal and informal, as even in the formal systems, informal mechanisms operate, and in counterpart, informal systems have widespread legitimacy and provide a sense of security.

ALTERNATIVES

An alternative basis for better understanding of formal and informal systems might be to use the classification proposed by the economic historian Karl Polanyi. According to him, there are three main systems of socio-economic integration: reciprocity, redistribution and the market. Polanyi defined reciprocity as movements between correlative points of symmetrical groupings, such as obligatory gift giving between kin and friends; redistribution as appropriational movements toward a centre and out again, such as obligatory payments to central, political, social or religious authorities; and market exchange as anonymous, price-based exchange through formalized markets (Dalton 1971).

Polanyi asserted that these exist in parallel, albeit with one form dominant. This is clearly applicable to the above situation of urban residential land access, where systems of reciprocity, redistribution and market exchange often work in parallel. Reciprocity in land access is expressed, for instance, through mutual assistance in occupation, where information on availability of land is channelled through kinship networks, and households rely on help from family and/or friends to obtain land.

The informal role of traditional chiefs and land holding families at the urban periphery, as well as that of the informal local political and administrative structures in the wider peri-urban area, is based on social redistribution. Land invasions, where households use social networks to establish security can also be seen as a socially based form of redistribution, as residents often pay the invasion leaders, but receive some form of protection as a result. The state land allocation system is also intended as a form of social redistribution, although there is strong evidence of it being a prime source of land commodification, whether intentionally or not. Politicians and state employees in land agencies who use the state system for their own benefit usually work through the market, although politicians may occasionally use land as rewards for votes.

As demonstrated in the findings above, the full monetary exchange market system for land is, however, quite restricted in operation in Mozambique, whether informal or not. There are several reasons for this. It is partly due to the economic costs, with low effective demand and affordability levels of the majority. It is also affected by the nature of land holdings, as both traditional and legal land holdings are concentrated in a minority. Legal and administrative processes are ill-defined, complex and represent high and generally unattainable standards, and hence are both exclusionary and open to abuse. This is also determined in great part by the nature of the political process. The more politicians need popular votes, the more likely they are to provide land for lower-income groups whether through the formal system or through informal alternatives. When this is not the case they may use land to bolster their power in other ways. In present day Mozambique the political elite use land allocation both as a means of patronage and also as a form of economic reward.

Given the declining incomes of increasing urban populations in many parts of the developing world, especially in Sub-Saharan Africa, it is unlikely that large proportions of the urban population will be able to afford land through formal land markets. This is compounded by the weak forms of political control which permit political and economic elites to almost exclusively benefit from the rise in land values associated with rapid urbanization. As such the tendency will be for informal forms of socio-economic interchange in land access to remain important for some time to come. The trend of monetarization of informal land allocation and transfer systems, however, essentially undermines the socially determined systems of control implicit in reciprocity and redistributive systems. There is also a danger that attempts by the state to incorporate informal markets with formal markets may only assist in more fully commoditising these informal access mechanisms, which may then also promote social exclusion due to the decreased purchasing power of parts of the urban population.

It is thus suggested that there is a need for alternative systems for land allocation, management and transfer that are not based primarily on the market or state mechanisms, although interacting with both where necessary. Rather than identifying these systems as informal and studying how these can be articulated with the formal state and market systems, alternative systems would rely more directly on socially controlled mechanisms as a more appropriate and socially inclusive base. This form of land access system is not seen as a replacement of monetarized land markets, but recognizes that the formal and informal markets will not in the foreseeable future act on behalf of many of the urban poor. It also recognizes that the attempt to develop redistributive land systems based exclusively on the state has severe limitations. This is partly due to market forces, increasingly acting at supra-national levels, but also to institutional and political constraints and weak systems of accountability between state and society. The weak link between the state and wider society in many developing countries has meant that these systems have seldom been designed to cater effectively to the needs of the majority. Hence it is suggested that apart from better state-market systems of land management, a socially based alternative could also be developed.

Some such mechanisms already exist where land is held on behalf of a community, and there is control by the community of allocation and/or exchange. It is important to note that such socially based systems can also be subverted and be exploitative, particularly for women and other traditionally disadvantaged groups, and they may also be undermined by market and/or state activity. They thus need clear socially accepted objectives and control, a legitimate and legal basis, and economic protection vis-à-vis the market. They can, however, provide, to use Stein's term, less alienating ways to achieve more inclusive access to land for the majority. The major difficulty in promoting such reforms is of course existing land owners or traditional elites who control land; state officials, politicians, land brokers and economic elites who benefit from the existing systems. However, with mobilization, the large proportions of urban dwellers who could potentially benefit from such socially based means of land management could be an extremely powerful social, if not political, force.

Urban Land Reform in Mozambique

Land still remains nationalized in Mozambique, and despite some recent changes, the Land Law and a draft Urban Land Regulation, it continues to be based on a usufruct title system. The law allows long-term leases and titling, but not land mortgaging. Economically and politically there is little incentive for the institutions officially responsible for land allocation and registry to service the urban poor, and the activities of these institutions, basically the municipalities, are increasingly oriented to raising finance for their most basic operations as successive central government transfers decrease in value (Jenkins 1999b and 2001a). These approaches have arguably led to greater polarization of the urban poor, in relation to their access to land and this is a basis for their livelihoods. Research has pointed to the urgent need both to protect the land which the urban poor have acquired for housing, through whatever process, and provide more land for residential use in accessible locations (Jenkins 2001a).

This action-research approach stresses the importance of maintaining the benefit of land nationalization for the public good. It argues that privatization of land would favour the politically and economically powerful, such as has happened to a great extent with the divestiture of the nationalized housing stock. The appropriation of urban land values is historically the basis for wealth creation, and wider social appropriation is an essential part of any sustainable social, economic and political base for urban development. In this sense Mozambique with its land nationalization has a unique opportunity, but civil society needs to seize the opportunity before it disappears. However, this requires new forms of perceiving and structuring the so-called informal land system and its interface with the formal land system.

The above research has shown that, since independence, formal state allocation has been a minor feature, and access to land with at least tacit approval of local level structures has been the major mode. This suggests that some form of decentralized land system, with local registry and protection through structures answerable at a neighbourhood level is most likely to be the most appropriate, supplemented by overall registry, guidance and supervision at municipal level. It should be possible under the new Land Law to allow regularization of existing occupation (of more than 10 years duration) of urban land, that is appropriately situated in terms of a land use or "urbanization plan, and permit some form of communal titling for local communities" (Garvey 1998). This would create the basis for more secure tenure, and even allow sub-allocation and transfers to individual families. Registration and possible subdivision of communal land titles could be handled through local level institutions. A vehicle for this could be some form of community land trust, as the exact legal persona of communities in terms of the Land Law is unclear. This institution could be used both to protect existing *de facto* land rights as well as develop new low-income residential areas.

The suggestion to create community land trusts is not only to provide an adequate legal persona for the local community. The recognition of such a semi-formal form of registration would not necessarily benefit those with land at present if there is no continued communal responsibility for land management. If residents in more attractive areas receive some form of individual and transferable title these could be sold at below market value to those with economic capacity, as a regulated market would not necessarily arise in these areas and the real urban land costs would be hidden through the state's allocation. The creation of community land trusts, with appropriate regulations to firstly safeguard community interests, would therefore be a means to safeguard the public good. This in itself would not exclude the possibility of land commodification, but would allow non-state forms of re-distribution and even reciprocal networks to operate as well. Full individual freehold land titling, on the other hand, would almost definitely lead to "land grabbing" by the better off.

The problem remains of how to develop the rights to use such a process for the poor and traditionally disadvantaged in peri-urban areas, and to ensure these groups will benefit proportionally. It is also important that the process does not become corrupted. This can only effectively be controlled at local level, particularly given the weak engagement of the majority in any formal form of representative governance to date. In the present context, neither the national nor the new local government may be interested in this process, nor the private sector, if the added value accrued remains for the benefit of the community. As such it will need to be a focus for non-state mobilization via the organizational elements of horizontal (intra-societal relations) and vertical (state-society relations) civil society. A key role could be played by the religious and other socio-cultural organizations that have survived the period of proto-socialism. However, given the weak role these have to date in social issues, there is a need to tap into the relatively strong horizontal civil society in Mozambique. Nevertheless, despite its strength in underpinning survival mechanisms (Mlay et al. 1998), little is known about how horizontal civil society operates, especially in urban areas. A first step in this process would be to investigate the evolving forms of horizontal civil society, and their actual and possible role in non-state redistribution.

In terms of vertical civil society, the activities of existing organizations could well be allied to those of the fledgling NGOs involved in physical urban upgrading and to the intellectual community associated with the higher education sector. This would be of particular importance in the interface with the local state. As noted above, the nature of local state power is still extremely unclear in Mozambique. As such there will need to be strong lobbying from civil society to ensure that mechanisms such as the above are at least attended to within the formal state structures. Other important institutions of vertical civil society that could support the political lobbying process would be the independent media and the churches, the former having a key role in lobbying the state to date, and the latter being often the only form of formal association at neighbourhood level. Finally support in the form of resources from other institutions such as international non-governmental organizations is likely to be crucial.

CONCLUSIONS

In the prevailing conditions of a weak state and weak market, such as in Mozambique, it is unlikely that the urban poor can get access to formal state and market land supply mechanisms. In addition, the weakness of the political system, allied to growing regionalization and economic globalization, undermines any effective political "voice" for the urban majority. Given the acute institutional and economic constraints, in the short or medium term it is not likely that the state or the market will effectively reach the urban poor in terms of formal access to land for housing. In contrast, it has been argued that when the state and the market are as weak as in Mozambique, both historically and actually, underlying social structures are more obviously, and crucially, engaged in economic activity, not only social and cultural activities. New approaches to land access and to development in general, thus need to be based on the very social mechanisms and structures whereby the majority of the population manage their survival.

This then is the starting point for a society-driven urban development policy, as opposed to a state or market-driven policy. In this perspective the organizations of civil society need to be able to adapt and strengthen to guide their own development, engaging with the state and the market where possible and desirable. There is no reason to assume however, as "Third Sector" theorists do, that these organizations will be modern, nor will they be exclusively vertically oriented organizations (Turner 1988; Fiori and Ramirez 1992). Modified traditional civil society and kinship structures have probably a more crucial role in Mozambique, given the weakness of modern and vertical civil society (Jenkins 2001c).

In this context direct reciprocity, through extended kinship, ethnic and related structures, and non-state redistribution, play important roles. They would appear to be the most productive means to assist the urban poor as the state and the market are increasingly unable and unwilling to do. It is thus suggested that working on the basis of these concepts can permit a more nuanced and appropriate analytical basis for understanding the perception of African urban dwellers, as well as mechanisms for consolidating urban development.

In conclusion, many African urban analysts may feel uncomfortable with the concept of formal-informal, but it has been very useful shorthand and we all, to a greater or lesser extent, use it. Whether we can find alternative analytical concepts that are broad enough to cross disciplines and sectors, while being adaptable to complex real and perceived situations, is a major challenge. It is necessary to avoid a simplistic definition of formality which has been appropriated to the often exclusive benefit of the urban-based elites. It is also necessary to find an alternative to the dominant state hegemony which has defined the formal to date, and whose legitimacy for the majority is rightly questioned.

References

Angel, S., R.W. Archer, S. Tanphiphat and E.A. Wegelin, 1983, *Land for Housing the Poor.* Singapore: Select Books.

Boucher, S., A. Francisco, L. Rose, M. Roth and F. Zaqueu, 1995, *Legal uncertainty and land disputes in the peri-urban areas of Mozambique: Land markets in transition.* Research Paper 121. Wisconsin Land Tenure Center.

Braathen, E. and B.V. Jörgensen, 1998, "Democracy without people? Local government reform and 1998 municipal elections in Mozambique", *Lusotopie* 1998, pp. 31–38.

Coquery-Vidrovitch, C., 1991, "The Process of Urbanization in Africa (From the Origins to the Beginning of Independence)", *African Studies Review*, Vol. 34/1:1–98.

Dalton, G. (ed.), 1971, *Primitive Archaic and Modern Economies: Essays of Karl Polanyi,* Boston: Beacon Press.

Durand-Lasserve, A., 1997, "Regularising Land Markets", *Habitat Debate*, Vol. 3/2, UNCHS.

Euroconsult, 1999, "Metropolitan Maputo Structure Plan, Maputo.

Fernandes, E. and A. Varley (eds), 1998, *Illegal cities: law and urban change in developing countries.* London: Zed Press.

Fiori, J. and R. Ramirez, 1992, "Notes on the Self-Help Housing Critique", in Mathey, K. (ed.), *Beyond Self-Help Housing.* London: Mansell.

Fourie, C., 1997, "Combining Informal Systems with Formal Systems", *Habitat Debate*, Vol. 3/2, UNCHS.

Friedmann, J., 1986, "The world city hypothesis", *Development and Change,* Vol. 17:69–83.

Garvey, J., 1998, "The nature of rights under Mozambique's reform land law". Paper delivered at the *International Conference on land tenure in the developing world, with a focus on Southern Africa,* University of Cape Town.

Harbeson, J.W., D. Rothchild and N. Chazan, 1994, *Civil Society and the State in Africa.* Boulder: Lynne Rienner.

Hirschmann, A.O., 1970, *Exit, voice and loyalty: Responses to decline in firms, organizations and states.* Cambridge: Harvard University Press.

Hyden, G. and M. Bratton, 1992, *Governance and politics in Africa.* Boulder: Lynne Rienner.

Jenkins, P., 2001a, *Emerging land markets for housing in Mozambique: The impact on the poor and alternatives to improve land access and urban development—an action research project in peri-urban Maputo.* Research Paper No. 75. Edinburgh College of Art/Heriot-Watt University, School of Planning and Housing.

—, 2001b, "Strengthening access to land for housing for the poor in Maputo, Mozambique", *International Journal of Urban and Regional Research,* Vol. 25/3.

—, 2001c, "When the state and market are weak—the role of civil society in shelter at the periphery. Experience from peri-urban communities, Maputo" in Carley, M., P. Jenkins and H. Smith, *Urban development and civil society: The role of communities in sustainable cities.* London: Earthscan.

—, 1999a, *Maputo city: The historical roots of under-development and the consequences in urban form.* Research Paper No. 71. Edinburgh College of Art/Heriot-Watt University, School of Planning and Housing.

—, 1999b, *Mozambique: Housing and land markets in Maputo.* Research Paper No. 72. Edinburgh College of Art/Heriot-Watt University, School of Planning and Housing.

—, 1998, *National and international shelter policy initiatives in Mozambique: Housing the urban poor at the periphery.* PhD thesis. Edinburgh College of Art/Heriot-Watt University, School of Planning and Housing.

—, 1990, "Mozambique" in Mathey, K., *Housing Policies in the Socialist Third World.* London: Mansell.

Knox, P.N. and P.J. Taylor (eds), 1995, *World Cities in a World System.* Cambridge: Cambridge University Press.

Lundin, I.B., 2001, *Reflections on the Dynamics of a Nation Building Process under Stress. The Case of Mozambique 1993–1998. Illustrated with Five Articles.* Fil lic dissertation, Department of Human and Economic Geography, Göteborg University.

—, 1991, *The Role of Kinship in an Urban Context—a Study of Survival Strategies in an Urban Context in a Situation of Generalized Crisis: The Special Case of Maputo City.* PhD draft, Department of Anthropology and Archaeology, Universidade Eduardo Mondlane, Maputo.

Mlay, G.I. et al., 1998, "Seasonality and Food Consumption Patterns in Mozambique". Paper presented at the *Conference on Food Security and Nutrition* in Maputo, October 1998.

Myers, G.W., 1994, "Competitive rights, competitive claims: Land access in post-war Mozambique", *Journal of Southern Africa Studies,* Vol. 20/4.

Payne, G., 1997, *Urban land tenure and property rights in developing countries: A review.* Oxford: ITDG.

—, 1989, *Informal housing and land subdivisions in Third World Cities: A review of the literature.* Oxford: ODA/Oxford Polytechnic.

Sassen, S., 1994, *Cities in a World Economy.* Thousand Oaks: Pine Forge.

—, 1991, *The Global City.* Princeton NJ: Princeton University Press.

Sinha, A.P., 1997, "Security of Land Tenure: From New Delhi to Istanbul", *Habitat Debate*, Vol. 3/2, UNCHS.

Stein, H., 1995, "Institutional Theories and Structural Adjustment in Africa", in Harriss, J., J. Hunter and C.M. Lewis, *The New Institutional Economics and Third World Development*. London: Routledge.

Turner, J.F.C., 1988, "Introduction" and "Conclusions" in Turner, B., *Building Community*. London: Building Community Books.

UNCHS, 1996, *An Urbanizing World: Global Report on Human Settlements 1996*. United Nations Centre for Human Settlements, Nairobi.

UNDP, 1998, *Mozambique—Peace and Economic Growth: Opportunities for human development*. National Human Development Report, Maputo.

White, G. (ed.), 1985, *Revolutionary Socialist Development in the Third World*. Brighton: Wheatsheaf Books.

World Bank, 1993, *Housing: Enabling Markets to Work*. Washington: World Bank.

Abbreviations

ANC	African National Congress
AVSI	Associazione volontari per il Servizio Internatiozionale/ Voluntary Association for International Service
CARDO	International Conference on Housing, Work and Development
CBD	Central Business District
CBO	Community-Based Organisations
CCJP	Catholic Commission for Justice and Peace
CCM	Chama Cha Mapinduzi
CCZ	Consumer Council of Zimbabwe
CETZAM	Christian Enterprise Trust of Zambia
CIDA	Canadian International Development Agency
CMC	Cape Metropolitan Council
CMDA	Cato Manor Development Association
CMRA	Cato Manor Residents' Association
COMESA	Common Market for Eastern and Southern Africa
CSO	Central Statistical Office
CZI	Confederation of Zimbabwe Industries
DCC	Dar es Salaam City Commission
DFID	Department for International Development
DHCS	Department of Housing and Community Services
DSEI	Department of State Enterprises and Indigenisation
EIU	Economist Intelligence Unit
EU	European Union
FAO	Food and Agricultural Organisation of the United Nations
FINNIDA	Finnish International Development Agency
FMPE	Family Mode of Production Enterprise
FRELIMO	Frente de Libertãçao de Moçambique
GDs	Grupos Dinamizadores ("Dynamising Groups")
GIMS	Geospatial Information Management System
GRZ	Government of the Republic of Zambia
HAVAZ	Hawkers and Vendors Association of Zimbabwe
HBE	Home Based Enterprises
HFCK	Housing Finance Company of Kenya
ILO	International Labour Organization
ILO/SATEP	International Labour Office/Southern African Team for Employment
IMF	International Monetary Fund
ITOA	Inanda Taxi Owners' Association
KCC	Kitwe City Council
KWSP	Kitwe Water Supply Project
LA	Land Act
LCC	Lusaka City Council
LR	Land Reference
LSPP	Directorate of Lands, Surveys and Physical Planning
MAJUDEA	Makongo Juu Development Association
MK	uMkhonto weSizwe (Spear of the Nation, the armed wing of the ANC)
MLC	Metropolitan Local Council
MLGRUD	Ministry of Local Government Rural and Urban Development
MPSLSW	Ministry of the Public Service, Labour and Social Welfare
NACHU	National Housing Cooperative Union

NCC	Nairobi City Council
NCDP	National Commission for Development Planning
NGO	Non Governmental Organisations
NIC	National Investment Corporation Ltd
NISCC	Nairobi Informal Settlement Coordinating Committee
NUDC	Nairobi Urban District Council
ODA	(British) Overseas Development Administration
PAIGC	Partido Africano para a Independencia da Guiné e Cabo Verde
PVC	Private and Voluntary Cooperation
RDP	Reconstruction and Development Programme
SANCO	South African National Civics Organization
SAP	Structural Adjustment Programme
SCP	Sustainable Cities Programme
SDA	Selected Development Area
SDP	Sustainable Dar es Salaam Project
SEDCO	Small Enterprises Development Corporation
SIDA	Swedish International Development Cooperation Agency
SME	Small and Medium Enterprise (sometimes MSE)
SNV	Stichting Nederlandse Vrijwilligers/Foundation of Netherlands Volunteers)
SSA	Sub-Saharan Africa
STD	Sexually Transmitted Disease
TCO	Town and Country Ordinance
TDF	Tabata Development Fund
UCLAS	University College of Lands and Architectural Studies at the University of Dar es Salaam
UCT	University of Cape Town
UDF	United Democratic Front
UNCHS	United Nations Centre for Human Settlements
UNCHS/HABITAT	United Nations Human Settlement Programme
UNDP	United Nations Development Programme
UNIP	United Independence Political Party
USAID	United States Agency for International Development
ViSP	Visual Settlement Planning
WRC	Water Research Commission of South Africa
ZARD	Zambia Association for Research and Development
ZCCM	Zambia Consolidated Copper Mines

Biographical Notes

John Abbott (b. 1947) obtained his Ph.D. degree from the University of the Witwatersrand, Johannesburg, South Africa, within the Faculty of Engineering and the Built Environment (1993). He is currently Independent Consultant Urbanist and was previously Professor of Urban Engineering, at the University of Cape Town, South Africa. He has developed an integrated upgrading methodology for application in the area of informal settlements. Other research interests include Urban GIS management, with a focus on developing cities and the use of GIS both in informal settlements and in urban areas that lack a formal cadastre.

Marco Burra (b. 1957) received his MA in architecture from the School of Architecture, Royal Danish Academy of Arts, Copenhagen, Denmark in 1987. He is currently a Ph.D. scholar at the University of Dar es Salaam, Tanzana and is employed at the University College of Lands and Architectural Studies (UCLAS), Dar es Salaam as lecturer in urban and regional planning. His research interests are urban planning and governance, housing, community and civil society initiatives in managing human settlements.

Rose Gatabaki-Kamau (b. 1956) was a Kenyan scholar with a Ph.D. degree from the School of Public Policy, the University of Birmingham, UK. Her research interests were housing, the urban informal economy and infrastructure and services. At the time of her death in 2002, she was a researcher with the Building Research Institute, the University of Nairobi, Kenya.

Karen Tranberg Hansen (b. 1945) obtained her Ph.D. in sociocultural anthropology from the University of Washington, Seattle, USA, in 1979. She is Professor of Anthropology at the Northwestern University, Illinois, USA. Her research interests are: third world urbanization, informal economy, gender relations, and consumption.

Paul Jenkins (b. 1953) is a Ph.D. in planning and housing at Heriot-Watt University, Edinburgh, Scotland. He is currently Director for the Centre for Environment and Human Settlements, School of the Built Environment, Heriot-Watt University. His research interests include planning during rapid urbanisation, housing development for low-income groups, policy advocacy and action research. He has more than 30 years experience in Central and Southern Africa

Amin Y. Kamete (b. 1967) obtained his M.Sc. in rural and urban planning from the University of Zimbabwe in 1994. He is a lecturer at the Department of Rural and Urban Planning, the University of Zimbabwe. His research interests include urban housing, urban management, urban governance, urban economies, local economic development, and sustainable human settlements. He has published widely in these areas. He is currently employed at the Nordic Africa Institute, Uppsala, Sweden, where he is coordinator of the research programme *Gender and Age in African Cities*.

Sarah Karirah-Gitau (b. 1961) obtained her Ph.D. degree in Urban Planning from the University of Central England in 1996. She is currently working as a project co-ordinator for the Gender Mainstreaming Unit, UN-HABITAT. Otherwise she is a senior lecturer in the Land Development Department, Faculty of Architecture, Design and Development at the University of Nairobi, Kenya.

Barbara Mwila Kazimbaya-Senkwe (b. 1969) is currently a Commonwealth Ph.D. Scholar in the School of Architecture, Planning and Landscape at the University of Newcastle Upon Tyne, UK. Her research interests are urban development and service provisions, notably privatisation of urban municipal services and informalisation of urban economic life.

Clement R. Leduka (b. 1961) received his Ph.D. in city and regional planning from Cardiff University, UK, in 2000. He is currently a senior lecturer at the Department of Geography, Urban and Regional Planning Programme, the National University of Lesotho. His research interests are urban land management and policy, informality and urban livelihood strategies, social justice in urban service delivery, urban management and governance, peri-urban change and urban agriculture, and politics of urban planning.

Ilda Lourenço-Lindell (b. 1965) obtained her Ph.D. degree in 2002, at the Department of Human Geography, Stockholm University, Sweden. She is currently employed as a researcher at the Nordic Africa Institute in Uppsala, Sweden. Her research interests are urban economies, urban livelihoods, social networks, associations, collective action, and urban politics.

Knut G. Nustad (b. 1968) received his Ph.D. in social anthropology from Cambridge University, UK. He is currently a lecturer at the Department of Social Anthropology, University of Oslo, Norway. His research interests include anthropology of the state, development, and local politics.

Gabriel Tati (b. 1959) received his Ph.D. in urban studies from the University of Bristol, UK, in 2000. He is currently a lecturer at the University of Swaziland. Research interests include the public-private partnership in the provision of urban services, urban sprawl and local institutions, the relationship between African immigrant entrepreneurship, ethnic networks and appropriation of public space. He is at present conducting research on labour resource allocation among male- and female-headed households in rural area, and social integration of self-settled refugees in an urban context. His geographical areas of research interests are Central and Southern Africa.

Mariken Vaa (b. 1937) obtained her Mag. Art. degree in sociology from the University of Oslo, Norway, in 1967, and is currently Professor of Development Studies at Oslo University College, Norway. From 1997 to 2002 she was coordinator of the programme *Cities, Governance and Civil Society* in Africa at the Nordic Africa Institute in Uppsala, Sweden. Her research interests include urban governance and service provision, development theory and poverty, and women and work.

Index

Abbott, John, 205
African National Congress (ANC), 47, 49, 52
aid agencies, urban policies, 14–17
apartheid, South Africa, 46–8

Bahatoglu, Deniz, 35
Bardouille, R., 104
Bayart, Jean-François, 53
Bigman, L., 88
bilateral agencies, 17
Bissau, informal trade, 81, 84–96
Black Local Authorities, South Africa, 47
black marketing, Zambia, 63–4
Bøe, Turid, 29
Botha, P.W., 53
Brazil, Belo Horizonte, 141, 193–4, 197–8, 203–4
'briefcase businesspeople', Harare, 124

Cape Town
    informal settlements, 141, 193–208
    local government, 195–6
    planning, 201–2
cashew nuts, Guinea-Bissau, 91–2
Cato Crest, South Africa
    community organizations, 26–7, 47–8, 50–5
    formal/informal dichotomy, 45–6, 52–5, 57–9
    registration numbers, 54–5
    squatter settlements, 46, 49–50
    taxi wars, 27, 55–7
Cato, George Christopher, 46
Cato Manor Development Association (CMDA), 48, 50–3
Cato Manor Residents' Association (CMRA), 48
children, home-based enterprises, 106–7
Chiluba, Frederick, 65
Chipondo, Enock, 75
Christian Enterprise Trust of Zambia (CETZAM), 111–12
CIDA, urban development strategy, 17
civic organizations, South Africa, 47–8, 53–5
colonial period, Kenya, 161–2
Common Market for Eastern and South-ern Africa (COMESA), 64
community based organizations (CBOs)

Dar es Salaam, 144–7, 151–2, 154–6
    see also civic organizations
Congo-Brazzaville
    conflicts, 12
    fishermen, 25–6, 28–44
    settlement patterns, 31–3
    space appropriation, 33–7, 40–4
Coquery-Vidrovitch, C., 211, 215
corruption, Guinea-Bissau, 88
courtyard developments, Congo, 34–5
credit see micro-credit
crisis, urban development, 18–19

Daka, Steven, 67, 68, 69
Dar es Salaam
    community based organizations, 144–7, 151–2, 154–6
    informal settlements, 143–4, 148–52
    land use, 139–40, 143–56
dependency rates, 13
Destro, Donald Giovanni, 164–5
Devas, Nick, 190
DFID, urban development strategy, 17
Dugard, Jackie, 56
Dyulas, Guinea-Bissau, 87, 88, 89–90

economic activities, women, 36–7
economy see informal economy
electricity supply, Congo fishing settle-ments, 34–5
Elf-Congo, and fishermen, 28, 31–3, 38–40
enablement, 15
European Union, Zambia development funding, 69–70

Fernandes, E., 210
Fernandes, R., 88
finance, home industries, 125, 134–5
fishermen, Congo, 25–6, 28–44
formal employment, Zambia, 99–100
formal sector
    definition, 8, 210–14
    interface with informal, 9, 42, 57, 203–8
formal/informal dichotomy
    Cato Crest, South Africa, 45–6, 52–5, 57–9
    home industries, 121
    land access, 210–24

'free market', informal economy, 62–3, 77
Friedman, Steven, 48
Funk, U., 89

Galli, R., 88, 89
gender relations
    fishing activities, 29, 36–7
    home-based enterprises, 105–6
    housing, 12
Geospatial Information Management
    Systems (GIMS), 197
GIS technology, 199, 204
Gomes, P., 92
Gough, Katherine, 112
government, power of, 12–13
Grey-Johnson, C., 85
Guinea-Bissau
    cashew nut trade, 91–2
    corruption, 88
    Dyulas, 87, 88, 89–90
    food shortages, 88–9
    independence, 86–7
    informal trade, 81, 84–96
    People's Stores, 87
    political disengagement, 87, 89–90
    'rice coup', 89
    structural adjustment programme, 90

Ha Mabote, Lesotho, 188–90
Habitat Agenda, 15
    see also United Nations Conference on
    Human Settlements
Halfani, Mohamed, 18
Hansen, Karen Tranberg, 100
Harare
    Department of Housing and Com-
    munity Services (DHCS), 133, 136
    home industries, 82–3, 120–36
    local authority, 131–4
    private sector, 130–1
Hart, Keith, 10–11, 19–20, 45, 58–9
Hawkers and Vendors Association of
    Zimbabwe (HAVAZ), 134
Hays-Mitchell, M., 100
Heymans, C., 48
Hirschmann, A.O., 211
HIV/AIDS, 13
Holland, Jeremy, 101
home industries
    definition, 120
    finance, 125, 134–5
    formal/informal dichotomy, 121
    Harare, 82–3, 120–36
    institutional reactions, 130–5

legality, 128
and local authority, 131–4
marketing, 127–8
types of, 120–1, 123–4
and urban development, 129–30
home-based enterprises (HBEs), 17
    advantages, 110–11
    difficulties of, 111–14
    gender differences, 105–6
    income from, 108–9
    and infrastructure, 113–14
    research, 100–1
    skills, 112
    start-up capital, 111–12
    types of, 104–5, 109–10
    Zambia, 82, 99–116
housing
    aid agencies, 14–15
    Congo fishermen, 34–6, 40–4
    privatization, 12
    see also informal settlements

informal
    definition, 7–8
    interface with formal, 9, 42, 57, 203–8
    see also formal/informal dichotomy
informal economy
    definition, 10–11, 19–20, 45–6, 58–9,
    86
    'free market', 62–3, 77
    Harare, 121–2
    see also home-based enterprises and
    informal sector
informal planning, Tanzania, 143–8
informal sector, 10, 11, 16, 81, 100–2,
    104–6, 111–2, 121–2, 134, 136
    see also informal economy
informal settlements, 9–10, 12–13
    Brazil, 193–4, 197–8, 203–4
    Congo fishermen, 34–6, 40–4
    development interventions, 49–55
    infrastructure, 10, 149–51
    Kenya, 140, 158–72
    Lesotho, 140–1, 176–91
    South Africa, 46, 49–50, 141, 193–208
    state planning, 152–4
    Tanzania, 139–40, 143–56
    upgrading, 193–208
    see also housing
informalization
    Guinea-Bissau, 81, 84–96
    Nairobi, 158
infrastructure
    and home-based enterprises, 113–14
    informal settlements, 10, 149–51

utilities, 34–5
interface, informal and formal, 9, 42, 57,
    121, 203–8
Intergraph, 199
International Labour Office (ILO), 10
International Labour Organization (ILO),
    16

Jones, J., 88, 89
Jul-Larsen, Eyolf, 29

Kabengo, John, 76
Kalipeni, Ezethel, 29
Kazimbaya-Senkwe, Barbara M., 101,
    102, 104
Kellett, P., 102, 110, 112
Kenya
    colonial period, 161–2
    informal settlements, 140, 158–72
Kesteloot, Christian, 29
kinship, social networks, 214
Kitwe, Zambia, home-based enterprises,
    102–11

land access
    legality, 176, 212–14
    Lesotho, 140–1, 176–91
    Mozambique, 141–2, 214–24
    Nairobi, 140, 164–7
land use planning, Dar es Salaam, 139–40,
    143–56
legality
    definition, 210–11
    home industries, 128
    land access, 176, 212–14
Leitmann, Josef, 35
Lesotho
    direct grants, 183–5
    formal rules, 181–90
    illegal settlements, 140–1, 176–91
    Land Act (1979), 176, 179–91
    peri-urban population, 178–9
    Selected Development Areas (SDAs),
        179–80, 181, 183–90
Lipton, M., 100–1, 110
loans *see* micro-credit
Lundin, I.B., 214
Lusaka
    Chibolya market, 67, 69
    foreign traders, 75
    Kamwala Market, 75
    Kaunda Square market, 72, 73
    New City Market, 62, 65–7, 69, 72–3
    'nuisance act', 74

shopping malls, 70
street vendors, 27, 62–78

Mabogunje, Akin, 19
Makongo Juu Development Association
    (MAJUDEA), 147, 149–52
Makongo settlement, Dar es Salaam, 148–
    56
Malama, Albert, 102, 104
Mapeleng/Maqalika Reservoir, Lesotho,
    186–8
Maputo, land access, 141–2, 214–24
marketing, home industries, 127–8
markets, Zambia, 63–78
Maseru
    growth of, 180–1
    informal settlements, 140–1
    peri-urban development, 185–90
Mayekiso, Mzwanele, 48
McAuslan, Patrick, 16–17
Meert, Hank, 29
micro-credit
    access to, 82–3
    home industries, 134–5
    home-based enterprises, 111–12
micro-enterprises, 17
migration
    fishermen, 31, 42–3
    interregional, 14
MK (uMkhonto weSizew), 56–7, 58
Monteiro, H., 91, 92
Moser, Caroline, 101
Mozambique, land access, 141–2, 214–24
Mtemvu, Zuberi, 153
Muneku, Austin, 99
Murray, Colin, 52
Mwale, Alexander, 101, 104
Mwanawasa, Levy, 76

Nairobi
    growth of, 159–60
    informal settlements, 140, 158–72
    land transfers, 164–7
    Zimmerman housing area, 158–9,
        164–72
Nairobi Informal Settlement Coordinating
    Committee (NISCC), 164
National Investment Corporation Ltd.
    (NIC), South Africa, 49–50
neo-liberal reforms, 11–12
neo-patrimonialism, 53
New Delhi Declaration, 213
New Rest, Cape Town, 193–208

New Roysambu Housing Company
  Limited, 165–7
non-compliance, 177–8
non-governmental organizations (NGOs)
  urban development strategies, 17
  Zimbabwe, 134–5

oil company, and Congo fishermen, 28,
  31–3, 38–40
Olufemi, O.A., 101, 112

participatory development, South Africa,
  26–7, 48
Peattie, L., 85
peri-urban areas, Lesotho, 178–9, 185–90
planning
  Cape Town, 201–2
  informal, 143–8
  state-led, 152–4
Pointe-Noire, Congo
  beach committee, 33, 41
  Chamber of Commerce and Industry,
    41
  fishermen, 25–6, 28–44
  housing development, 34–6, 40
  institutional responses, 40–1
  and oil company, 28, 31–3, 38–40
  pollution, 39
  space appropriation, 33–4, 40–4
  utilities, 34–5
  women's role, 36–7
Polanyi, Karl, 219–20
pollution, marine, 39
population, youth bulge, 13–14
poverty, 100–01, 114–6, 133
  and informal sector, 8
  see also urban poverty
power, changing, 12–13
privatization, housing, 12

Rakodi, C., 159
Razzaz, Omar, 177
rental housing, informal settlements, 10
research priorities, 18, 19–20
roads
  Makongo, Dar es Salaam, 150–1
  New Rest, Cape Town, 200
Robben, Antonius, 35
Robinson, P.S., 50
Rubia, Charles, 170

Scott, James C., 177–8
Seekings, Jeremy, 48
settlements *see* informal settlements

Shubane, K., 48
SIDA, urban development strategy, 17
small and medium enterprises (SMEs), 17
Smit, Warren, 48
SNV, urban development strategy, 17
Soto, H. de, 17, 84
South Africa
  civic organizations, 47–8, 53–5
  informal settlements, 26–7, 45–59, 141,
    193–208
  local government, 195–6
  taxi wars, 27, 55–7
South Africa National Civic Organization
  (SANCO), 47–8
space
  appropriation, 29–30, 33–7, 40–4
  transformation of, 11–14
squatter settlements, South Africa, 46, 49–
  50
Stein, Howard, 213
Strassman, Paul, 101
street vendors, 13
  Lusaka, 27, 62–78
Stren, R., 7, 19, 170
Structural Adjustment Programmes
  (SAPs), 11–12
  Guinea-Bissau, 90
  informalization, 85
  Zambia, 64, 101
Sustainable Dar es Salaam Project (SDP),
  144

Tabata Development Fund (TDF), 147
Tanzania
  informal planning, 143–8
  land use, 139–40
  state planning system, 152–4
taxi wars, South Africa, 27, 55–7
Theko, Makalo, 188–90
Tipple, A.G., 102, 110, 112
trade, informalization, 84–96
Tripp, Aili Mari, 177–8

United Democratic Front (UDF), South
  Africa, 47
United Nations Centre for Human Settle-
  ments (UNCHS/Habitat), 15
United Nations Conference on Human
  Settlements (Habitat I, 1976), 14–15
United Nations Conference on Human
  Settlements (Habitat II, 1996), 15, 16
United Nations Development Programme
  (UNDP), urban development agenda,
  15–16

Untari, R., 112
upgrading, informal settlements, 193–208
urban crisis, 18–19
urban development, 17–9, 129–30, 139–
    40, 222–4
urban poverty, 16–7, 99–100, 129, 194
    see also poverty
utilities, access to, 34–5

Varley, A., 210
Visual Settlement Planning (ViSP), 197

water supply
    Congo fishing settlements, 34–5
    Makongo, Dar es Salaam, 150
'weapons of the weak', 177
Whitehouse, George, 159
Williams, Gavin, 52
women
    artisanal fisheries, 29
    Congo fishing community, 36–7
    home-based enterprises, 82, 105–6
    housing, 12
    informal trade, 81
    informalization, 92–94
    settlement of fishermen, 31
    street vendors, 70
World Bank, urban development strategy,
    15–16

young people, 13–14

Zambia
    Copperbelt Province, 101–2
    economic restructuring, 64, 99–100
    foreign investment, 64, 69–70
    home-based enterprises (HBEs), 82,
    99–116
    housing, 12
    street vendors, 27, 62–78
Zambuko Trust, Zimbabwe, 134–5
Zeleza, Paul, 29
Zimbabwe
    home industries, 82–3, 120–36
    non-governmental organizations
    (NGOs), 134–5
Zimmerman, Nairobi
    control of growth, 167–71
    informal settlement, 158–9, 164–72
    land transfers, 164–7